Housing Partnerships

Housing Partnerships

A New Approach to a Market
at a Crossroads

Andrew Caplin,
Sewin Chan,
Charles Freeman,
Joseph Tracy

The MIT Press
Cambridge, Massachusetts
London, England

HD
7293
Z9
H695
1997

This book was set in Palatino on the Monotype "Prism Plus" PostScript Imagesetter by Asco Trade Typesetting Ltd., Hong Kong.

Printed and bound in the United States of America.

Library of Congress Cataloging-in-Publication Data

Housing partnerships : a new approach to a market at a crossroads / by
  Andrew Caplin ... [et al.].
    p. cm.
  Includes index.
  ISBN 0-262-03243-0 (hardcover : alk. paper)
    1. Housing—United States—Finance. I. Caplin, Andrew.
  HD7293.Z9H695   1997
  338.4'36908'0973—dc21   96-37852
                                                        CIP

PREFER and SCEPTRE are service marks of Charles Freeman.
"The second half of your house may be the worst purchase you will ever make" is a service mark of Charles Freeman.

Contents

Preface   xi

1 Introduction   1
   1.1   Overview   1
   1.2   Guide to Chapter 2: Buy or Rent?   3
   1.3   Guide to Chapter 3: The Mortgage Market and the Budget
         Set   4
   1.4   Guide to Chapter 4: Home Ownership and the Life Cycle   4
   1.5   Guide to Chapter 5: Home Ownership and Risk   5
   1.6   Guide to Chapter 6: Introduction to the Partnership
         Market   6
   1.7   Guide to Chapter 7: New Options for Home Ownership   7
   1.8   Guide to Chapter 8: Partnerships and the Life Cycle   8
   1.9   Guide to Chapter 9: The Partnership Contract   9
   1.10 Guide to Chapter 10: Secondary Partnership Markets   10
   1.11 Guide to Chapters 11 and 12: The Primary Markets   11
   1.12 Guide to Chapter 13: Pricing Partnerships   12
   1.13 Guide to Chapter 14: Partnerships and Purchasing a
         Home   13
   1.14 Guide to Chapter 15: Partnerships and the Ownership
         Experience   14
   1.15 Guide to Chapter 16: Partnerships and Federal Policy   15
   1.16 Guide to Chapter 17: Partnerships and the Broader
         Economy   16
   1.17 Guide to Chapter 18: Institutional Angles on Partnership
         Markets   16
   1.18 Concluding Remarks   18

I   The Mortgage Market and Housing Market   19

2   Buy or Rent?   21
    2.1   Some Facts   21
    2.2   Household Preferences   23
    2.3   Introduction to the Mortgage Market   28
    2.4   The Affordability Approach   33

3   The Mortgage Market and the Budget Set   37
    3.1   A Simple Guide to the A Mortgage Market   37
    3.2   The Three Basic Products   39
    3.3   The Computations: Simplifying Assumptions   41
    3.4   The Costs of Purchasing a $100,000 Home   43
    3.5   The Feasible Set of Houses   45

4   Home Ownership and the Life Cycle   49
    4.1   The Early Years: A Time of High Pressure   49
    4.2   Time to Save and the House Poor: Some Numerical
          Examples   53
    4.3   The Later Years: Inertia   57
    4.4   The Liquidity of Housing Wealth and Consumption
          Possibilities   61
    4.5   The Middle Years: Ownership and Anxiety   65

5   Home Ownership and Risk   71
    5.1   The Variability of House Prices   71
    5.2   The Correlation between House Price Risk and Income
          Risk   73
    5.3   Mortgages and the Problem of Indebtedness   76
    5.4   Housing Investment and the Asset Portfolio   79

II The Partnership Market and the Housing Market   83

6   Introduction to the Partnership Market   85
    6.1   Overview of the Partnership Market   85
    6.2   Will There Be Any Demand for Limited Partnerships?   87
    6.3   The Managing Partner's Portfolio   90
    6.4   The Managing Partner's Valuation of the Second Half of the
          House   93
    6.5   The Limited Partner's Valuation of the Second Half of the
          House   96

7 New Options for Home Ownership   99
   7.1 Partnerships and the Costs of a $100,000 Home   99
   7.2 Partnerships and Trading Up   102
   7.3 Mixed Motives   105
   7.4 The Impact of Price   108
   7.5 Appendix   108

8 Partnerships and the Life Cycle   113
   8.1 Easing the Transition to Ownership: Illustrative
        Examples   113
   8.2 Partnerships and the Middle Years   119
   8.3 Partnerships and the Later Years   121
   8.4 Dynamics and Adjustment in the Partnership Market   123

III The Supply Side   127

9 The Partnership Contract   129
   9.1 Guide to the Contract   129
   9.2 Clauses Covering the Purchase   130
   9.3 Clauses that Ensure Adequate Maintenance   131
   9.4 Alterations   133
   9.5 The Sales Process   136
   9.6 Breach   139
   9.7 The Partnership Contract and the Mortgage Contract   140

10 Secondary Partnership Market for Trading Real Estate
   (SCEPTRE)   143
   10.1 The Secondary Mortgage Market   143
   10.2 The Secondary Partnership Market   145
   10.3 SCEPTRE and New Investment Vehicles   146

11 The Primary Mortgage Market   149
   11.1 The Household's Search-and-Application Process   149
   11.2 Screening by the Mortgage Originator   150
   11.3 The Variety of Mortgage Products   152
   11.4 The Structure of the Primary Mortgage Industry   155

12 The Primary Partnership Market   157
   12.1 The Household's Search-and-Application Process   157

12.2 Screening by the Partnership Originator and the Mortgage
      Originator   158
12.3 The Range of Partnership Products   161
12.4 The Structure of the Primary Partnership Industry   163

13 Pricing Partnerships   165
    13.1 Measuring House Prices   165
    13.2 Real Estate in the Limited Partner's Asset Portfolio: The
          Literature   168
    13.3 Simple Estimates of the Demand for Residential Real Estate
          Assets   170
    13.4 From Real Estate Price Indices to Partnership Funds   178
    13.5 New Opportunities for Diversification   179
    13.6 Self-Selection Effects   180
    13.7 Transactions Costs   181

IV Partnerships and the Housing Experience   183

14 Partnerships and the Home Purchase   185
    14.1 The Searcher's Problem and the Real Estate Agent   185
    14.2 Incentive Problems and Networks   187
    14.3 The Right Home?   188
    14.4 The Right Price?   190
    14.5 From Contract to Closing: More Players, More Games   191
    14.6 Partnerships and the Buying Experience   195

15 Partnerships and the Ownership Experience   199
    15.1 Partnerships and Life at Home   199
    15.2 Partnerships, Breach, and Default   201
    15.3 Partnerships and the Sales Process   203

V Partnerships, Policy, and the Big Picture   207

16 Partnerships and the Federal Government   209
    16.1 Federal Housing Policy: The Status Quo   209
    16.2 Targeted Partnership Subsidies and Community
          Reinvestment   211
    16.3 Precedents for TAPS   212
    16.4 The Agencies and the Evolution of the Housing Finance
          Market   216

17 Partnership Markets and the Broader Economy   219
    17.1 The Housing Market Equilibrium and Housing Finance
          Markets   219
    17.2 Macroeconomic Effects of Partnership Markets   222
    17.3 "Optimal" Housing Finance Markets   225

18 Institutional Angles on Partnership Markets   229
    18.1 The Institutional Infrastructure of Partnership Markets   229
    18.2 Inertia in the Housing Finance Market   232
    18.3 The Importance of Market Leadership   237
    18.4 The Agencies: Part of the Problem or Part of the
          Solution?   240

    Concluding Remarks   243
    Notes   245
    Acronyms   255
    References   257
    Index   263

Preface

In this book we propose the development of a new set of markets, called Partnership Markets, that would open up many new financial options for home buyers. The proposal developed out of some simple questions. Why do households have to choose between renting their homes and buying them outright? A household that occupies and owns a house is holding and maintaining the whole of a valuable asset. Why can't the household take part ownership of the home and sell off an equity stake to a financial institution? A large corporation has a far wider range of options when considering how to finance capital investment. Why is the asset market most important to U.S. households, the housing market, the only one in which there is no way to sell any part of the return stream to other investors?

When we first posed these questions, we did so in something of an impish spirit. It was intriguing and stimulating for academic economists and business practitioners to pool their knowledge bases and speculate on why the market functions as it does, rather than in the naive alternative manner that we hypothesized. We started our exploration believing that there is a strong enough market in ideas to ensure that "if this were such a good idea, it would already be here."

As we delved deeper into the theory and practice of the housing market, we began to see things in a very different light. We began to believe not only that these equity markets are feasible but also that they will develop in the United States in the not-too-distant future. In fact, we now view our proposal as providing the conceptual basis for a natural next step in the evolution in the housing finance market. This book is designed to present to the reader the reasons for our change in perspective as openly as possible.

To understand the background to our proposal, consider the difference between purchases of two of the key necessities in life: food and shelter.

Every day we decide exactly what we would like to eat based on our preferences and budgets. We can make different choices each day, and little time elapses between when we pay for our food and when we eat it.

In contrast, the purchase of shelter in the form of an owned home involves a purchase of the entire supply of shelter that the house will provide into the indefinite future. We have to pay up front not only for our own future shelter in the house but also for the shelter of the household that follows us in the home, and the household that follows them, and so on indefinitely. Given that we must make such a massive purchase, we must borrow money to buy the home, and may be kept out of the market because of our inability to pay for something that we do not even want: the perpetual shelter that the house provides.

In essence, our proposal is designed to reduce the extent of the asymmetry between purchases of food and purchases of shelter. One way to do this would be to open markets in which people could buy perpetual supplies of bacon and eggs before letting them qualify to eat breakfast, and then setting up a market with a very high commission rate in which they could sell their supply of bacon and eggs if they decided that they preferred cereal. But we feel that this market would not be very popular. So we have set about this in the other direction, looking for a method that allows households to consume shelter without having to buy the entire home. In doing this, we have to recognize the forces that account for the existence of the ownership sector in the first place, such as the various problems of maintenance involved in the rental market. In essence our proposed markets are designed to reduce the financial hurdle involved in home ownership while ensuring that households have adequate interest in maintaining their homes.

As a method of raising equity we propose a rather specific form of Limited Partnership Contract, and we therefore refer to this new market structure as the Partnership Market. To convince the reader that Partnership Markets are an idea whose time has (almost) come, we need to take not only a long tour of the existing market structure, but also a "virtual tour" of an alternative market structure with some form of equity market.

The tour must extend well beyond the housing finance market itself, because our proposal has far wider ramifications than the specification of a new contract. It involves changes not only in the way homes are financed, but also in the way homes are sold, in the form and structure of the secondary market, in the government's role in the housing market, in the composition of assets held by institutions, and in the general level of risk for individuals. More broadly, for readers to get a rounded view of our reform proposal, they must be aware of the economic theory of the housing market and the housing finance market and key facts concerning the institutional structure and performance record of the current market.

How best to arrange such an intricate tour through both the current institutional realities and a hypothetical vision of an alternative market structure? Given the differing backgrounds of the co-authors, it can be no surprise that the book represents something of a hybrid between the theoretical and statistical approaches of the economics profession and the pragmatic approach of business practitioners. It can also be no surprise that the organization of the book is sufficiently intricate to necessitate our using the first chapter to provide something of a road map for the reader. While many readers will prefer to embark on the journey without reading the map, they may find themselves using it at a later stage to check their coordinates.

If we are correct in our assessment of the potential for equity-type markets in residential housing, this raises a number of very provocative questions. The first is: How could a small group of people with no secret weapons and without need of any flashes of inspiration spot such a huge gap in the market? This is really a reiteration of the point that initially convinced us we would reach a negative conclusion on the potential of these markets: "If this is such a good idea, why has nobody done it already?" Of course there can be no simple one-line answer to such a profound question, but it is nevertheless worth pondering.

One part of the answer is that the potential for the development of Partnership Markets rests on recent technological advances, and in particular, the widespread computerization of financial services. We believe that in financial markets as well as production applications, the United States and other advanced industrialized countries are now entering the more mature part of the innovation phase, in which the new possibilities opened up by the information age can be explored at greater depth. The Partnership Market is in this sense just a small part of a far broader set of changes the information age has made possible.

But the connection between technological change and institutional change is not a simple one. As individuals we can each get stuck in outmoded patterns of behavior, and to think that the institutions with which we live will be inertia free is to miss a painful amount of the action (and inaction) with which we are surrounded. Practices and customs, once they form, often prove hard to change, and there is resistance to change unless it can be convincingly demonstrated that the new model significantly outperforms the old. While some inertia is rational, we believe that there are times and places in which there is excessive inertia, the institutions of housing finance being a case in point.

Very high levels of inertia are at once a major problem for the economy, a major challenge for economic theorists, and a major opportunity for dedicated students and proponents of rational reform. Our deepest hope is that this book and the response to it provide a positive example of how responsible discussion of a reform proposal can lower resistance to change and also how the political and institutional structure can respond with an open mind to the challenge a new idea represents.

Of course, it is also possible that our ideas are wrong or poorly timed, and that someone out there will discover their fatal flaw. Either way, writing the book was a profoundly engaging experience and was (almost) reward enough for the authors. We hope that some of our excitement rubs off on the reader.

Acknowledgments

We would like to thank Jan Brueckner, William Goetzmann, John Leahy, and Robert Shiller for their valuable contributions to the ideas developed in this book. We would also like to thank Terry Vaughn of The MIT Press for his constant support for our efforts, as well as Victoria Richardson, Melissa Vaughn, and their colleagues at The MIT Press for their significant and imaginative work on our behalf. We also thank Bob Reed for his creativity in developing and executing a marketing strategy for our ideas. Finally, we thank Ed Moed, Steve Cody, and Pete Harris of Peppercom for helping us to communicate our ideas to the widest possible audience.

Andrew dedicates the book to his wife Ruth Wyatt in celebration of their new joint life, which includes sharing in the development of the ideas in the book, and to his brother Adam with love, understanding, and optimism. Sewin dedicates the book to Mama and Baba with much love and gratitude for their endless support and understanding. Charlie dedicates the book to his wife Mary Ann, and to his children, Heather and Thomas, without whose love and support none of this work would have been possible. Joe dedicates the book to the memory of Truman G. Tracy, a great educator and a great father, to his wife Ellen Carter, and to his children, Matthew, Audrey, and Phillip.

1   Introduction

1.1   Overview

The book has five parts. Part 1 lays out core aspects of the current housing and housing finance market.

• Chapter 2 describes the nature of the choice between renting and buying a home in the current U.S. housing market.

• Chapter 3 describes the structure of the U.S. primary mortgage market.

• Chapter 4 describes the broader economic context of housing market decisions.

• Chapter 5 describes the financial risks involved in owning a home.

Chapters 4 and 5 give the most complete description of the economic impact of the current U.S. housing and housing finance market and provide the most complete picture of the many motivations underlying the reform proposal. They stress three factors that get short shrift in classical treatments of the economic structure of the housing market: the fundamental indivisibility between ownership and rental, the relation of housing to the life-cycle pattern of consumption, and the interaction between housing choices and the profile of portfolio risk for households over the course of the life cycle.

With this groundwork in place, part 2 provides an introduction to the Partnership Market.

• Chapter 6 introduces the market and outlines the basic gains from trade on which the market would rest.

• Chapter 7 illustrates the new options the Partnership Market would make available to potential home owners.

• Chapter 8 outlines some of the many different ways households might use Partnership Markets to alter their pattern of housing consumption, nonhousing consumption, and portfolio risk over the course of their life cycle.

With the basic contractual and economic background in place, part 3 continues the virtual tour of the Partnership Market by providing details of the institutional structure of its supply side.

• Chapter 9 presents details of the proposed Partnership Contract.

• Chapter 10 outlines a secondary market structure for Partnerships that builds on the model set by the existing secondary mortgage market.

• Chapters 11 and 12 outline both the current primary mortgage market structure and the proposed structure of the primary Partnership Market.

• Chapter 13 surveys and extends theoretical and empirical studies relevant to the pricing of Partnership Contracts.

The profound change in financing we are proposing would significantly change the nature of transactions, incentives, and information flows, and the balance of power in the market. To continue our virtual tour of the Partnership Market, part 4 describes these changes according to the stage of home ownership in which they would occur.

• Chapter 14 outlines the impact of Partnership Agreements on the process of buying a home.

• Chapter 15 outlines the impact of Partnership Agreements on life while the home is occupied and at the point of sale.

Part 5 outlines the impact of Partnership Markets on federal housing policy and also steps back to examine how the markets would affect the broader economy.

• Chapter 16 explores the intriguing possibilities for using Partnership Agreements to further the goals of federal housing policy.

• Chapter 17 addresses the impact of Partnership Markets on the behavior of the broader housing market and also of asset markets.

• Chapter 18 speculates on institutional aspects of Partnership Markets. Why do we believe the United States is ready for Partnership Markets, and are there other reforms that one can envisage taking place as the institutions of housing finance develop?

In concluding remarks, we question whether the housing finance market is the only market at a crossroads.

1.2 Guide to Chapter 2: Buy or Rent?

One of our goals is to assess the nature of the choice among owning a home outright, partially owning the home, and renting the home in the U.S. housing market. To begin our assessment, Chapter 2 focuses on what is known about the forces that determine tenure choice in the current housing market. Section 2.1 presents facts about tenure choice drawn from the 1990 census. The analysis centers on the age-tenure profile, which shows that the ownership rate peaks for households in their late fifties, with a steep falloff for households aged forty and younger. We also outline some dynamic aspects of the ownership structure, including the recent decline in ownership rates for younger households.

In section 2.2 we catalog the forces widely believed to exert important influences on household preferences between owning and renting a home. Home owners with a mortgage receive two rather obvious financial benefits: housing appreciation in the medium term and the tax advantage provided by the mortgage interest deduction and the nontaxation of imputed rents. Owning a home also has many nonfinancial advantages including the quality of owner-occupied housing, which is typically higher than that of rental accommodations, as it is hard to provide sufficient incentives for tenants to adequately take care of rental property.

Given the advantages of ownership, why do 36% of U.S. households rent homes (according to the 1990 census)? For some short-term residents of an area, renting is preferable given ownership's high transactions costs. Some others simply prefer the simplicity of life in rental accommodation, and still others benefit from special deals such as low-price public housing or rent controls that keep payments artificially low. Another large group of "frustrated renters," however, are keen to leave the rental sector but find themselves unable because of the difficulties they encounter in the market for housing finance. Section 2.3 outlines the constraints on ownership of residential homes in the current housing finance market and introduces readers to the complexities of the current mortgage market.

Section 2.4 introduces the idea of housing affordability, which forms the basis for existing approaches to the economics of home ownership, by studying whether a given household can afford a "reasonably priced" home in the area in which they live. Although limited, this approach is historically important as a guide to whether proposed policies would increase the number of potential home owners.

1.3   Guide to Chapter 3: The Mortgage Market and the Budget Set

What is the overall household budget set in the current U.S. mortgage market? Chapter 3 presents a broad picture of how the current U.S. mortgage market functions, with primary focus on the highly standardized A-paper mortgage market. In sections 3.1 through 3.3 we present the basic set of mortgage products available in the housing finance market. We pay particular attention to the most standardized part of the market, comprising primarily conventional mortgages with and without private mortgage insurance (PMI), and the various low-down-payment Federal Housing Administration (FHA) mortgages.

In section 3.4 we provide quantitative assumptions for a series of examples that formalize the qualification criteria for these types of mortgages. In section 3.5 we diagram which households are able to afford a house costing $100,000. Section 3.6 is concerned with how to determine the largest house a given household can afford. We use the diagrams introduced in sections 3.5 and 3.6 in chapter 6 to compare the options open to households in the current market with those that would become available in the Partnership Market.

1.4   Guide to Chapter 4: Home Ownership and the Life Cycle

Chapter 4 explores the impact of ownership's costs and risks on the household's broader consumption and asset allocation decisions. We adopt a perspective based on following a household over the course of the life cycle, commensurate with our stress on the age-tenure relationship in chapter 2.

Section 4.1 discusses precisely how the housing market affects the behavior of younger households, which for purposes of statistical illustration we take to be those less than forty years of age. We document both these households' very high loan-to-value (LTV) ratios on their home and their very high annual payments of principal, interest, taxes, and insurance on the house in proportion to income (the PITI ratio). We discuss the familiar phenomenon of young, "house poor" households living in enforced frugality in a valuable house, as often happens when they have managed to buy. There is evidence of an even more severe squeeze on consumption in the period leading up to home occupation, as the household struggles to acquire an adequate down payment. Just how severely the household must restrict consumption to save for the down payment is, in fact, one of the most important determinants of who can own a home.

Section 4.2 presents examples to illustrate how this decision might look to the household. It documents just how much saving for a down payment can strain a young household, and the resulting long stay in the rental sector.

Sections 4.3 and 4.4 outline the experience of households in their later years, focusing on older owners' apparently high levels of inertia, which manifest themselves in occupancy times far longer than average. But more significantly, a sizable set of older owners live in valuable homes, do not take out any second mortgages, and appear to have very little income and therefore very low levels of consumption.

Section 4.5 documents the nature of the housing market experience for households in their middle years (forty to fifty-nine). Once the young household has lived in the house a while, the consumption squeeze can be expected to lessen as income rises and the burdensome expenses of the initial home purchase become a distant memory. But even at this stage, the housing market involves profound risks, and there is evidence that payment problems may continue well into the middle years.

1.5   Guide to Chapter 5: Home Ownership and Risk

Chapter 5 documents the great risks involved in owning a home. We provide information on the high variability of individual house prices in section 5.1. Section 5.2 addresses the correlation between house price risk and income risk, which results from the fact that the negative shocks to an area that cause house prices to fall frequently have an adverse impact on earnings also, as in the Texas oil bust of the early 1980s.

Section 5.3 introduces the many risks households face because of high leverage. Many households take on an uncomfortably high level of debt to buy a house. If income falls and the household has trouble making the mortgage payments, they risk a significant consumption squeeze and may even be forced to default on the mortgage. The volatility of house prices heightens the danger of default or even bankruptcy, so that the house at times is worth less than the outstanding mortgage. Besides default and bankruptcy, a fall in house value of this kind can lead to such problems as the inability to refinance the home to take advantage of a reduction in interest rates, as occurred in many states in the early 1990s, and inability to relocate to take advantage of superior income prospects. Section 5.4 documents that many households hold a massive proportion of their asset portfolio in owner-occupied housing.

1.6   Guide to Chapter 6: Introduction to the Partnership Market

The "all-or-nothing" constraint on home ownership forces households to make the stark choice between rental accommodations' disadvantages and complete ownership's harsh financial realities. In classical economic terminology, the current housing market has a major indivisibility. Because one cannot own only part of a house, owners are forced to tie their housing consumption decision to their asset accumulation and portfolio decisions. Households may wish to live in large houses without wanting either to spend a vast proportion of their income on housing or risk a large proportion of their wealth on the fate of their property and the surrounding housing market. Simply stated, our proposal involves relaxing this constraint.

We propose that housing be financed with not only a mortgage but also an institutional investor that provides equity capital for the house in exchange for a proportion of the ultimate sale price.[1] We believe the Limited Partnership, briefly introduced in section 6.1, is the institutional and legal structure best suited to this market. One of its advantages is that casting the investor as a Limited Partner removes any personal liability arising from ownership. Hereafter we refer to the household that takes occupancy of the home as the Managing Partner, and the financial institution that co-owns the asset as the Limited Partner.

In the simplest Partnership Contracts, the basic financial transaction would involve the Managing Partner's supplying funds up front in exchange for a fixed proportion of the ultimate sale price of the house, with no other monetary payments made between the parties. From the household's viewpoint, it is key that obtaining Partnership finance not dilute their fundamental need for control over the property they occupy. The Managing Partner would retain complete control and use of the space for an unlimited time and would be penalized only for decisions that harm the Limited Partner, such as failing to maintain the property.

The broad goals of the Partnership Contract are outlined in section 6.1, as is a market structure in which the broad financial community would supply funds to the Partnership Market in exchange for securities comprising bundles of Limited Partnership Agreements.

Although many households might be pleased to sell part of their home to reduce their mortgage costs and financial risks, exactly who would buy these shares is not immediately apparent. Why would anyone be willing to pay a reasonable price for the Limited Partner's share of the property, especially if they would have no rights of occupation? Why do we believe there would be a natural market in shares in residential homes?

To answer this question, we must identify the gains from trade in the Partnership Market. The simplest way to see these gains is to note that the household that currently owns 100% of the property in which they reside will place a lower value on the "second half" of the home than will many other asset holders, especially the institutional investors whom we see as the ultimate suppliers of Partnership funds. In section 6.2, we expand on the importance of three key factors in explaining why institutional investors might actually be willing to pay more for what appears to be less than a pro-rata share of the house: household risk aversion, household impatience, and institutional demand for residential real estate returns.

Sections 6.3 and 6.4 illustrate through numerical exercises the significant quantitative importance of the gains from trade identified in section 6.2. In many cases, the second half of ownership in a given housing asset may prove to have considerably more value to institutional portfolio investors than to the individual home owner. In this light, Partnership Markets offer a far better vehicle for investing in residential property than is currently available, in part because the home owner is a highly efficient and well-incentivized property manager.

As the illustration of the gains from trade does not directly enable us to predict the actual prices of Limited Partnerships, we classify them according to potential payout. *Partnerships at par* offer to pay a pro-rata proportion of the property's initial appraisal value, *partnerships at discount* offer to pay less than a pro-rata proportion, and *partnerships at premium* offer to pay more.

Chapter 13 takes up Partnership pricing in more detail, but in chapters 7 and 8 we concentrate on Partnerships at par.

1.7   Guide to Chapter 7: New Options for Home Ownership

Chapter 7 provides a series of numerical examples to illustrate the various uses to which households can put Partnership Agreements and should help the reader gauge Partnership financing's potential to enable households to cut the costs of a given home and raise nonhousing consumption, move to a better home, and reduce portfolio risk.

Section 7.1 takes up cost savings, using numerical examples first introduced in chapter 3 to illustrate the options available to households seeking to buy a $100,000 home in the current mortgage market. A simple method is presented for graphing the Partnership Market's potential reduction in both down payment and annual carrying costs.

Section 7.2 explores trade-up possibilities with Partnerships, building on the analysis in section 3.4, which characterized the houses a household can afford according to cash available at closing and annual income. Many households, as the section makes abundantly clear, could afford far larger houses with Partnership finance than in the existing market. Section 7.3 presents a quantitative analysis of hybrid options, in which the home buyer decides to both trade up to a larger home and spend less up front and in annual installment payments. Section 7.4 illustrates how the price of the Partnership Agreement would affect the household's available savings and trade-up possibilities.

1.8   Guide to Chapter 8: Partnerships and the Life Cycle

Over the course of the life cycle, households would probably use Partnerships for different reasons. When young, the household would care most about using the Partnership to speed up the transition from rental to ownership and to spend less on the mortgage, freeing resources for consumption. For those in the middle years, risk reduction might be more important as they look for a portfolio less dominated by an idiosyncratic housing asset. The Partnership would offer older households the ability to consume more without losing owner occupation and incurring debt. Chapter 8 considers these themes both quantitatively and qualitatively.

Section 8.1 illustrates the potential for partnerships to ease the household's transition from renting to owner occupation. Beginning with chapter 5's numerical illustrations of current-market waiting time, the section shows that in many cases Partnerships could cut in half the time required for a young household to save for a home while also allowing them greater levels of consumption. Section 8.2 explores how Partnerships could reduce the risk of negative equity and negative net worth in a household's middle years.

Section 8.3 uses historical data to show how much Partnerships would offer older households by highlighting the potential differences between the retirement portfolios of an older household that buys a home under a

Partnership Contract, and one that uses a regular mortgage. The household using a Partnership would have additional funds to invest in other assets, and would wind up having not only a significantly higher level of wealth but also a greater concentration in forms more liquid than the owner-occupied home. Section 8.4 provides a qualitative overview of the dynamic nature of the Partnership Market. It raises the issue of how a household would determine its optimal use of the Partnership Market over the life cycle.

1.9   Guide to Chapter 9: The Partnership Contract

In chapter 9 we provide details of the Partnership Contract. The chapter opens with a more detailed institutional and legal introduction to the Limited Partnership format that underlies our contractual proposal. It is important to recognize that although the Partnership Contract involves several new clauses, it breaks no new ground in a legal or a conceptual sense but is simply a customized form of a standard contract concerning joint ownership. As such, it can be based almost entirely on clauses standard in a wide variety of existing markets in which joint ownership is common. The only subtle issue would be the need to customize certain parts of the standard partnership agreement to cover incentive issues particular to the residential real estate market.

In Section 9.2 we present details of the contract clauses that would apply at the time of home purchase and formation of the agreement. These primarily concern information both parties would require to enter into the contract, including information on the Limited Partner's past financial and housing market behavior and on the house itself. Section 9.3 presents the clauses designed to ensure that the Managing Partner would maintain the house properly, and Section 9.4 presents those relating to home improvements. In summary, the Managing Partner would be required to

• remain in occupation of the property until sold,

• not encumber or borrow against the Limited Partner's ownership share in the property, and

• go through appropriate certification procedures to adjust the ownership share for improvements made to the property.

Section 9.5 details clauses that would relate to the sales process for the house, and section 9.6 details clauses and procedures that would be relevant to breach of contract and its remedies. These clauses cover such issues as preventing "fire sales" and artificially low-priced sales to related parties, and the procedure for dissolving the Partnership should either party breach their obligations under the Partnership Agreement.

Section 9.7 covers some important questions relating to the interaction between the Partnership Contract and the mortgage contract.

In our view, the issues of additional control and notification required of the Managing Partner would be unlikely to be of serious importance to most potential home owners. In fact, the implicit restrictions in the proposed Partnership Contract are less severe than those that currently exist for housing units having common property.[2] Even for traditional single-owner properties, local zoning and other regulations also provide various, and sometimes severe, limitations on the home owner's complete freedom of action.

1.10   Guide to Chapter 10: Secondary Partnership Markets

At the point of origination, the Limited Partner would own an investment with acceptable return properties but an uncertain maturity. So one of the Limited Partner's first concerns would be the ability to recognize financial gain by selling off the Partnership Agreement at a fair price to a mass market without waiting for the uncertain termination. This would require the development of an active secondary market in Partnerships with many similarities to the existing secondary mortgage market. This market is described in Chapter 10.

Section 10.1 describes the current U.S. secondary mortgage market, which provides the institutional model for the secondary Partnership Market. In the United States today, huge volumes of individual mortgages are purchased by market-making intermediaries, primarily the three federally sponsored agencies: the Federal National Mortgage Association (FNMA), Government National Mortgage Association (GNMA), and Federal Home Loan Mortgage Association (Freddie Mac). These mortgages are then grouped into larger pools and sold to institutional investors. The large institutional investors thus end up providing funds for residential mortgages.

Section 10.2 presents our proposal for developing secondary markets in Partnership Agreements. As in the secondary mortgage market, it would be necessary for a specialist to "bundle" individual Limited Partnership Contracts into larger, well-defined investment pools in which investors could buy shares. We envision the specialist's buying the Partnership

Contracts, holding them in portfolio, and issuing shares on the underlying baskets (fund shares). The specialist could choose to split up the portfolio into geographic baskets (region, state, metropolitan statistical area (MSA), zip code) or along a variety of other dimensions depending on the desires of the fund shares' institutional holders and any pertinent guidelines provided by government policy makers.

Section 10.3 presents our reasons for believing that the development of secondary markets in Limited Partnerships would have exciting side benefits. The secondary market would offer an intriguing set of new investment vehicles with potential appeal not only to institutional investors but also to households interested in hedging their bets in the housing market or saving for a larger house. Specifically, we would expect a market to develop for the trading of futures, forwards, and derivatives in Partnership fund shares. Many parties in the housing market anticipate changing their exposure to the market at some point (e.g., a home buyer or builder who has contracted to purchase or sell in six months). We believe the natural evolution of options on Partnership fund shares would allow such hedging.

1.11   Guide to Chapters 11 and 12: The Primary Markets

One of the important issues should the Partnership Markets take off is that the process of applying for Partnership finance not be radically more costly, time consuming, or complex than the process in the current mortgage market. Before explicitly suggesting an outline of just such a simple application procedure in chapter 12, we look at the current primary mortgage market in chapter 11.

In section 11.1 we describe how a household is prequalified, selects a mortgage and so forth in the existing market and also outline the mortgage application process. Section 11.2 describes the screening, verification, and other behind-the-scenes activities from the time the application has been submitted and reviewed through to the process's conclusion: either a granted mortgage or a withdrawal from the mortgage market. Section 11.3 provides a picture of the massive range of products available to a mortgage applicant. Section 11.4 provides a glimpse of the industry structure that has developed to fill the roles required for the efficient functioning of the U.S. primary mortgage market.

Sections 12.1 through 12.4 run analogous discussions in the context of the proposed primary Partnership Market. Section 12.1 covers issues until the point of application for the Partnership; section 12.2 looks behind the scenes as the application is processed and the reply is given; section 12.3 outlines the range of potential Partnership products, standardized and nonstandardized, and also looks at the precise contract clauses and ultimate equity shares; and section 12.4 comments on the industry structure likely to emerge to ensure efficient functioning of the Partnership Market. One of the chapter's important themes is that there would be no single unified Partnership Market, but rather a complex of markets at least as diverse as the existing mortgage market.

1.12   Guide to Chapter 13: Pricing Partnerships

Chapter 13 studies the pricing of Partnerships, combining a highly empirical analysis aimed at exploring the lessons of historical real estate returns for potential Limited Partners with a set of theoretical considerations as to how these historically based exercises would have to be adapted to analyze Partnership pricing more accurately. We find that the assumption of a price at or close to par for Partnerships is not an unreasonable starting point, but we also acknowledge the many difficulties involved in any more detailed attempt to estimate Partnership prices.

Since much of the analysis involves understanding the past behavior of real estate price indices, we outline the profound measurement problems in the real estate market. In section 13.1 we discuss the conceptual difficulties involved in measuring real estate prices to encourage caution in reading the empirical analyses that follow. In section 13.2 we survey existing literature on the potential role of real estate in asset portfolios, prominently featuring the work of Goetzmann (Goetzmann 1993 and Goetzmann and Ibbotson 1990). In section 13.3 we provide simple adaptations of Goetzmann's approach to estimate that the potential demand for residential Limited Partnerships at a price close to par is potentially very large: one reason for this is that the risks in the real estate market have a relatively low historical correlation with those in the stock market. Real estate is also a good hedge against inflation.

Section 13.4 outlines the adjustments necessary to estimate Limited Partnership prices from our estimates of historical housing returns. Sections 13.5 through 13.7 then discuss three specific adjustments in somewhat greater detail.

Section 13.5 explores whether Partnerships might be more valuable than historical estimates suggest because they would open up new forms of insurance and classes of investment opportunity. Section 13.6 outlines some issues of self-selection that might cause Partnership values to follow a somewhat different dynamic than the average pattern of house prices. Section 13.7 explores various transactions costs that might reduce the value of Partnership Agreements.

1.13   Guide to Chapter 14: Partnerships and Purchasing a Home

Chapter 14 explores the impact of Partnership Markets on searching for and buying a home. The introduction of Partnership Markets would profoundly change the microeconomic structure of the housing market. The most obvious issue is that the Partnership Contract would involve a somewhat altered contractual setting for the home's occupant because of differences between the clauses of the Partnership Contract outlined in chapter 9 and those of existing mortgage contracts. But some potentially even more significant changes would take place. To describe the housing market experience with Partnerships in a rounded manner, we focus not only on the changes Partnerships would create during home occupation but also on the profound potential changes in other aspects of the housing market.

In section 14.1 we describe key aspects of the home search in the current residential real estate market. For most buyers, the key guide in the search is the real estate broker. Unfortunately, the buyer's real estate broker typically is paid by the seller a percentage of the house's final sales price. The broker's basic incentive is to make the deal happen and at as high a price as possible. While using a buyer's agent can somewhat offset this agency problem, we document the numerous incentive and informational problems that remain even with the use of such an agent, problems that run from agent to appraiser to structural engineer to mortgage banker.

Sections 14.2 through 14.4 detail the problems buyers face in the current housing market. These incentive problems provide the cornerstone of a common experience known as "buyer's remorse." Section 14.5 describes how the Partnership Market would mitigate many of the incentive problems. We believe that in the end the house purchase experience would change profoundly, because in most circumstances, the Managing Partner and the Limited Partner would share many interests, such as the desire to pay as little as possible for the house. A basic realignment of incentives would occur in the presence of a Limited Partner with financial interests closely aligned with those of the home owner, real estate expertise and a powerful position as supplier of capital in the real estate market. In the current housing and housing finance markets no one has incentives that align this well with the household's.

1.14   Guide to Chapter 15: Partnerships and the Ownership Experience

Chapter 15 continues tracing changes Partnerships would generate in the housing market. Section 15.1 assesses the changes that would take place during normal occupation of the home, with the most significant alteration being the need to supply additional information if the household decided to undertake major upgrades to the property. In return for this, the household would obtain increased information about the probable resale value of these upgrades.

Section 15.2 addresses issues concerning breach of the Partnership Contract. Such a situation would in many ways be very similar to what currently happens when households default on a mortgage. One difference would be that the presence of a Limited Partner might allow the parties involved in the breach to arrive at a more cooperative agreement than obtains in the current market. In the existing market, for example, households who have defaulted on their mortgage commonly declare bankruptcy and try to stay in the home as long as possible. It is well known in the real estate finance industry that this final period of home occupation can involve a very rapid deterioration in the property, since the occupants have lost all incentives for even minimal maintenance. In fact, in some cases damage is deliberately inflicted on the property by delinquent tenants, who may reason that a damaged property is less of a priority in eviction proceedings. Since the Limited Partner would have an incentive to make a reasonable offer to buy out the Managing Partner and provide rental accommodation, Partnership Markets might prevent such episodes of deterioration and destruction.

Section 15.3 contrasts the sales process with and without Partnerships. The Partnership Contract would add a structure to the sales process that would make it less likely for the property to be sold at a "fire sale" price when the Managing Partner wished to sell. This might be of particular value if the Managing Partner experienced a liquidity squeeze because they were forced to relocate and their housing market was slow. On the other hand, the Partnership Agreement would make the sales process even more complex than it currently is. Our overall view is that there are real trade-offs in the housing market experience with and without Partnerships. For those powerfully averse to engaging in any new and unfamiliar transactions, the Partnership Market might not be appealing. On the other hand, many potential home owners might prefer the risk reduction involved in having a Limited Partner join them in purchasing their home.

1.15   Guide to Chapter 16: Partnerships and Federal Policy

The federal government has a long history of involvement in the U.S. residential housing market. One of the fundamental tenets underlying federal policy has been the desire to increase home ownership. In chapter 16 we lay out some opportunities for Partnership Agreements to improve the direction of federal housing-market policy.

Section 16.1 outlines the main tools of current U.S. housing market policy, including the very costly mortgage interest deduction, the many federally subsidized loan programs offered by FHA and by the Veterans' Administration (VA), and the subsidies to various types of public housing. In all cases, Partnership Markets could be used to improve the performance of these policies without any increase in cost. For example, the ability to interest Limited Partners in investing in properties with FHA borrowers depends on policies the federal government sets through the Department of Housing and Urban Development (HUD) and through its own influence on the agencies. What appears certain is that if the federal agencies involved responded wisely, Partnership Markets would open possibilities to expand opportunities for first-time home buyers without increasing the subsidies.

Section 16.2 presents our basic idea that applying various types of federal subsidy to Partnership schemes would introduce a new method for supporting the development of affordable housing and helping neighborhoods and population groups targeted by specific federal initiatives. In fact, a simple variant of the Partnership idea has already been tried in several other countries to reduce some problems in public housing projects. In several countries, Partnership-like structures have been used both to encourage the occupants of previously public housing projects to make the transition to ownership and to offer young households a cheaper alternative to classical home ownership.

Section 16.3 outlines publicly subsidized shared ownership schemes introduced in the United Kingdom. Although these schemes are young, the evidence suggests that the households that benefit from the scheme

are more than happy with their part ownership. While the publicly subsidized U.K. system differs significantly from our conception, we nevertheless find the U.K. experience encouraging.

Section 16.4 presents an altogether different viewpoint on the history
of federal policy in the residential housing market, which in our view
includes some interesting success stories along with the standard litany
of failures. Specifically, a strong argument can be made that some of the
market innovations the federal agencies initially pushed have strongly and
positively affected the market. The FHA mortgage program first introduced the thirty-year fixed-rate mortgage, and only after the program
was established as successful did private thirty-year mortgages take off. In
addition, the huge secondary market in mortgages resulted from several
federal interventions in the market. We end the section by suggesting that
the federal government might also play an important leadership role in
the Partnership Market, a topic taken up in more detail in chapter 18.

1.16   Guide to Chapter 17: Partnerships and the Broader Economy

Partnerships are such a major innovation that important impacts would be
felt everywhere in the economy. Chapter 17 takes up the issues raised by
these effects in the appropriately speculative fashion, beginning with a
discussion of the impacts on the broader housing market and the housing
finance market. The discussion of these markets in section 17.1 involves
outlining the short- and long-run impacts of Partnership Markets on supply and demand. But a number of more unusual impacts would be worthy
of discussion. What impact would Partnerships have on the volatility of
the housing market? What impact would Partnership Markets have on the
evolution of rental markets? We provide some highly tentative comments
on these questions in section 17.2. Section 17.2 also outlines some of the
broader asset-market impacts of Partnership Markets.

In section 17.3 we present an introductory analysis of the determinants
of an optimal set of housing finance institutions. One of the most valuable
aspects of this highly preliminary exercise is that it may help pinpoint
some directions in which the housing finance market will evolve.

**1.17   Guide to Chapter 18: Institutional Angles on Partnership
Markets**

The current housing finance market is a complex web of institutions. The
Partnership Markets we suggest are equally complex but very different. It

is not possible to fully understand the role these markets would play without explicitly recognizing the broad importance of market institutions and the forces that determine the evolution of these institutions. Chapter 18 outlines some important angles suggested when one focuses on the institutional aspects of Partnership Markets.

Section 18.1 outlines some technological determinants of the structure of market institutions and explains some reasons the advent of the information age is a key reason Partnership Markets seem far more plausible today than they would have in past decades. This section also presents our view that the United States today already possesses an institutional infrastructure particularly well suited to the development of Partnership Markets.

Two markets in particular are at an advanced stage in the United States that we view as critical to the successful introduction of Partnership Agreements: first, the massive secondary mortgage market that distinguishes the United States from most other countries, and second, the vast information services that exist in the U.S. credit market. The development of these information services has been key to that of a standardized market for consumer lending that is not based on a close relationship between the individual and the banker. This impersonal information structure is crucial to the development of a commodity market in residential housing equity.

It is important to recognize that technology alone does not determine the nature of the current institutions of housing finance. Another important determining factor is the complex amalgam of historically based institutions, many of which have survived virtually unchanged for many years in the face of a rapidly changing environment. In section 18.2 we outline the institutional inertia in the U.S. housing finance market that has resulted in many failed efforts to reform the market.

Will this inertia act as an impenetrable barrier to Partnership Markets? This is certainly one possibility in light of the history sketched in section 18.2. Moreover, we are well aware of the unprecedented scale of the changes we are proposing. The successful introduction of Partnerships would involve a vast and interlocking set of market adjustments. For this reason, we believe a key feature of the path to development of Partnership Markets is the need for some player to take a leading role in coordinating market developments, as we outline in section 18.3.

In the United States, the obvious candidates for market leaders are FNMA, Freddie Mac, and HUD: the "Big Three" of the housing finance market. Since all three were set up by Congress, they can largely be considered appendages of the federal government. Their efforts at housing market reform are largely driven by federal suggestion, and this makes the federal role vital in housing finance reform. We believe the Partnership Market presents a major opportunity for the federal government, possibly through the three existing housing market agencies, FNMA, GNMA, and Freddie Mac, to become a coordinator and leader of a significant effort to encourage innovation. The issue of whether the federal role in the housing market is part of the problem or part of the solution is addressed in section 18.4.

1.18 Concluding Remarks

Our concluding remarks address what we see as the main contributions of this book in the broad context of policy and institutional analysis. We then discuss what we feel is new about our approach to the housing finance market, and why we believe that many markets other than the housing finance market are at their own crossroads.

I The Mortgage Market and the Housing Market

2   Buy or Rent?

2.1 Some Facts

A useful way to gain insight into the pattern of tenure choice in the United States is to plot the basic age-tenure profile extracted from the 1990 census data. Figure 2.1 shows the proportion of households that own rather than rent homes according to the age of the head of household. There is only a 10% ownership rate among households headed by twenty-year-olds, with a rapid increase in the ownership rate for older households and a rate of close to 70% for households headed by forty-year-olds. The ownership rate peaks at roughly 80% when the head of household is about sixty, and thereafter shows a gradual decline to below 70% when the head of household is older than 80.

Another factor affecting the ownership rate is household status.[1] In the United States, getting married and having young children are important life-cycle events that spur households to try to enter the ownership sector of the housing market. Figure 2.2 shows that according to the 1990 census, the age-tenure profile for unmarried households lies everywhere below the age-tenure profile for the married population.

In addition to demographic factors, evidence clearly shows economic factors influence the ownership rate. Households that have higher levels of income have higher ownership rates. Figure 2.3 provides one simple illustration by showing that the higher quintiles in the income distribution have higher ownership rates across all age groups.

More broadly, it appears that among households, a subtle mix of economic and demographic forces influence tenure choice. Supply side factors also play an interesting role. Urban and nonurban areas in the United States show very different ownership rates, and there are also wide differences across urban areas. In 1980 home ownership rates varied across standard metropolitan statistical areas (SMSAs) from a low of 29.7% in

Percentage of
owners

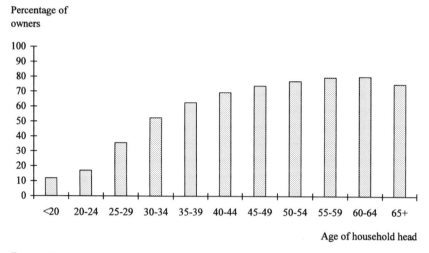

Age of household head

Figure 2.1
Home ownership rates by age
Source: The 1990 census.

Percentage of
owners

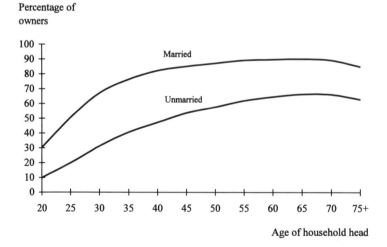

Age of household head

Figure 2.2
Home ownership rates by age and family type
Source: The 1990 census.

Percentage of
owners

Figure 2.3
Home ownership rates by age and family income quintile
Source: The 1990 census.

New York to a high of 79.4% (see Eilbott and Binkowski 1985). This variation partly reflects differences in the populations and partly the comparative strength of rental markets in, say, New York as opposed to most other parts of the country.

In the United States as in many other countries, home ownership is viewed not only as conferring certain private economic advantages to owners, but also as creating positive social spillovers. This has prompted considerable interest in the prospective changes in the ownership rate, and many policies have been developed with the aim of increasing it. Figure 2.4 provides basic data on postwar changes in home ownership. The pattern involves a steady increase in the ownership rate from 1945 to 1975, followed by a leveling off since then, with even the hint of a slight decline in the most recent period.

Despite the stable ownership rate overall, the composition of owners has shifted significantly since 1975. Older households have shown an increased ownership rate, while younger households have had significant declines.

2.2   Household Preferences

How do we explain the pattern of home ownership? One key component is to understand the factors that influence household preferences between

Percentage of owners

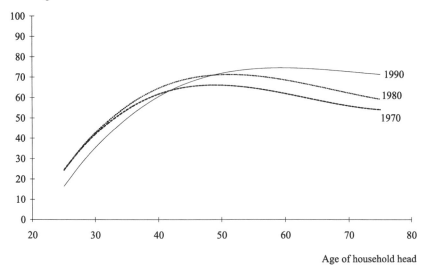

Figure 2.4
Home ownership rates by age
Source: The 1970, 1980, and 1990 census.

owning and renting. We briefly outline the factors that typically contribute to forming a household's desire to make the leap from the rental market to the ownership sector.

Financial Incentives
Among the most easily recognized and important factors are the financial incentives provided by the federal, state, and local tax codes. These tax codes provide important incentives for owning a home, including the mortgage interest deduction, nontaxation of imputed rent, deductibility of property taxes, deductibility of points, and the deferral and partial exemption of house price gains from the capital gains tax.

Households can claim both the interest paid on residential mortgages and property taxes as a deduction against federal as well as most state and local income taxes. These deductions allow households to lower their tax bill at the same time they take ownership of the housing asset. The mortgage interest deduction results in something of a bias against renters as opposed to owners within the tax codes.[2] These deductions also cost a great deal in lost tax revenues, with the latest Congressional Budget Office (CBO) estimate that the interest deduction costs the federal government $60 billion annually.[3]

Another financial incentive stressed by many (especially real estate brokers) is that renting a property may be seen as throwing money away relative to owning a home, under the premise that the home owner gradually builds financial equity as the mortgage is paid down. While it is indeed true that over the long haul, national real estate indices show a reasonable pattern of appreciation, the risks of ownership are nevertheless very significant, making it something of a two-edged sword. Chapters 4 and 5 take up the financial implications of home ownership in more detail.

Transactions Costs
Buying and selling a home involves many transactions costs, some of which are paid at purchase and the remainder at sale. The main transactions costs at point of purchase include costs of closing on the mortgage, title insurance, origination fee, and lawyers' fees. Together, these costs range from 3% to 5% of the price of the typical house purchased with a mortgage. At point of sale, there are many additional transactions costs including the sales commission to the real estate agents and their brokers. In combination, these two-sided transactions costs are commonly estimated to range from 6% to 9% of the home's value; see Dipasquale and Wheaton (1995). Not included in this estimate are the costs of moving and the time costs of searching for a home, which can be very significant at both point of purchase and point of sale. The result is that few people will consider a move lightly.

Transactions costs associated with moving to a rental accommodation are typically far lower. Renting is therefore likely to be the preferred option for households that do not anticipate staying in an area long enough to amortize the fixed costs of purchasing a house. In addition, households new to an area that wish to carry out an extended search for the locality that offers the mix of services and amenities that best suits their needs are likely to rent during this search period. As a result of these forces, renters are more mobile than owners. Figure 2.5 plots data from the 1990 census showing renters' and owners' average time in the current accommodation across all age groups. Not surprisingly, renters have consistently shorter average length of stay in the residence.

The connection between mobility and choice of tenure helps in understanding some of the key qualitative features of the age-tenure profile. Those who are young, single, and without children are frequently very mobile and at this stage often find all the transactions costs associated with ownership an unnecessary burden. The advantages of owning a

Years in current
address

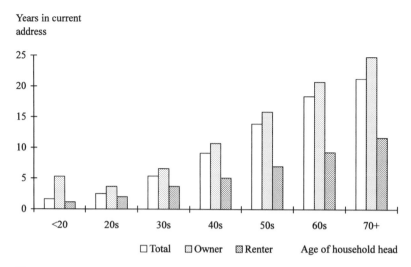

Figure 2.5
Average years in the current address by age
Source: The 1990 census.

home speak loudest to those more settled in their career and lifestyle choices, typically following events such as getting married and having young children.

The Incentive to Retain Control
For many households, the desire to own a home arises not only from an economic calculation involving their taxes and asset position but also from the fact that housing is not a simple, homogeneous commodity. One aspect of this is that rental accommodation offers limitations in control over the space, security of tenure, and security of terms. Standard rental agreements are of a relatively short term (typically annual or monthly) and therefore create uncertainty concerning security of tenure as well as the potential for an increase in rent if an extension is offered.

That these fundamental control rights rest with the landlord is an important issue for many households and has an impact on public policy. Ex post problems arising when landlords choose not to offer contract extensions to existing tenants tend to lead to governmental actions restricting landlords' freedom of action, which in turn give rise to other economic and legal problems. On the other side of this, for some households, the responsibility involved in controlling the property is more of a burden than it is worth, and for these, rental properties have an advantage.

Maintenance Incentives

In terms of the quality of the living units, powerful moral hazard problems in the rental market make it hard to ensure that tenants will invest in the property's upkeep. It is rather difficult to write rental contracts in a manner that will ensure a high standard of maintenance given that the tenant has no ownership interest in the property. Renters therefore must often pay an implicit premium based on the rational anticipation that they will treat the property poorly. This moral hazard issue may also give rise to adverse selection, whereby those who occupy rental property have the least concern for the quality of any property in which they live (Miceli 1989). Adverse selection is often reinforced by the fact that the young, the poor, and the transient residents of an area end up renting.

In fact, problems arising from behavior by tenants who are less than fully responsible are so serious that landlords commonly find it advantageous to periodically monitor properties to prevent damage. The need for a great deal of monitoring and the poor incentives for tenant upkeep of property result in a high proportion of rental properties being in large multifamily units, whose amenities are highly standardized and somewhat spartan. The problems involved in maintaining rental property create an important form of heterogeneity in housing, since these problems often limit the supply of rental homes. As a result, the most desirable homes are in many cases very hard, if not impossible, to rent.

The connection between monitoring problems and the nature of the supply of rental housing helps in understanding some of the exceptions to the rule. Very high quality rental accommodations can be found in some of the more expensive parts of big cities such as Chicago and New York. The very high density of wealthy households that cluster in the neighborhood seems to make these areas exceptional, as well as the fact that the apartment building rather than the single-family detached home is the primary form of residence. This makes these areas logically very well suited to high quality rental accommodation, because a rental high-rise is very easy to maintain. Issues of adverse selection may also be somewhat mitigated by the fact that many of the buildings have monthly rentals in excess of $3,000 per month. However, even within this exception, the story of the nightmare neighbor whom the landlord is unable to control remains legendary.

The Membership Incentive

Owned homes cluster at the higher end of the market not only in quality of the actual housing unit but also in amenities available in the neighborhood.

Ownership is therefore a way to buy into a desirable community with a high level of public services, such as schools, and easy access to work. Communities have an incentive to use zoning regulations to remain predominantly composed of higher-income households that make a net financial contribution to the community by paying high taxes and using few services. Among the common zoning rules are minimum lot-size requirements and maximum density restrictions (i.e. restrictions against multifamily accommodation). Many of these restrictions reduce (or eliminate) the supply of long-term rental housing in many areas with good amenities, making ownership all the more important.

The resulting restriction on the supply of rental housing may please many communities, since owners are widely viewed as better neighbors than renters. Evidence of this sentiment can be found in the survey conducted by Fannie Mae (1994). Roughly 70% of those surveyed would prefer to live in a community with at least 80% owners. Most cited stability of owners as a primary reason. At least half the respondents felt that increased home ownership rates would create and preserve better neighborhoods, increase local voting, and improve neighborhood safety.

In addition, having renters as neighbors is strongly perceived as lowering property values. This question was addressed in a paper by Wang, Grissom, Webb, and Spellman (1991), who carried out an empirical investigation of the determinants of property values in the San Antonio area. They conclude that rental properties on average are valued 3.7% lower than owned properties that are otherwise similar. Further, if at least two of the houses surrounding an owned property are rental, then the value of the owned property is lowered on average by 2%.[4]

2.3 Introduction to the Mortgage Market

As in any market, household preferences only partly explain the observed pattern of choice in the housing market. Costs are the other key component, and the peculiarities of the housing market show up most clearly there. One feature that differentiates housing from most other commodities is the intricate process of qualification required to buy a particular house. Very few households have sufficient wealth to buy their homes outright and so must obtain credit from the mortgage market. Naturally, lenders take steps to assure their loans are reasonably safe, and this ends up locking out many potential buyers.

The procedures put in place to ensure this level of safety constrain many households in their ability to own homes. In broad terms, the current market is structured so that households need three things to qualify for a mortgage:

• *Evidence of willingness to pay*: an acceptable credit history

• *Cash at closing*: enough liquid assets to cover the closing costs, the moving expenses, and the down payment

• *Evidence of ability to pay*: enough income to afford the payments

A deficiency in any one of these areas can rule a household out of the high-quality A-paper mortgage market. It is far more difficult and expensive to obtain loans once rejected from the A mortgage market. Lower-quality B, C, and D markets can be used but are significantly more expensive. The degree of this increased expense is reflected in the small number of loans closed in these higher-risk markets; the B and C markets have an estimated share of about 4.2% of the total mortgage market (see Groves and Prigal 1995).[5]

Credit History as a Constraint
A potential borrower can have several types of problems with their credit history that can constrain their ability to access funding. In the credit test, the borrower and co-borrower (if applicable) have their credit records checked according to several criteria to determine whether they have an A credit rating.[6] The first stage is to call for a report from one of the credit bureaus that specialize in providing information on an individual's credit history. Some common factors demonstrating a borrower's lack of willingness to pay are

• *Bankruptcies and judgments.* Any court judgment or filing is a strong negative indicator. Bankruptcies are supposed to be removed from the credit file after seven years.

• *Derogatory credit lines.* Any recent delinquency on some form of credit, particularly if it is still delinquent, is a serious indicator. Usually some items are excluded, such as amounts under $100, medical bills, or membership fees, since these more often than not represent disputed charges, not a lack of willingness to pay.

• *Inquiries.* A high number of recent inquiries is an indicator of fraud.

• *Credit usage.* Recent higher than normal usage is a negative indicator because people often tap credit when they anticipate financial problems.

Credit bureaus collect information on these and other factors over time. The household's eligibility for A credit is determined using either a

Table 2.1
Freddie Mac industry letter on credit scoring

If the Bureau score is:	Then the recommended approach to reviewing credit is:
Over 660	Underwrite the file as required to confirm the borrower's willingness to repay as agreed.
620 to 660	Underwrite all aspects of the borrower's credit history to establish the borrower's willingness to repay as agreed.
Less than 620	Perform a particularly detailed review of all aspects of the borrower's credit history to ensure that you have satisfactorily established the borrower's willingness to repay as agreed. Unless there are extenuating circumstances, a credit score in this range should be viewed as a strong indication that the borrower does not show sufficient willingness to repay as agreed.

judgmental credit review by an underwriter, who evaluates the information in the credit report against the mortgage bank's credit guidelines, or a more quantitative treatment based on the summary credit scores the credit bureaus report.

Currently lenders place great emphasis on credit scores as the first step in determining whether the household can qualify for an A mortgage. In table 2.1 we reproduce the Freddie Mac industry letter that outlines their suggestion for how these credit scores should be used in determining whether to grant a loan.

Mortgages for some who apply are difficult to underwrite because they either do not have a credit file ("no hits") or lack sufficient data in their credit history to generate a credit score ("thin files"). This is particularly common for groups with little credit history, such as many poor households, younger households, and immigrants.

Income as a Constraint
For those who pass the credit check, a debt/income test follows. The debt/income test checks that the household earns enough to pay off the mortgage in a timely manner. The bank first looks at the household's statements of earnings for the past few years and comes up with its own calculation of adjusted gross income based on these statements. This calculation is trivial if there is a steady job and steady income but involves significant elements of judgment when income shows considerable fluctuations, as it does for many who are self-employed, earn commissions, have substantial overtime, or are in similar situations.

Once this measure of income has been computed, the bank can mechanically compute the borrower's expected level of principal, interest, taxes, and insurance payments (PITI) as a proportion of their income, thereby computing the "front-end ratio." The bank also computes a "back-end ratio" by adding to PITI any recurring monthly obligations, such as debt or lease payments, and measuring this sum as a proportion of income. Applications with front- or back-end ratios above set limits are generally rejected (as an example, 28% for the front, 36% for the back on conforming conventional mortgages). Although the ratios are rarely changed, even in recessions, underwriters have considerable latitude within the definition of what qualifies as income. How much weight one gives to bonuses, overtime, child support, self-employment income, and so on can have a significant impact on the volume of loan approvals.[7]

Liquid Assets as a Constraint

Borrowers are also constrained in their mortgage borrowing activity by their level of liquid assets, which must be sufficient to cover closing costs, moving costs, and the chosen down payment. Liquid assets are also important because any excess in this area can be used as a compensating factor for other borrowing constraints.

One reason that the lender usually requires that the borrower make a down payment on the property is the bonding benefit of having the borrower suffer 100% of the marginal losses if the collateral decreases in value. To ensure this bonding effect, the lender hires an appraiser to value the property. The lender uses the appraised value to calculate the loan-to-value ratio (LTV). A loan application with an LTV at or below 80% is routinely accepted in the A-paper market. As we detail in chapter 3, some A loans allow far lower down payments, involving either private mortgage insurance (PMI), or federally subsidized Federal Housing Administration (FHA) and Veterans Administration (VA) mortgages.

While FHA and VA loans allow the household to relax the liquid-asset constraint to a certain extent, these alternatives are not without cost for the household. Even with federal assistance, there is no free lunch. When one adds all the transactions and closing costs, it is almost impossible for a household to buy a home without available liquid assets of at least 10% of the home's value, and even in this range the market will severely penalize the household for having so few assets available.[8]

Evidence on the Constraints

Overall, the inverted U-shaped age-ownership profile in figure 2.1 reflects differences both in preferences toward ownership and affordability of ownership over the life cycle. A variety of evidence, though, points to affordability as a primary reason households rent instead of own their home, especially younger households.

Varady and Lipman (1994) present survey evidence on the importance of the constraints. They report the findings of a large and careful survey of renter attitudes carried out for the National Association of Realtors (NAR). One of the key questions asked of the sample of renters was whether they planned to buy, and if so, how soon. The responses showed that roughly one in six renters planned to buy within the next two years, and fully two in three planned to buy at some future date. One quarter of those who planned to buy reported that they had already been saving for at least three years to attain their goal of home ownership. This is just one of several questions that showed the strong desire and willingness to sacrifice on the part of households that currently rent but would like to own a home.

Other interesting survey data suggest the important role that saving for the down payment takes in delaying ownership for those who wish to leave the rental sector:

• In the NAR survey, more than 50% of renters reported that their main reason for renting was inability to afford either the mortgage payment or the down payment on an owned home.

• The Fannie Mae *National Housing Survey* (NHS) (1994) also provides general evidence on the importance of the down payment constraint.[9] In the NHS, among renters not likely to buy in the next three years, 74% indicated down payment as an important reason, 65% indicated affordability, and 39% indicated credit problems.

• The time it typically takes a young household to save for a down payment has increased over the past fifteen years. The Chicago Title & Trust Co. conducts regular surveys of first-time and repeat home buyers.[10] For the period from 1976 to 1978, the average time to save among first-time buyers was 2.4 years. For the period from 1991 to 1993, the average time to save increased to 2.8 years. Over this same period, the average down payment fell from 16.5% to 14.3%.

Econometric studies also point to the down payment constraint's importance. Engelhardt and Mayer (1994), using the Chicago Title & Trust data, document the increasing role of gifts in helping first-time buyers overcome the down payment constraint. The data indicate that 22% of first-time buyers receive some gift assistance for the down payment and that the average gift exceeds half the total down payment. Households receiving gifts spend on average ten months less saving for a purchase, have higher debt/income ratios (0.27 for gift recipients vs. 0.24 for non-recipients), and have lower down payment percentages (10% vs. 15%). This evidence is consistent with the view that gifts are an attempt to relax a binding down payment constraint.

An econometric study by Linneman and Wachter (1989), examining data from the 1977 *Survey of Consumer Credit* and the 1983 *Survey of Consumer Finances*, estimated the impact of wealth and income constraints for households that moved in the periods 1975–77 and 1981–83. The wealth constraint was predicted to be binding on 45% of movers in the early period and 40% of movers in the later period. In contrast, the income constraint was predicted to be binding for only 15% of movers in the early period and 27% of movers in the later period. Binding wealth constraints were predicted to lower the probability of buying a house to a much greater extent than binding income constraints.[11]

2.4 The Affordability Approach

A number of studies aim to assess the impact of housing costs on home ownership rates. These studies tend to focus on measuring a concept of "housing affordability" by assessing what percentage of the renting households that live in a given area can afford the estimated costs of an average, or even a "modestly priced," home in the area in which they live. For many reasons, the results of such studies should be interpreted with caution, including the large number of measurement problems and the conceptual problem in matching a renting household with their intended house. For our purposes, these studies' chief value is that they suggest the home ownership rate may not be easy to change absent some fundamental realignment in the relative costs of rental versus owned accommodation.

The most widely known affordability index is published by the NAR. This index, constructed so that a value of 100 implies that the median-income family qualifies for the median-value home, suffers from several problems. First, it considers only income requirements and ignores down payment constraints. Second, it selects an arbitrary household income and household quality (both median) which may not be relevant for particular policy questions (such as housing affordability for young and poor households).

Housing affordability indices are also compiled by the Census Bureau using data from the Survey of Income and Program Participation (SIPP).

The census looks at income, assets and debt to determine the maximum-priced house each household can afford. This is compared to a "criterion" home in the household's area of residence[12] defined as the median-priced home or a modestly priced home (25th percentile). Affordability depends on mortgage type, and both thirty-year conventional fixed-rate mortgages (FRMs) and FHAs are considered (the appropriate average interest rates are used). The standard qualification rules for conforming conventional and FHA loans are used.

Table 2.2 gives tabulations for 1991, the most recent year for which calculations are available. Overall 84% of renters cannot afford a modestly priced home in their area. This figure declines from a high of 95.5% for rental households aged less than twenty-five to 66% for rental households

Table 2.2
1991 Bureau of Census housing affordability

	Housing affordability using FHA fixed-rate thirty-year mortgage			
	Median-priced home		Modestly priced home	
	Owners	Renters	Owners	Renters
% households that cannot afford in their area				
All age groups	33.5	89.7	21.6	84.0
<25	87.7	98.0	78.5	95.5
25–34	55.0	92.2	40.0	87.0
35–44	33.9	89.4	22.3	82.8
45–54	27.8	85.9	17.3	78.7
55–64	22.9	82.4	12.8	76.3
65+	23.4	74.6	10.4	66.0
Reason household cannot afford				
	100.0	100.0	100.0	100.0
Debts too high	17.4	10.5	37.1	20.3
Cannot afford down payment	12.6	18.3	13.4	27.2
Cannot afford monthly payments	39.9	6.7	28.1	4.9
Debts too high and cannot afford monthly payments	14.3	34.4	13.8	29.2
Cannot afford down payment and cannot afford monthly payment	15.8	30.1	7.5	18.3

aged 65 and older. These data suggest that while renting becomes more of a lifestyle choice with age, the current housing finance market imposes significant financial constraints.

A study by Gyourko and Linneman (1993) uses the affordability approach to shed light on why the ownership rate has fallen among younger and less-educated households. The authors measure affordability over time by comparing relative real house prices to relative real incomes for a particular demographic group. They carefully match the demographic group with its particular concentration in the housing quality spectrum. They find that over the past fifteen years, real home prices have appreciated across the quality spectrum. However, real wages have fallen for younger and less-educated households. This suggests the decline in ownership among these households reflects a worsening affordability situation. They conclude that many households in the baby boom generation will only be able to afford homes later in the life cycle than was true for previous generations and that a significant portion may never be able to afford to own a house.

3   The Mortgage Market and the Budget Set

The studies of housing affordability reported in the last chapter hint at the importance of housing costs for the ownership rate, but they provide too incomplete a picture of the housing finance market for our purposes. In this chapter we analyze affordability in more detail by showing how to construct each household's budget set in the current market. Specifically, we construct simple and realistic examples that show how a given household can answer two basic questions. Which houses can we afford to buy? For a house that we can afford, what are the costs involved?

To construct the budget set in full generality, we would have to account for the entire set of different mortgage products available, such as FRMs and adjustable rate mortgages (ARMs), in combination with all the different variables such as household income and mortgage interest rates. The profound complexity of the products and the institutions that constitute the U.S. mortgage market would make this task all the more difficult.

Fortunately, it is enough for our purposes to develop a reasonable first approximation to the current budget set rather than a precise version with all of the bells and whistles. In addition, despite the complexity of the mortgage market, most households choose from a relatively small group of highly standardized products, and in our quantitative analysis we limit attention to these. Specifically, we concentrate exclusively on mortgages in the high-quality A mortgage market introduced in chapter 2. We also limit attention to mortgages on owner-occupied, single-family homes, as opposed to second homes, investor properties, condos, multifamily units, or cooperatives.

3.1   A Simple Guide to the A Mortgage Market

In this section we provide an introductory description of the key products in the A mortgage market, leaving the issue of which household will choose which product for the next section.

The two general categories of mortgage loans are government mortgages and conventional mortgages. Government loans are insured by the FHA or guaranteed by the VA, while conventional loans are not insured or guaranteed by the U.S. government. The FHA and VA are part of the Department of Housing and Urban Development (HUD). The FHA and VA impose a maximum mortgage amount for individual loans and require adherence to their underwriting standards. Although FHA and VA loans are often classed together, they are conceptually distinct. VA loans are restricted to veterans, while FHA loans are available to all.

Government-sponsored mortgages are commonly sold on the secondary mortgage market as Government National Mortgage Association (GNMA) securities. In contrast to government mortgages, not all conventional loans can be sold into the secondary markets. This gives rise to the important distinction between conforming and nonconforming conventional mortgages. The defining characteristic of conforming mortgages is that they can be sold by a lender to the secondary market using guarantees from one of the federally sponsored agencies, the Federal National Mortgage Association (Fannie Mae) or the Federal Home Loan Mortgage Association (Freddie Mac).[1]

A conforming mortgage must meet certain rather detailed guidelines set out by each of the agencies to determine that the mortgage meets their investors' standards of quality, and is an acceptable insurance risk for the agency. The three agencies publish guidelines in the respective seller's guides, which are typically several inches thick.[2] There is a separate book for servicing pools of mortgages.[3]

Nonconforming loans are ineligible for sale to a government-sponsored enterprise (GSE). The most common example is a loan whose principal exceeds the ceiling established by the GSEs (jumbo loans).[4] Additional examples are loans that vary because of financial terms (e.g., below-market teaser rates), property type (e.g., co-ops with fewer than ten units), or due to credit exceptions (e.g., mortgages granted under credit guidelines more lenient than those of the agencies).

An important special class of conforming mortgages are conventional conforming mortgages with private mortgage insurance (PMI). Whether mortgages are offered with or without PMI is determined by the LTV and the desire to sell the mortgage to investors. PMI is typically required on loans with an LTV ratio above 80% and sold to an agency or to a private conduit.

In addition to the basic categorization of products introduced above, there is massive variation in the terms of mortgage products, such as the period of amortization (thirty years and fifteen years being the two most common), and whether the interest rate is fixed or variable (in most periods, fixed-rate mortgages have formed the larger market segment). In the quantitative analysis that follows, we restrict attention to thirty-year mortgages with a fixed interest rate. Chapter 12 paints a more complete picture of the wide variety of different terms available on different mortgage products.

3.2 The Three Basic Products

In the analysis that follows, we restrict attention to three key products that are widely available and that cover the full range of options in terms of qualification criteria and costs:

- conventional conforming mortgages without PMI,
- conventional conforming mortgages with PMI,
- FHA mortgages.

To understand the household budget set, we expand somewhat on the costs and the qualification criteria of these mortgage products. As we will see, the LTV on the loan is a key determinant of product selection, as well as the maximum size constraint in the case of FHA loans.

Conventional Conforming Mortgages without PMI

For those who can afford large down payments, conventional conforming mortgages without PMI are the most economical type. The household must satisfy three conditions to qualify for this type of mortgage:

- passing the A credit test (as outlined in section 2.3),
- passing the front-end and back-end PITI ratio tests (as outlined in section 2.3),
- having sufficient cash at closing to afford a 20% down payment.

Conventional Conforming Mortgages with PMI

Consider a household that has A credit and sufficient income to pass the front-end and back-end PITI tests, but has only enough cash at closing for a 15% down payment. Given that the LTV on the house is above 80%, the agencies insist the household provide some additional assurance against default. Specifically, the agencies insist that the borrower seeking a conventional mortgage with an LTV above 80% and below a maximum of 95% pay the additional fees involved in obtaining PMI. The PMI company insures the holder of the mortgage against losses on the first 20% of the original assessed value of the house.[5] This shifts most of the risk involved in securitizing the mortgage onto the PMI company. Canner, Passmore and Mittal (1994) survey the PMI industry.

The PMI company provides valuable services and charges the mortgage applicant a commensurate fee. One of the more subtle services that the PMI company provides is reviewing the entire mortgage application.[6] If the PMI company accepts the application, they set and charge an additional nonrefundable cost for the household. Apart from enabling the PMI company to profit from their role in the market, these fees help screen applicants by discouraging borrowers who are high risks for quick default.

The pricing of PMI is rather intricate, and varies with the LTV ratio of the underlying mortgage, the level of coverage (the proportion of the debt for which the PMI company is liable), and the underlying property and mortgage type. Fortunately, the agencies specify the minimum level of coverage that the household must purchase across different LTV ratios, and it is these products that we are interested in pricing. We also limit attention to thirty-year fixed-rate mortgages on single-family residences, which further simplifies the pricing.

Even within this narrow category of mortgages, the PMI price will vary with the geographic location of the property, whether the fee is paid up-front or in annual payments (or even a combination of both), how much of the fee gets refunded if the house is sold at an early date, and by the particular PMI company involved. We restrict our attention to the basic price for most of the country. To keep the analysis simple, we also restrict our attention to the pure up-front cost method of payment. We also use refundable premiums because this is what the vast majority of borrowers choose.

In table 3.1 we list the charges for the various different PMI products according to the LTV on the underlying mortgage. We use pricing sheets (as of August 1996) of three of the biggest suppliers of PMI: MGIC, CMAC, and Amerin.

Table 3.1
PMI pricing

Up-front cost	80.1–85% LTV	85.1–90% LTV	90.1–95% LTV
MGIC	2.45	3.35	N.A.
Amerin	2.2	3.05	4.5
CMAC	2.15	2.85	4.1

FHA Mortgages

The FHA offers a wide variety of mortgage programs of special interest to borrowers who require high LTV mortgages. There are some important qualitative differences between FHA mortgages and conventional mortgages, including the fact that FHA loans allow for higher debt ratios, and that the down payment can be borrowed from relatives.[7] In addition, there are standard FHA mortgages that allow the LTV to rise as high as 97%, as against a maximum of 95% for mortgages with PMI.[8] Finally, the FHA offers mortgages only up to a fixed maximum value, which differs across locations and changes over time. In 1995, the maximum FHA loan in high-cost areas was $151,725.

There is also a significant difference between the pricing of FHA mortgages and the pricing of conventional mortgages with PMI, and it is this price difference on which we focus in our description of the household budget set. For the standard thirty-year fixed-rate mortgage on a single-family residence, the FHA charges an up-front fee of 2.25% of the principal for all loans regardless of LTV. For loans with an LTV of 80% or above, there is also an annual increment of 0.5% on the interest rate. This 0.5% increment continues for eleven years for loans with LTV below 90%, and for thirty years for loans with LTV above 90%.

3.3   The Computations: Simplifying Assumptions

To move from the product descriptions above to representations of the household budget set, we must make a number of simplifying assumptions. Some key qualitative assumptions concern the household's choice of mortgage product and the house appraisal. We assume that

• the household wishes to obtain a thirty-year fixed-rate mortgage,

• the household has no debts other than the mortgage,

• interest rates are constant over time,

• the house price is identical to its appraised value,

• the household decides not to pay any additional up-front points, and

• the household cannot go outside the mortgage market to borrow for the down payment.

The assumption that the household is applying for a thirty-year fixed-rate mortgage simplifies matters by allowing us to apply the simplest of the PITI calculations to determine affordability. Assuming that the household has no debts other than the mortgage implies that only the front-end PITI test can ever be binding. Together with constancy of the interest rate over time, it also ensures that calculating the costs of buying the home is simple and two-dimensional: an up-front cost and an annual carrying cost. The assumption that the house price is identical to its appraised value allows us to apply the simplest of LTV tests, and assuming that the household pays no up-front points pins down the amount of resources required up front to buy the house, as does the assumption that the household has no ability to borrow funds (from say, relatives). The assumptions are easy enough to relax, although the analysis becomes commensurately more complex.

We also make a number of numerical assumptions to be more concrete:

• *Closing costs.* Closing costs typically range from 2% to 4% of the house's appraised value. We assume closing costs amounting to 3% of the house value; see Jones and Hart 1995, and First American Title Insurance 1996.

• *Taxes and insurance.* Annual property tax rates range widely from close to zero to 3.5% of the appraised value annually. Annual insurance costs are typically in the range of 0.25% of the house value and are paid for out of net as opposed to gross income. The annual level of taxes and insurance combined that must be paid from gross income come out somewhere in the range of 0.25% to 3.75% of the house value. Again, in our illustrative examples we work with the intermediate level, with taxes and insurance amounting to 2% of the house value each year.

• *Principal and interest.* As for the annual principal and interest payments, the annual interest rate on a thirty-year fixed-rate mortgage has varied widely over the years. We choose an algebraically simple intermediate case in which the annual interest rate is about 9.6%, so that principal and interest payments as a proportion of gross income can be rounded to 10% of the loan amount each year.

• *Low down payment mortgages.* For convenience, we have chosen to work with the pure up-front cost version of PMI and the FHA mortgage. We make assumptions about up-front costs based on LTV according to the following schedule:
PMI:
  • 80%–85% LTV: a fixed incremental 2.25% up-front cost
  • 85%–90% LTV: a fixed incremental 3% up-front cost
  • 90%–95% LTV: a fixed incremental 4% up-front cost.

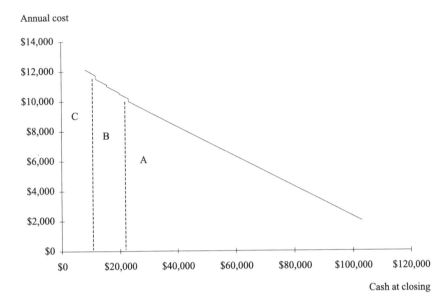

Figure 3.1
The costs of housing ($100,000 house)

FHA:

- 80%–97% LTV: a fixed incremental 2.25% up-front cost plus an annual interest rate premium of 0.5 percentage points.

3.4 The Costs of Purchasing a $100,000 Home

In this section we show how to use the information above to calculate the costs of a given house purchase. These costs are composed of some combination of up-front and annual carrying costs. In figure 3.1, we illustrate the options available to the household in a simple graph, with the up-front cost on the horizontal axis and the annual cost on the vertical axis. To be concrete, we consider the costs involved in buying a $100,000 home.

The graph consists of three different segments:

- Segment A corresponds to the options available using a conventional mortgage without PMI.

- Segment B illustrates the options available using a mortgage with an LTV in the range of 80% to 95%—either a conventional mortgage with PMI or an FHA.

• Segment C illustrates the options available using an FHA mortgage with an LTV greater than 95%.

As the figure shows, if the household has the financial resources and pays the entire $103,000 up front, which includes the closing costs, the home buyer can purchase the house with no mortgage and be left with only $2,000 of taxes and insurance as annual carrying costs.

If the household chooses to take out a conforming conventional mortgage with a 20% down payment, they will need to pay $23,000 in upfront costs. This covers the closing cost of $3,000 and a down payment of $20,000, so that the remaining $80,000 is financed with a mortgage. This leaves the household with annual costs amounting to $10,000: $8,000 in the form of principal and interest on the loan, and $2,000 in the form of taxes and insurance on the house.

Segments B and C of the feasible set, which involve low down payment mortgages, present a somewhat more intricate range of options. Figure 3.2 gives a more detailed picture of the feasible set in the low down payment region.

The amount of cash at closing that will allow a household to buy a $100,000 home falls from $23,000 with an 80% LTV mortgage to $15,700 with a 90% LTV mortgage with PMI and all the way to $8,194 with a

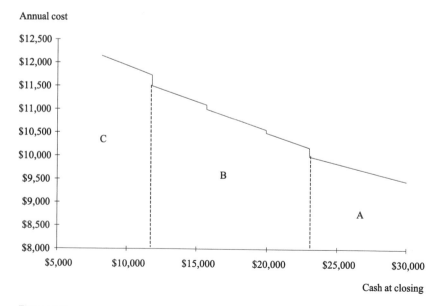

Figure 3.2
The costs of housing, low down payment mortgages ($100,000 house)

97% LTV FHA loan ($3,000 down payment, $3,000 closing costs, and $2,194 to the FHA).

This example can be readily modified to reflect different assumptions. An increase in the price of the house shifts the entire graph outward in a parallel fashion. If closing costs increase, the graph shifts to the right as up-front costs increase uniformly for a given level of annual cost. Higher interest rates rotate the graph clockwise as annual costs are now higher for a given up-front cost.

3.5   The Feasible Set of Houses

We now indicate the upper limit on housing affordability for different households in the current U.S. mortgage market under the assumptions in section 3.4. Two major economic factors limit the amount of housing that households can purchase: the amount of money available at the time of closing to split between closing costs and down payment (cash available at closing), and annual income as computed by potential lenders (adjusted annual income).

For applicants in the existing mortgage market who apply for the specific thirty-year fixed-rate mortgages outlined above, it is relatively simple to identify the most expensive maximum house that they can afford to buy as a function of cash available at closing and adjusted annual income. To illustrate this function in a simple two-dimensional manner, we consider the maximum affordable house for a household with a given amount of cash available at closing and variable levels of adjusted annual income. Specifically, we consider a fixed level of cash available at closing ($25,000), and annual income ranging from $10,000 to $100,000 per annum.

Under these assumptions, figure 3.3 plots the maximum house value that the household can afford as a function of their income. To compute the maximum house value, we begin by limiting attention to a household that seeks a conventional mortgage without PMI. Note that at low income levels, the payment-to-income constraint will restrict the maximum house value that the household can afford.

The maximum a household with income of $30,000 will be able to afford is a house costing slightly under $90,000. To see this, note that the household's maximum payments are $8,400, and annual taxes and insurance on the house amount to 2% of the purchase price, which is $1,800. Thus the household can afford to pay principal and interest of $6,600. This translates into a loan amount of $66,000.

Maximum house value

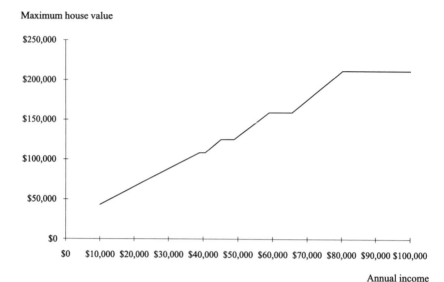

Figure 3.3
Housing possibility function ($25,000 available up front)

Maximum payments (0.28 · income)	$8,400
Less annual taxes and insurance	($1,800)
Maximum principal and interest	$6,600
Equivalent loan amount	$66,000

Since the 3% closing costs on a $90,000 house total $2,700, this leaves $22,300 available for the down payment.

Cash for closing	$25,000
Less closing costs	($2,700)
Cash for down payment	$22,300

Together with the maximum loan of $66,000, the household can afford a house worth close to $90,000.

Cash for down payment	$22,300
Mortgage	$66,000
House value	$88,300

For different levels of cash available at closing, the housing possibility function of figure 3.3 remains valid with some rescaling of the axes: with

$12,500 up front, the figure remains valid if the numbers on both axes are divided by two, and with $50,000 up front, the figure remains valid if the numbers on both axes are multiplied by two.

Appendix

For a conventional mortgage without PMI, the formula linking the maximum house value H to annual income Y, mortgage payments M, and cash for closing C, within the income range in which the PITI constraint binds, is

$$M = 0.28Y - 0.02H \tag{3.1}$$

$$C = D + 0.03H \tag{3.2}$$

$$H = L + D. \tag{3.3}$$

The first equation says that mortgage payments M must be equal to 28% of annual income less the 2% taxes and insurance. Under our interest rate assumptions, the loan amount L is equal to 10 times the annual mortgage payments, M. The second equation says that all the cash C is used up between the down payment D and the 3% closing costs. The third says that the maximum house value is equal to the loan balance and the down payment. With a small amount of rearrangement and substitution, this reduces to the single equation:

$$H = 2.28Y + 0.81C \tag{3.4}$$

Once income exceeds a certain level, the LTV constraint rather than the PITI constraint becomes binding. When the LTV constraint is binding (e.g., at 80%), the down payment (cash less closing costs) amounts to one fifth of the house value:

$$H = 5(C - 0.03H)$$
$$\tag{3.5}$$
$$H = 4.35C.$$

With cash of $25,000, the maximum house value would be $108,750. Of the $25,000 cash, roughly $3,250 goes to closing costs, and $21,750 is left for the down payment, so that the mortgage is $87,000. Given these data, the PITI test is passed provided the annual mortgage payments of $8,700 and the annual taxes and insurance of roughly $2,175 can be afforded according to the PITI test. This is true provided the following inequality is satisfied,

$$Y > (8{,}700 + 2{,}175)/0.28$$

$$Y > 38{,}800. \tag{3.6}$$

For income levels between \$10,000 and the critical level of \$38,800, the maximum affordable value rises as in equation (3.4). Above \$38,800 it follows equation (3.5), that is, the maximum house value is constant.

The use of conventional mortgages with PMI or FHA mortgages will allow the LTV to exceed 80%, and the equations will have to be modified to reflect this. Equations (3.4) and (3.5) will contain a number of conditioning statements that depend on the LTV chosen.

4   Home Ownership and the Life Cycle

How do the high costs of housing affect a household's economic experiences over the course of the life cycle? Although each household has a unique experience, there are important common factors at work at three critical life stages outlined in this chapter:

- younger households with head of household aged forty or less,
- a middle period from ages forty to fifty-nine,
- older households aged sixty and above.

4.1   The Early Years: A Time of High Pressure

Ownership introduces a broad set of financial strains for young households. The nature of these strains changes significantly from an early period in which the key is to save enough to afford the home, to the later period of occupation of the home.

The Pressures on Young Home Owners

For most young households, owning a home involves very high mortgage installment payments and a very high level of mortgage debt. When the household has finally saved enough to buy a house, they typically will be able to afford only a starter home, and will frequently be at or close to the maximum allowable PITI. As a reward for years of sacrifice, they can join the "house poor" and "cash poor" class.

In addition to these purely economic strains come all the new responsibilities involved in owning and maintaining the home. What makes the strains all the more telling is that they typically coincide with even more profound changes in lifestyle, such as getting married and bringing up young children. "High pressure" is a mild phrase for this period.

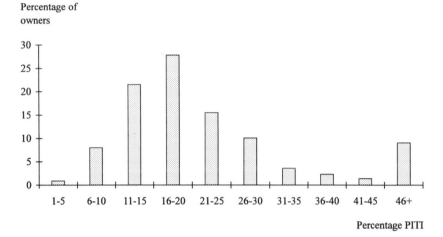

Figure 4.1
Distribution of current PITI for twenty- to thirty-nine-year-old owners with a mortgage
(mean = 26.5%)
Source: Consumer Expenditure Survey (1990).

A glance at the data reveals just how profound are the pressures many
households face when they become owners. We use data from the 1990
Consumer Expenditure Survey (CES). Like the 1990 Census of Population
data, the CES is a cross-section survey with self-reported house values.[1]
However, the CES contains much more detailed household asset and liability information. A more detailed discussion of the CES is presented in
the Appendix to this chapter.

Figure 4.1 shows the distribution of current PITI ratios for these
younger households. Note that nearly one in three of these families is
paying out at least 25% of their income in PITI. Close to 9% of young
households devote more than 45% of their income to covering these basic
ongoing housing costs.

It can be no surprise to anyone who has bought a home to know that
young home owners generally have very few assets other than their
house. Figure 4.2 plots the ratio of current house value to total assets for
younger home owners.[2] The striking feature is that housing accounts for
over 90% of the gross assets of the average household.

Adding to the stress is the high level of mortgage debt. For many
young households, home ownership means living under the shadow of a
high LTV and/or PITI ratio. Figure 4.3 shows the distribution of LTV

Percentage of households

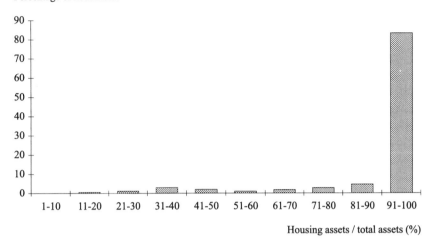

Figure 4.2
Distribution of housing assets[1] to total nonpension assets for younger home owners
1. Primary residence only
Source: Consumer Expenditure Survey (1990).

Percentage of
owners

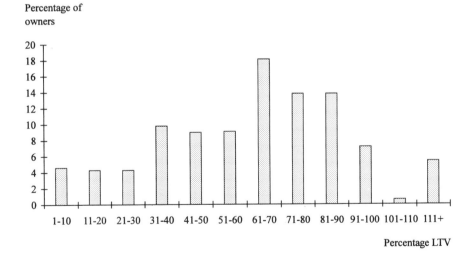

Figure 4.3
Distribution of current LTV for twenty- to thirty-nine-year-old owners with a mortgage
(mean = 71.4%)
Source: Consumer Expenditures Survey (1990).

ratios for households aged twenty to thirty-nine that own a home and have a mortgage outstanding.[3]

Note that some 30% of these households have LTV ratios above 80%. Nearly 7% have LTV ratios exceeding 100%, meaning they have perceived negative equity in the home. In fact, the debt side of the household balance sheet is dominated by the mortgage.

Overall, young home owners have very few assets other than their house and very few liabilities other than their mortgage. This means that these households keep their level of expenditures very close to income, less taxes and mortgage payments. They are liquidity constrained in the language of economic theory, and under tremendous stress in the language of popular psychology.

The Pressures Involved in Becoming an Owner

The desire for home ownership affects a young household's consumption expenditures long before they actually take ownership. For most young households, the desire to switch from rental accommodation to ownership involves a broad set of financial strains. Many intending owners have reasonable current income levels and future income prospects, but very weak current net asset positions, which means they will have to struggle for several years to save a down payment, as section 2.4 suggests.

It is hard to interpret the survey questions on how long it takes households to save for the down payment. A family that was willing to use one of the low down payment FHA mortgages, borrow the closing costs, eat bread and water, and move into a tiny house could save for the down payment in a short time. More realistically, the savings period will depend on what the family considers a minimally acceptable level of consumption and house size and how many additional expenses they are willing to incur to reduce the down payment.

There is some evidence available on the extent of the squeeze on consumption spending during the period in which the household is saving for the down payment.[4] Using food consumption data from the *Panel Study of Income Dynamics*, Engelhardt (1994) estimates the magnitude of the down payment consumption squeeze among households making the transition to home ownership. His preferred estimate is that two-year real food consumption growth is 10% lower during periods when a household is saving for a first house as compared to after the house purchase.

To clarify the strains involved in becoming an owner, we present a series of examples of the transition from renting to ownership. We deal separately with households with no substantial outside debts when they decide to become owners and those that have a relatively high level of non-mortgage debt.

4.2   Time to Save and the House Poor: Some Numerical Examples

A Household with No Education Debt

We make a number of assumptions in analyzing both the housing and nonhousing consumption of a household with no education debt (NED) that decides to make the transition from the rental market to the home ownership sector:

- They make the decision to move to ownership with no assets and no liabilities.
- They wish to buy a starter house worth at least $60,000.
- Their annual income is $24,000.
- They seek a 90% LTV loan with PMI.
- The mortgage has all of the characteristics introduced in section 3.4, with closing costs of 3% of the appraised house value, taxes and insurance of 2%, principal and interest amounting to 10% of the loan amount, and three additional up-front points for PMI.

Given that the household is buying a $60,000 house with a 90% LTV loan, they will take out a $54,000 mortgage. This mortgage requires principal and interest payments of $5,400 annually. This, combined with the $1,200 of taxes and insurance (2% of $60,000), creates a PITI ratio of 27.5% (6.6/24), which just passes the front-end PITI test. The household must save for closing costs of $9,420 consisting of the 10% down payment ($6,000), the three up-front PMI points on the $54,000 mortgage ($1,620), and the closing costs of 3% of $60,000 ($1,800).

To pin down the time it will take the household to purchase, we need to specify the household's disposable income and the amount they spend on rent and nonhousing consumption prior to moving into the ownership sector. To accomplish this, we further assume that the household faces a combined federal and state average income tax rate of 25%, and their minimum acceptable expenditure level on nonhousing consumption and rent is $16,000 per annum. These assumptions imply that the household's maximum annual savings is $2,000. Thus the household will have to wait five years to move to the ownership sector.

Another variable of interest is the disposable income left over for consumption expenditures once the household has moved in. This can be computed as follows:

Gross income	$24,000
Less tax payments[5] (24,000 − 5,400) · 0.25	($4,650)
Annual after-tax income	$19,350
Less annual mortgage payments	($5,400)
Less annual taxes and insurance	($1,200)
Less annual house maintenance (1% of house value)	($ 600)
Net income available for nonhousing consumption	$12,150

To summarize, during the five-year period of saving for the down payment, the household has annual income of $24,000 and spends $16,000 on combined rental and nonhousing consumption expenditure. After five years, the household purchases a $60,000 home and ends up with a net income of $12,150 available for nonhousing consumption. Note that unless the household makes rental payments less than $3,850 per year while saving for the down payment, their income available for nonhousing consumption expenditures rises when they move to an owned home.

The above example can readily be generalized. To begin with, we vary the level of income alone and consider a household identical in every way to NED but allow their income to vary between $24,000 and $30,000. Figure 4.4 illustrates the relationship between household income and the time required for the household to move into the $60,000 home.

Time to save, years

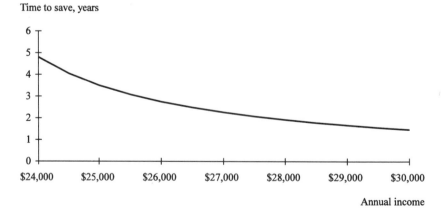

Annual income

Figure 4.4
Time to save for a down payment (household with no education debt)
Note: Calculations are based on these assumptions: house price = $60,000, minimum consumption = $16,000 per annum, front-end payment ratio = 32%, interest rate = 9.6%.

The time it takes the household to move from renting to owning declines rapidly as income increases. With an income of $28,000, the period of saving falls to two years, since this income allows the household to save an additional $3,000 per annum. Note, though, that this example is a little unrealistic since the household would strain to somehow save $5,000 after taxes from a moderate income. More realistically, this higher-income household would also likely increase their nonhousing expenditures while renting. In addition, the household might increase the size of the starter home they consider minimally acceptable to a level above $60,000. Either adjustment would extend the saving period beyond two years.

A Household with Education Debt

We now consider the case of a household that has education debt (ED), with characteristics as follows:

• They make the decision to move to ownership with no assets and education debt of $40,000.

• They wish to buy a starter house worth at least $100,000.

• Their annual income is $40,000.

• The annual payment of principal and interest on the education debt is $6,000.

• The mortgage has all of the characteristics introduced in section 3.4, with closing costs of 3% of the house value, taxes and insurance of 2%, and principal and interest of 10% of the loan amount.

For this household the situation is very different. Their critical problem is passing the back-end PITI ratio, which limits the total level of debt the household can hold. They are already paying off a heavy education debt, with principal and interest payments amounting to 15% of gross income. In addition, the $100,000 house will involve annual tax and insurance payments of $2,000.

We assume that the lender uses a liberal back-end ratio of 37.5%. With the household income at $40,000, the maximum level of principal and interest they can afford under the PITI test is $7,000, which brings their total payments of principal, interest, taxes, and insurance to $15,000. This is precisely 37.5% of their gross annual income and translates to a loan amount of $70,000. Thus the household must save a total of $33,000 to buy the home, with $30,000 going toward the down payment and $3,000 in closing costs.

What remains is to see how long the household will take to save this amount. Again, this depends on the household's disposable income, and the amount they spend on rent and nonhousing consumption before moving into the ownership sector. To illustrate this more clearly, we further assume that the household faces an average federal and state income tax rate of 25%, and the household does not wish to spend less than $18,000 per year on rent and nonhousing consumption combined.

With these assumptions, the household has net income of $30,000, of which $6,000 is used for paying principal and interest on the education debt. Deducting their annual rental and consumption expenditures leaves the household with $6,000 in annual savings, which means they will have to wait five and a half years to move from renting to owning.

We can also compute the level of disposable income left over for consumption expenditures when the household has moved into their starter home.

Gross income	$40,000
Less tax payments[5] (40,000 − 7,000) · 0.25	($8,250)
Annual after-tax income	$31,750
Less payments on the education debt	($6,000)
Less annual mortgage payments	($7,000)
Less annual taxes and insurance	($2,000)
Less incremental maintenance	($1,000)
Net income available for nonhousing consumption	$15,750

To summarize, the household has an annual income of $40,000 and spends $18,000 per annum on combined rental and nonhousing consumption expenditures. After five and a half years, the household moves into a $100,000 home, which leaves them with $15,750 per annum available for nonhousing consumption. Note that the income available for nonhousing consumption rises when the family buys a home, unless the annual rent payments while saving for the down payment are less than $2,250.

The simplest generalization considers variations in income while keeping all other parameters the same. We consider a household identical to ED but allow annual income to vary between $37,500 and $42,500.

Figure 4.5 illustrates the connection between household income and the time it takes the household to move into the $100,000 home. The time it

Time to save, years

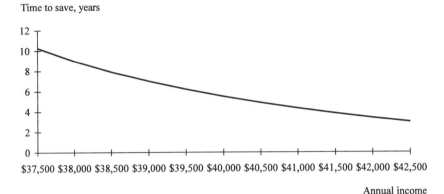

Annual income

Figure 4.5
Time to save for a down payment (household with education debt)
Note: Calculations are based on these assumptions: house price = $100,000, minimum consumption = $18,000 per annum, student loan balance = $40,000, student loan payments = $6,000 per annum, back-end payment ratio = 37.5%, interest rate = 9.6%.

takes to save the necessary cash for closing gradually declines from ten years at an income of $37,500 to three years at $42,500.

Income affects the time it takes to move into the ownership sector through two channels. First, as income rises, the back-end PITI ratio places less of a constraint on the amount that can be borrowed. Second, the increased income means more can be saved each year to accumulate the lower savings needed (since more can be borrowed). Again, the example is not completely realistic, since higher-income households would likely increase their expenditures while in the rental sector as well as the size of the starter home they consider minimally acceptable.

4.3   The Later Years: Inertia

The data on housing tenure for the elderly suggest the theme of ownership in the later years is inertia. Figure 4.6 shows that the average duration of home owners in the current home rises monotonically with age from less than five years for the youngest households to close to thirty years for households over age seventy-five.

Other reflections of the increasing inertia as the household ages show up in many other aspects of the household's behavior. For example, figure 4.7 shows that older owners have extremely low levels of debt in absolute dollar terms. Fully 50% of owners above aged sixty have *no* gross debt.

Duration, years

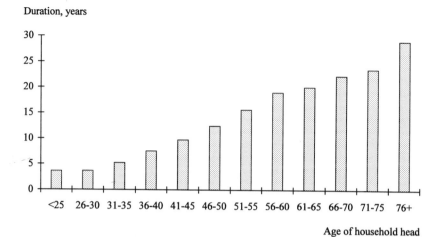

Figure 4.6
Average duration in current home for all home owners, by age
Source: Consumer Expenditure Survey (1990).

Percentage of
owners

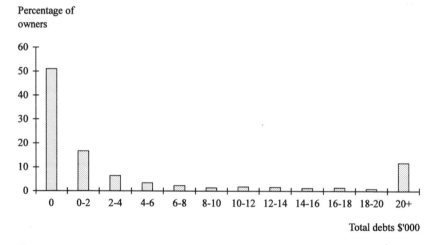

Figure 4.7
Distribution of total debts for owners over sixty (mean = $8,100, median = $0)
Source: Consumer Expenditure Survey (1990).

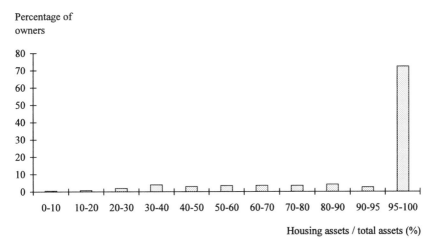

Figure 4.8
Distribution of housing assets as a proportion of total nonpension assets for owners over sixty (mean = 88.7%)
Source: Consumer Expenditure Survey (1990).

The asset side of the story is equally striking. Figure 4.8 shows the distribution of the ratio of housing assets to total nonpension assets for all elderly owners. The distribution has a long tail but a massive spike at the extreme level of concentration, with almost three out of every four older owners having 95%–100% of their gross nonpension assets tied up in their house.

These statistics illustrate that many elderly households remain in their homes with minimal other nonpension assets and minimal debt and simply consume very close to their current income—a little disturbing given the low income level of many of these households. Figure 4.9 shows a wide dispersion in the level of income among older owners, with fully 50% receiving less than $15,000 per year.

To gain a little more insight into the behavior of older owners, we define two groups of older owners as subjects of particular interest:

• *The financially inert*: those home owners who have 98% or more of their assets in the house and debt of no more than $3,000

• *The low-income financially inert*: the inert who have incomes of $12,000 or less.

Figure 4.10 shows the breakdown of older home owners into non-inert, low-income inert, and other. Almost 50% of elderly owners fit our

Percentage of
owners

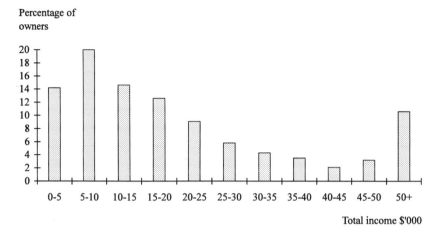

Figure 4.9
Distribution of total income for owners over sixty (mean = $22,900, median = $16,100)
Source: Consumer Expenditure Survey (1990).

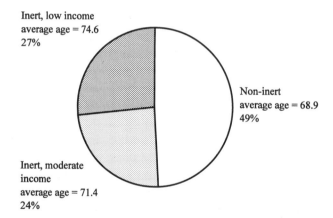

Figure 4.10
Percentage of inert, low-income inert, and non-inert older households
Source: Consumer Expenditure Survey (1990).

definition as inert, roughly half of whom also have low incomes. The figure also includes each group's average age. The low-income inert are the oldest, followed by the moderate-income inert and the non-inert. The gap in average age between the low-income inert and the non-inert is roughly five years.

Figure 4.11 presents further information on the demographic breakdown of these elderly owners. Almost 70% of non-inert households are couples, and the head of household's average age is sixty-nine. Only 50% of inert households are couples, with an additional 40% being single females. Of the inert low-income households, only 36% are couples, and more than 55% are single females. The single females in this last category have an average age over seventy-six.

The population of low-income inert households has several other striking features. They derive the vast majority of their income from Social Security. Furthermore, their house value represents an average of nearly seven years of annual expenditures, as opposed to an average of five and a half years of annual expenditures for all older households.

4.4 The Liquidity of Housing Wealth and Consumption Possibilities

In principle, it would seem that many older households are consuming far less than their wealth allows, if only they would adopt a flexible attitude to their housing wealth. Rather than borrow against their home or move to a smaller home, it appears that older households often chose to stay in their current home, borrow nothing, and live off of their relatively low level of pension and other income. Many older owners seem to find it difficult to turn their house into cash, treating it as an illiquid, and hence very inconvenient, form of asset.

A simple way to understand the potential significance of increased liquidity of the housing asset is to calculate the ratio of the value of the house to the total annual household expenditures. Figure 4.12 gives the distribution of this ratio. The average older household lives in a home worth more than five and a half years of total expenditures, and for a significant proportion of older households, the ratio exceeds ten years.

Similar calculations have appeared in the literature on reverse mortgages. To evaluate the potential benefit from such a mortgage, researchers have attempted, using a variety of data sources, to estimate the potential increase in monthly disposable income to elderly households available through the annuity value of their housing assets.

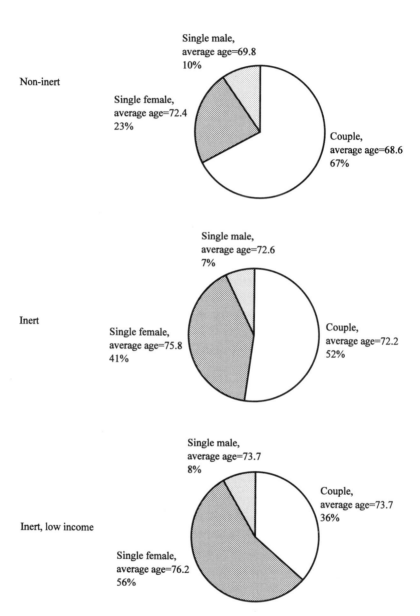

Figure 4.11
Family types for households over sixty
Source: Consumer Expenditure Survey (1990).

Percentage of
owners

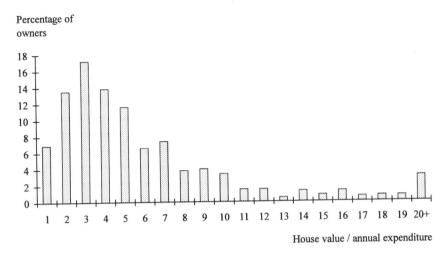

Figure 4.12
Distribution of house value to annual expenditure ratios for owners over sixty (mean = 5.54, median = 3.95)
Source: Consumer Expenditure Survey (1990).

Venti and Wise (1991) first proposed examining the potential impact of reverse mortgages on the income availability of elderly households using data from the SIPP, an ongoing rolling survey of the U.S. population. Each panel consists of eight interview waves every four months. The first panel in 1984 involved 20,000 households. Subsequent panels have involved roughly 12,000 households. Venti and Wise use waves 4 (autumn 1984) and 7 (autumn 1985), which contain information on housing costs.

They provide detailed summaries of the wealth composition of the elderly, finding that most elderly households enter retirement with little financial wealth other than housing equity (where private pension and Social Security wealth are not included). For example, for households aged sixty to sixty-five, the median liquid wealth is $6,600 and the median house equity is $43,000.[6] This is consistent with the CES data discussed above.

The SIPP permits estimation of total pension wealth only for those households currently receiving benefits. For households aged sixty-five to seventy, 59% receive private pension payments and 89% receive Social Security payments. Using reasonable assumptions, Venti and Wise calculate the present value of the flow of expected payments over the household's expected lifetime. For households aged sixty-five to seventy, the median total pension wealth is $113,400. Renters have less overall wealth than home owners. The overall medians are $170,400 for home owners and $59,300 for renters. The basic conclusion is that most elderly households live on fixed annuity (i.e., pension) income, and housing equity is the only asset available that could potentially increase consumption.

Venti and Wise consider a simple tenure-reverse mortgage that promises to pay a fixed annuity until the household dies. Their simulations indicate that the median increase in annual income from such an annuity is around 10%, but its impact varies widely along several dimensions. The gain is modest for married elderly couples, whose median income is $24,625 and median annuity is $1,358. This low annuity level reflects in part the longer expected payout period, since the annuity continues until both members of the household die. Similarly, the impact rises with the household's age. For low-income households aged fifty-five to sixty, the median gain is 4%, while for low-income households aged sixty-five to seventy, the median gain is 10%. Finally, single men have a larger gain than single women, reflecting women's longer life expectancy. For single men the median gain is 50%; for single women it is 36%.

Venti and Wise infer from the overall low median impact of 10% that the market for reverse mortgages is unlikely to be large. Their evidence suggests that freeing the elderly's housing equity would not significantly affect their consumption possibilities. Several papers have reexamined this issue and arrived at more optimistic conclusions.

Merrill, Finkel, and Kutty (1994) use *American Housing Survey* data and consider households aged sixty-nine or older with incomes less than $30,000 and housing equity between $100,000 and $200,000. They estimate that 933,000 households (10% of total households aged sixty-nine or older) have home equity in that range. Merrill, Finkel, and Kutty justify their age, income, and equity restrictions by citing the fact that annuity values increase with age and equity and affect low-income households more. They further restrict the sample to households with a tenure in the current house of ten or more years under the rationale that reverse mortgages are most attractive to households "attached" to their current residence. This final restriction leads to a 14% reduction in the number of targeted households (down to 800,000 out of an original 12 million).

Rasmussen, Megbolugbe, and Morgan (1995) argue that Merrill, Finkel, and Kutty impose overly stringent tenure and equity restrictions. The latter group's own simulation results indicate that among households sixty-nine or older with income less than $30,000, 4.9 million would gain at least 10%, while 3 million would gain at least 25% from the annuity reverse mortgage.

Mayer and Simons (1994) use 1990 SIPP data and simulate the gain from an annuity product similarly to Merrill, Finkel, and Kutty. They do not require that the household own the house without a mortgage. Their simulations allow a household to use a reverse mortgage first to pay off the remaining mortgage and the balance to purchase an annuity. They find that 60% of households aged sixty-two or older would gain at least 10%, 33% would gain at least 20%, and 13% would gain at least 50% from an annuity reverse mortgage. Around 3 million households (out of a total of 9 million aged sixty-two or older) are estimated to gain at least 20% in their monthly income.

The above calculations are certainly revealing in terms of the predicament of older owners in the current market. A reverse mortgage may not be the best way to increase the liquidity of housing assets. Specifically, a reverse mortgage is a form of debt, and there is little evidence that older households will be comfortable taking on additional debt for any reason. However, the unwillingness of these households to go into debt is costing them dearly in terms of foregone consumption. But this does not mean that they should be encouraged to go into debt. A concern for being in debt is completely rational, and inertia cannot be wished away since it is such a fundamental part of all of our lives. A real solution to these problems will have to take account of inertia. Just such a solution, based on the new markets that we propose, is outlined in chapter 8.

4.5   The Middle Years: Ownership and Anxiety

By the middle years many households have made the transition to home ownership and are set on a steady path of accumulating savings toward major expenses like a larger home, college for their children, and retirement. Avoiding negative shocks to their wealth portfolio becomes an important concern.

The life-cycle data show that the middle years commonly bring more moderate LTV ratios than the early years, and that the same is true of the average PITI for a household, since many households get wealthier as the equity in their home increases and expenditure on the mortgage and other housing expenses falls as a proportion of income.

But this central tendency masks some very dangerous outcomes that still affect some households during this phase of life. Equity problems may result from the interaction between the initial LTV on the mortgage and the subsequent house price changes. Similarly, cash flow problems may arise from the interaction between the initial PITI on the mortgage and the subsequent household income changes. Figures 4.13 and 4.14 show

Percentage of
owners

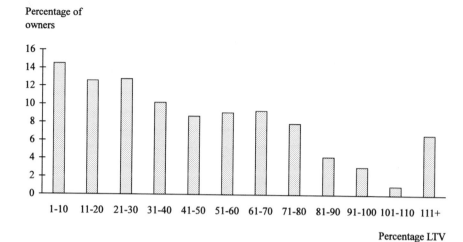

Percentage LTV

Figure 4.13
Distribution of current LTV for forty to fifty-nine-year-old owners with a mortgage
(mean = 52.3%)
Source: Consumer Expenditure Survey (1990).

Percentage of
owners

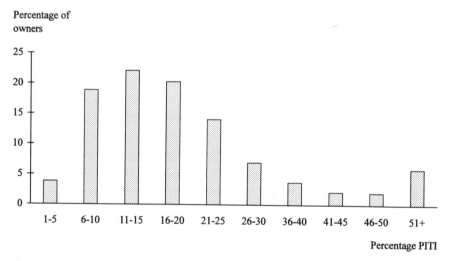

Percentage PITI

Figure 4.14
Distribution of PITI for forty- to fifty-nine-year-old owners with a mortgage (mean = 18.1%)
Source: Consumer Expenditure Survey (1990).

Percentage of
owners

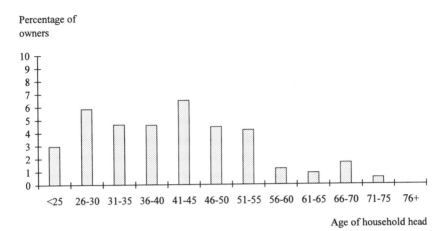

Figure 4.15
Proportion of all homeowners with negative equity, by age
Source: Consumer Expenditure Survey (1990).

the distribution of current LTV and PITI ratios for households in the age range forty to fifty-nine. More than 15% of households in this age bracket report current LTV ratios greater than 80%. In addition, a very significant minority of the households are paying more than 25% of their income on the house.

As figure 4.15 shows, the proportion of households with perceived negative equity positions in their house stays at or above 4% until the cohorts in their mid-fifties and older. One of the chief reasons equity problems can persist well into middle age is that housing equity builds up very slowly in a thirty-year mortgage. If a household starts with a 90% LTV mortgage, a 20% fall in the house price will produce a negative equity position even after the household has been in the home for a decade. Amortization of the underlying mortgage provides the household with a cushion against price declines that builds very slowly over time.

The Survey of Consumer Attitudes records the proportion of indebted households that experience any payment difficulty during a given year. Some of the data for 1993–94 are reproduced in figures 4.16 and 4.17. Figure 4.16 shows that of households aged less than fifty-five, more than 10% reported they had difficulty paying the mortgage during the prior year. Note that this proportion does not fall significantly until the households are above age fifty-five. Figure 4.17 shows, as expected, that the extent of these payment difficulties rises dramatically for households that have high PITI ratios.

Percentage of
indebted
households

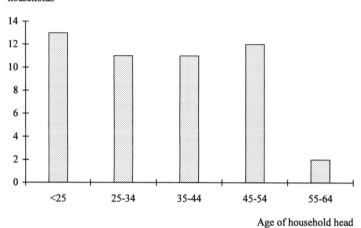

Age of household head

Figure 4.16
Proportion of indebted households with mortgage payment difficulties
Source: Survey of Consumer Attitudes, 1993–1994.

Percentage of
indebted
households

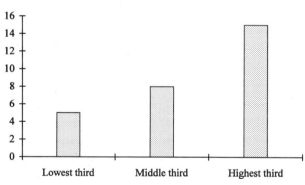

Payment-income ratio

Figure 4.17
Proportion of indebted households with mortgage payment difficulties by payment-income
ratio
Source: Survey of Consumer Attitudes, 1993–1994.

These figures provide a first indication on the riskiness of home owner-ship. The dream of owning a home for some households turns into a financial nightmare. This is a massive and important topic that we now turn to in far greater detail.

Data Appendix: The Consumer Expenditure Survey 1990

The Consumer Expenditure Survey (CES) is a rotating panel of approx-imately 7,000 households interviewed four times over the course of one year. Each quarter, 25% of the sample is replaced by new households. The sample is representative of the civilian population of the United States and each household is assigned an appropriate weight. The sample unit is the "consumer unit" that we call a household. It includes all members of a particular housing unit who are related, but may include individuals who are unrelated, provided that they share responsibility for two of three major categories of expenses: food, housing, and other expenses.

Some of the variables of interest are asked at each of the four inter-views, whereas some are asked only once or twice. In the cases where more than one quarter of information is available, we take the mean value of the responses.

Income Data
The measure of income used in the analysis is before taxes and includes: wages and salary, business income, social security, unemployment bene-fits, workers' compensation, welfare, interest, dividends and royalties, pen-sions, rental income, alimony and child support, and the face value of foodstamps. A topcode of $100,000 exists for each category of income.

Wealth Data
Total assets include funds held in saving and checking accounts, the esti-mated market value of all stocks, bonds, mutual funds, and other such secu-rities, as well as self-reported house values; the value of vehicles is not included. A topcode of $100,000 exists for each category of wealth, except for property values, which is topped at $300,000. Total debts include re-volving credit accounts (e.g., credit cards), installment loans, student loans, and mortgages. Pension wealth is not included.

Housing Data
The analysis looks at the principal residence only. Property values are self-reported market values, and the loan-to-value ratios are based on

this measure. The original mortgage amount as well as the remaining principal is topcoded at $200,000, whereas the property value is topcoded at $300,000; thus, for expensive properties, original and current LTVs may be biased. Payment to income ratios are calculated from the payments made on all mortgages for the owner-occupied property.

Socioeconomic Variables
Individual information such as age are based on the household head.

5   Home Ownership and Risk

The common picture of home ownership is that although it is costly, it brings the household the financial benefits of owning their place of residence, including any house price appreciation. What receives less discussion is that home ownership is a highly risky financial transaction, as we detail in this chapter.

Two key facts about housing risk stand out. First is its scale: by any reasonable measure housing risk is of massive importance to the typical owner. The second is that the risk is multifaceted: there is no simple single statistic that will do to summarize the risk level. Instead, to appreciate the many facets of housing market risk we need to tell a complex story. In a nutshell:

• House values are highly volatile, as documented in section 5.1.

• House values and labor market earnings are positively related, as documented in section 5.2.

• Many households are highly leveraged in real estate, as documented in section 5.3.

• Housing is the dominant asset in the household's portfolio, as documented in section 5.4.

The result of all these forces is that housing risk is worthy of far more attention than it receives. Before making a house purchase, the household would do well to review the risks to which the purchase exposes them, and possibly to adjust their purchase in light of this information.

5.1   The Variability of House Prices

What are the risk properties of individual house prices? Important as this question is, it is not easy to answer. In fact, it is hard to accurately define house price risk given the tremendous heterogeneity in housing, the fact that individual houses sell infrequently, as well as the costly and complex trading process.

Even if we ignore the complexities that arise due to the idiosyncrasies of the transactions process of selling a house, house valuation remains extremely complex. Reasons for changes in the value of a home range all the way: (1) from such large-scale issues as changes in the overall national real estate market; (2) to regional shocks such as oil prices in Texas, the defense industry in Southern California, and finance in New York City; (3) to neighborhood shocks such as the siting of waste facilities; (4) to purely idiosyncratic aspects of the individual property and its condition. We concentrate on issues of local and individual house price appreciation.

Patterns of Local House Price Appreciation

Our analysis of local house price behavior is based on the Freddie Mac repeat sale house price indices. Specifically, we use the Freddie Mac indices published for forty-two large standard metropolitan statistical areas (SMSA's) over the period 1975–1994. To gain insight into the variability of house prices, we select a time horizon of five years, and compute payoffs for all five-year holding periods in each of the forty-two SMSA's between 1975 and 1994. Figure 5.1 gives a smoothed empirical distribution of these returns.

To understand the risks of loss implicit in these five-year returns, it is important to keep in mind that the average turnover cost for buying and selling a house is around 10% of the house value. Figure 5.1 shows that 5% of the five-year *nominal* holding period returns were negative, and 20% were below the 10% turnover cost. So even if the household intends to remain in a house for five years, they still incur a significant chance of a financial loss.

From SMSA returns to Individual House Price Risk

The distribution of SMSA-level returns significantly underestimates the true level of risk at the individual home-owner level. The underlying housing returns used to estimate the distribution are SMSA averages, which one would expect to realize only if one held a diversified portfolio of real estate in the SMSA. Households typically own a single house, which is subject to a much greater price variability.

Case and Shiller (1987) develop a statistical model for individual house price risk. They assume that the transactions price for a house reflects the "true" value with error, and further that the true value depends on the

Percentage of
returns

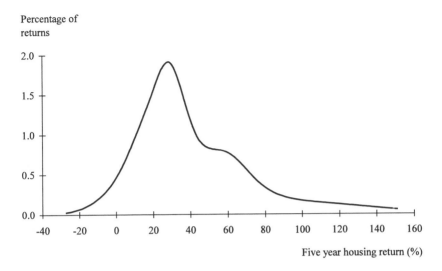

Five year housing return (%)

Figure 5.1
Smoothed distribution of housing returns
Source: Freddie Mac repeat sale house price indices, 1975–1994.

market-level value of real estate and an individual house price drift term. This decomposition can be used to calculate the percentage of the total individual house price risk picked up by the market risk (i.e., what is measured by variations in the price index). They apply this statistical model to repeat-sale house price data from four SMSAs.

The resulting percentages range from a low of 16% for Atlanta to a high of 50% for San Francisco (Dallas 36% and Chicago 27%). These results suggest multiplying the market risk by roughly a factor of three or four to approximate the individual home owner's risk. Consistent with this, Goetzmann and Ibbotson (1990, 69 n.14) estimate that while the market risk in the Case and Shiller data is 3%, the home owner risk is around 12%. Also, individual homes have other idiosyncratic risk factors such as gaps in insurance coverage.

5.2   The Correlation between House Price Risk and Income Risk

The house is an important asset, but it is far from the only asset for the typical household. For many households, especially younger households, their "human capital," representing the present value of future labor income, is their most valuable asset. A fall in house value will be least damaging to a household if it comes at the same time as an increase in the value of their human capital, and most damaging if it comes at the same time as a decrease in the value of their human capital. Unfortunately, the second scenario involving simultaneous falls in the values of both assets is far more characteristic. House price collapses often coincide with and reinforce other hardships that affect the local labor market.

A positive correlation between house values and incomes is quite intuitive. On average, house prices in a local housing market will be determined by the local supply of and demand for housing. In the short run, the supply of owner-occupied housing is quite inelastic. The demand for housing is determined by both the services and amenities provided in the community, as well as the level of income of the residents. A decline in local business opportunities leads to a reduction in income (wages) and an inward shift in the demand for housing. Given the inelastic supply of housing, this leads to a decline in local house values. Over time if the downturn persists, net migration of workers out of this labor market will mitigate the decline in wages and house prices.

There have been many examples of towns and even broader regions in which the housing market and the labor market suffer recessions at the same time, commonly because of a shock to some major industry in the area. The collapse of a major local industry is associated with decreases in both the value of houses and the level of labor income in the region. The problem of positive covariance risk between a household's "housing capital" and human capital is magnified in one-company towns, as when IBM slashed its level of employment in Dutchess County, New York.[1]

The connection between the labor market and the housing market is a general phenomenon not restricted to specific times and places. To document this connection between housing returns and labor market returns, we computed for each of the forty-two SMSAs used in figure 5.1 the annual house price appreciation and the annual appreciation in average nominal wages paid to manufacturing workers in the SMSA.[2] Figure 5.2 presents a simple scatter plot of these housing and wage returns.

The overall correlation between the annual housing and wage returns is 0.23, and is significantly different from zero. Computing the correlations by city gives a similar picture. Of the statistically significant correlations, all are positive. The highest correlation is for Philadelphia, with a correlation of 0.74 (probability value 0.001). The corresponding correlation for Los Angeles is 0.51 (probability value 0.09). Figure 5.3 plots the SMSA-specific correlations and their associated significance levels.

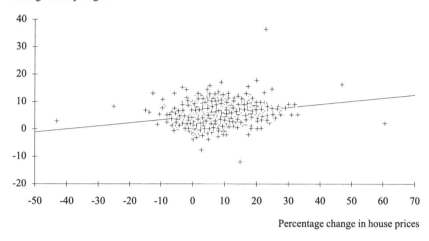

Figure 5.2
Annual wage and house price changes by SMSA
Sources: Freddie Mac repeat sale house price indices and Bureau of Labor Statistics' manufacturing wage series, 1975–1994.

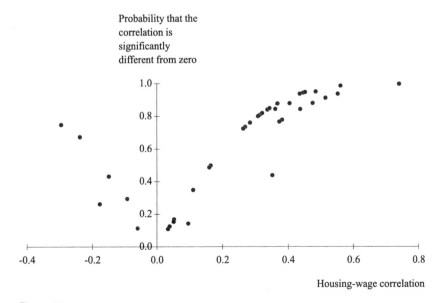

Figure 5.3
Housing-wage correlations
Source: Freddie Mac repeat sale house price indices and Bureau of Labor Statistics' manufacturing wage series, 1975–1994.

Percentage of
housing debts

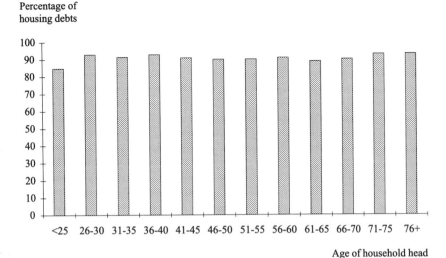

Age of household head

Figure 5.4
Average proportion of housing debts[1] to total debts for home owners with a mortgage, by
age
1. Primary residence only
Source: Consumer Expenditure Survey (1990).

5.3   Mortgages and the Problem of Indebtedness

Many of the risks of ownership are associated with the need to keep up
payments on the mortgage. Mortgages are the dominant form of household debt. Figure 5.4 shows the average proportion of gross liabilities
accounted for by housing debt for households that own their home and
have a mortgage. The proportion is over 85% for all age groups.

It is striking that the dominance of mortgage debt in total liabilities
survives when we aggregate across the entire population, including both
those who own their home without a mortgage and those who own no
home. Figure 5.5 shows by age group the ratio of mortgage debt to gross
household debts. This ratio lies in the 80%–90% range for most age
cohorts. A noteworthy feature of figure 5.5 is the high ratio for elderly
households given that only 10%–20% of these households both own a
home and have an outstanding mortgage. This indicates that nonhousing
debt must also be sharply decreasing for older households.

Indebtedness is more widespread among younger and middle-aged
households than among older home owners. Figure 5.6 plots by age the
proportion of home owners who have a first mortgage. Note that this
proportion falls monotonically with age for households over age fifty.

Percentage held as
residential debt

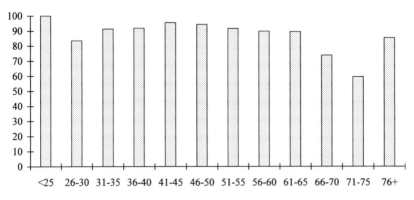

Figure 5.5
Proportion of total household debts held as residential debts,[1] by age
1. Primary residence only
Source: Consumer Expenditure Survey (1990).

Percentage of
owners

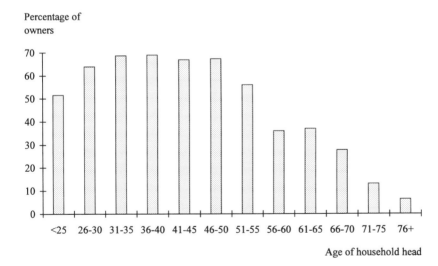

Figure 5.6
Proportion of home owners with a mortgage, by age
Source: Consumer Expenditure Survey (1990).

Next, we explore the risks associated with housing exposure in order of severity. Keep in mind that fear of extreme trouble often motivates behavior even in more moderate circumstances.

Default and Bankruptcy

Defaulting on a mortgage is not a step households take lightly, because it involves being forced to leave their home and possibly risking a creditor's willingness to pursue the household for any of their other assets. To gain as much protection as possible, households that default very commonly also declare bankruptcy.[3] Again, this is not a step that most take lightly, in part because of:

- damage to one's credit history,[4]
- the sense of personal failure that it may contribute,
- certain limitations on repeated bankruptcies,
- legal and other one-time costs,[5] and
- possible social stigma.[6]

We know from the previously cited examples within the last decade that the combination of a bad housing and labor market is not uncommon. Because of the gravity of default, financial institutions such as the ratings agencies have analyzed the subject extensively. The impact of various mortgage characteristics on the default rate is commonly measured by expressing them as multiplicative factors relative to a baseline case.[7] To give a general idea of the risks involved, table 5.1 shows the importance of LTV from Duff and Phelps's national figures. The data show a significant proportion of mortgages will default, with especially high default rates for high-LTV mortgages.

Lenders' extreme care in monitoring applicants for mortgages and checking that they can afford to buy reflects their awareness of ownership's

Table 5.1
Duff & Phelps default factors

Product feature	Factor
LTV 100%	4.25 X
LTV 90%	2.6 X
LTV 80%	1.4 X
LTV 75%	1 X
LTV 70%	.6 X
LTV 60%	.3 X

financial stress. While default is the most visible indication of trouble and the best studied (after all, it affects agency profits), households may endure other related and less extreme hardships as a result of owning their homes, as we now detail.

Lock-in and Negative Feedback
In less extreme cases, a fall in house values may lead to a lock-in effect whereby the household can no longer obtain the down payment on a new home by selling their current home. The household may thereby be locked out of alternative labor markets with better income prospects. In this way, falling house prices may impede residential mobility.[8]

As a result, oil workers in Texas in the early 1980s might have found their house values and labor incomes collapsing at the same time, leaving them with little or no equity in their houses. Such a lock-in effect can decrease future labor income. The regional collapse can lower the value of future human capital by restricting geographic mobility. By being tied to their houses, workers become tied to their current labor market. Consequently, high leverage, a lack of asset diversification, and positive covariance risk can cause tremendous hardship, even in the absence of actual default.

Continued Constraints on Housing and Nonhousing Consumption
The most common risk facing home owners, while less dramatic than default or lock-in, is nonetheless still difficult. For many home owners, a consumption squeeze continues well beyond the purchase of their first home, as the high level of mortgage payments and the difficulty in raising significant other funds restrict household consumption to near-term income.

Declines in property values can exacerbate this continuing consumption squeeze. Loss of equity in a house can lead not only to lock-in effects that limit job mobility, but also to lock-out effects whereby the household is denied access to the refinance market. Declines in house values may prevent households from paying off their current fixed-rate mortgages and taking advantage of falling interest rates through refinancing. As a result, the household cannot reduce financing costs to relax the consumption squeeze.[9]

5.4   Housing Investment and the Asset Portfolio

Given that house prices are risky and positively correlated with labor market income, there are clear diversification disincentives to placing a

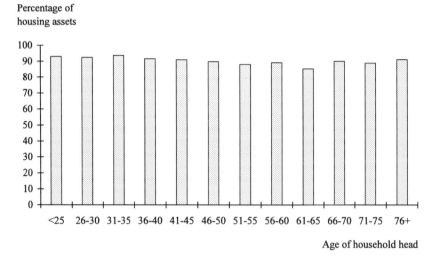

Figure 5.7
Average proportion of housing assets[1] to total assets for home owners, by age
1. Primary residence only
Source: Consumer Expenditure Survey (1990).

high proportion of total assets in housing. But the current market does not allow a household to separate its housing investment decision from its housing consumption decision. A household that wishes to increase their housing consumption must also increase their housing investment. That is, a household must own *at least* as much housing as they consume. This ends up causing massive concentration on housing in investment portfolios.

Using the CES data discussed earlier, we calculated for home owners the proportion of their nonpension assets due to their primary residence. These calculations are displayed for different age groups in figure 5.7. Across the age spectrum, the average proportion of household assets tied up in housing is extremely high, exceeding 90% for younger households and never dropping below 85% for older households. A direct implication is that for a great many households, housing is the *only* significant asset in their portfolio.

The qualitative features of figure 5.7 have been documented by other researchers using a variety of data sources. Engelhardt and Mayer (1996) look at the 1985–1990 waves of the Panel Study of Income Dynamics data. They measure "net housing wealth" as a proportion of overall net wealth for first-time home buyers, and find a median value of 90.6%. Net housing wealth (often called "housing equity") is defined as the value of the housing asset less the outstanding mortgage, and total net wealth is defined as the value of all assets less the value of all debts. As such, their numbers are not directly comparable with figure 5.7, which plots gross housing assets as a proportion of gross wealth. To provide a simple basis for comparison, suppose that the house value is the same as the price paid for the house, that the LTV for first-time buyers is 80%, and that the mortgage is their only debt. With these additional assumptions, the calculations of Engelhardt and Mayer imply that the gross housing asset is roughly 98% of gross assets, which is even larger than the figures that we derive for our sample of young home owners from the CEX.

Wealth figures for older households can be found in Mayer and Simons (1994). The authors use Survey of Income and Program Participation data to tabulate wealth composition for households aged sixty-two and older. For 1990, they report that the median housing equity for all elderly households is $39,347, and the median liquid assets are $9,093. The ratio of the median housing equity to the sum of the median housing equity and median liquid assets is 0.81. Although this is not a valid estimate of the median ratio of housing equity to total nonpension wealth for elderly households, it is consistent with the view that housing remains a dominant component of the nonpension wealth of elderly households.

A similar picture emerges from the Survey of Consumer Finance data. Kennickell and Shack-Marquez (1992) tabulate median household assets using the 1989 data. They report both median housing assets and median financial assets by age groups. We use their estimates to calculate the ratio of the median housing assets to the sum of the median housing assets and median financial assets by each age group. For households that are less than thirty-five years old, this ratio is 96.3%. For households that range from thirty-five to fifty-four years of age, the ratio is above 85%. Finally, for households that range from fifty-five to seventy-four years of age, the ratio remains above 75%.

Apart from the fact that we use different data series and somewhat different sample definitions, the main difference between our computations and those reported above is that we focus on gross assets as opposed to net assets. In our view, it is generally inappropriate to net out the mortgage from the value of the house. The cost of servicing the mortgage applies to the gross level of mortgage debt. Similarly, the risk and return properties of residential real estate apply to the gross asset value, not to the net asset value. The only time there is any specific connection between the value of the house and the value of the mortgage is when the household defaults on the mortgage and simultaneously reduces its housing assets and mortgage liabilities to zero. In all other circumstances the two are entirely separate, with the household receiving 100% of the capital gain (or loss) on the house, and being fully responsible for paying off the mortgage debt.

II

The Partnership Market
and the Housing Market

6

Introduction to the Partnership Market

6.1 Overview of the Partnership Market

The all-or-nothing constraint on home ownership forces households to make the stark choice between the disadvantages of rental accommodation and the harsh financial realities of complete home ownership. In classical economic terminology, the current housing market has a major indivisibility because one can not own only part of a house. This indivisibility forces owners to tie their housing consumption decision to their asset accumulation and portfolio decisions. Households may wish to live in large houses without wanting to risk a large proportion of their wealth on the fate of their property and the surrounding housing market. We have designed our proposed Partnership Markets to help overcome this constraint.

We propose that housing be financed not only with a mortgage, but also with an institutional investor that provides equity capital for the house in exchange for a proportion of the ultimate sale price. We propose to use the partnership rather than the corporate form of joint ownership in this market to avoid the additional expenses, tax issues, and complexities of the corporate format. We further believe the limited partnership format is the most appropriate of the various forms of partnership available. One of this format's advantages is that casting the investor as a limited partner removes any personal liability arising from ownership of the property, thereby retaining the key limited liability aspect of the corporate format.

Limited partnership agreements have recently gained much popularity in the commercial property market. In recent years a legal code, "the Uniform Limited Partnership Act," has been formulated to provide the basic body of law relating to such limited partnership agreements. In the context of the residential housing market, we refer to the household that takes occupancy of the home as the Managing Partner, and the financial institution that co-owns the asset as the Limited Partner. The distinction is that while the ultimate sale price would be split pro rata between the two, a written agreement would explicitly state that the basic occupancy rights and several other general rights relating to the commonly held asset were left to the Managing Partner.

In chapter 9 we provide a detailed outline of the proposed Partnership Contract. In the simplest of these Partnership Contracts, the basic financial transaction would be that the Managing Partner would supply funds up front in exchange for a fixed proportion of the house's ultimate sale price, with no other monetary payments made between the parties. The contract would leave the Managing Partner in control of the property they occupied while providing them with incentives to protect the Limited Partner's interests. Key decisions delegated to the Managing Partner would include when to sell, what additions to make to the property and when, and how much maintenance to perform. In return, the Managing Partner would have several responsibilities such as maintaining the home in good condition, and paying all operating expenses (including taxes).

In response to these common goals, all Partnership Agreements would have to provide a careful and specific assignment of both parties' financial and managerial obligations while aligning the Managing Partner's incentives for maintenance and home improvement as closely as possible with those of the Limited Partner.

We do not view Partnership finance as an alternative to the standard mortgage, but rather as a complementary form of finance. We therefore regard it as important to structure the Partnership Agreement so that the Limited and Managing Partners are each able to borrow against their equity holding in the Partnership. In this way, the Managing Partner could also obtain a mortgage against the value of the asset they purchased, which is an equity stake in the home's final sale value. One institutional requirement for such borrowing would be written certification of the relevant Partnership ownership interests that each party could use as collateral against other loans.

As important to the Limited Partner as the borrowing rights would be the right to sell the Partnership to third parties. In fact, we believe a liquid secondary market in Limited Partnerships is crucial to the success of the Partnership Market, since it allows for the maximum degree of diversification of ownership of the risky housing asset. In chapter 10 we outline proposals for a secondary Partnership Market to obtain Limited Partnership funds from the broadest possible investment community. On the institutional side, it might be prudent to have some form of registration and an extension of the Securities and Exchange Commission disclosure regulations.

The Partnership Market would involve some additional transactions. Extra information presented to the Limited Partner at purchase, sale, and times of major home improvement would all add transactions costs. This flow of information might not be altogether a bad thing, since it might help improve Managing Partners' decision making, as we outline in chapters 14 and 15.

6.2 Will There Be Any Demand for Limited Partnerships?

If a liquid secondary market develops in Limited Partnerships, the broad financial community, including pension funds, insurance companies, and wealthier households, will indirectly provide funds to the Limited Partnership Market. The price these potential Limited Partners would be willing to pay for their portion of the house's final sales price is an important issue and can be used to classify Partnerships as follows:

- *Partnerships at par.* The Limited Partner pays a pro rata proportion of the property's initial appraised value.
- *Partnerships at discount.* The Limited Partner offers to pay less.
- *Partnerships at premium.* The Limited Partner offers to pay more.

We address the subtle quantitative question of whether Partnerships would normally be priced at par, discount, or premium, and what degree of discount or premium would be offered in chapter 13, where we find evidence of a high potential demand in the financial markets for Limited Partnerships at a price close to par.

At first sight, par pricing for Limited Partnerships seems to be something of a paradox. The Managing Partner would get to live in the house, make all major decisions and receive half the sale price. The Limited Partner would get none of the accommodation benefits, be passive in the decision making, and receive the same half of the sale price. How would it be possible to get a par price for the Limited Partnership? Why pay half the money for less than half the benefits? To understand how this could happen, we must first remind ourselves of the basic economic motivation for developing the Partnership Market.

The key to understanding the forces that determine the price of Partnerships as in any market is to understand first *the gains from trade*. In the current housing finance market, the home owner must own the entire asset corresponding to the home in which they reside. The fundamental reason for developing the Partnership Market is that the asset defined by the *second half* of the house is worth less to the current home owner than to the financial community. The wedge between the value of this asset to the home owner and its value to the broad financial community defines the gains from trade and rationalizes our later estimates that make par pricing of Limited Partnerships a quite reasonable starting point.

These are the key forces that determine the difference between the value of the second half of the housing asset to the current home owner and the broader financial community:

• the home owner's desire to diversify investment away from the individual housing asset,

• the financial community's desire to diversify investment into residential real estate,

• the home owner's greater impatience for up-front funds.

Diversification for the Home Owner
We have seen the overwhelming role the housing asset plays in the asset portfolio of the vast majority of home owners and that housing is an extremely risky investment. Together, these facts imply that a household that owns the whole of the housing asset should place very little value on their ownership of the second half. After all, the second half of the home asset is perfectly correlated with the first half and is therefore the worst possible form of investment for asset diversification.

While this picture of highly risk-averse Managing Partners is likely to be accurate for the vast majority of owners, some households may have greater ambivalence concerning ownership risks. Consider in particular a young household settled in the area in which they wish to live and that believes they are on the way up the housing ladder. Such a household may regard owning the second half of the home as providing a certain amount of insurance against increases in the price of local property, although they are also subject to the idiosyncratic risk from owning their individual home. At best, given the great idiosyncrasy of home prices, owning is a highly imperfect insurance against the cost of future moves.

The extent this insurance role plays depends on the household's stage in the life cycle, any expectations they have of when and where they might move, and the common component of house price variation between their current home and the home to which they anticipate moving. These factors will differ from household to household, which is likely to lead to a certain amount of self-selection as to who will become Managing Partners, and this might well feed back into the housing return pattern.

It is also worth noting the role that secondary Partnership Markets might play in improving households' ability to prepare for moving to a new home. The existence of secondary Partnership Markets would make it possible for the household to buy an ownership interest in the relevant local housing market while diversifying away from the individualized risk associated with their own house.

Diversification for the Financial Community

Simple portfolio theory argues that there is scope for a Pareto improvement if the owner-occupant sells a proportion of their home's asset value to a large, well-diversified financial institution. For the financial community, a single house is a minute proportion of their portfolio. Given the asset's minuscule scale, the financial community would be risk neutral with respect to all the idiosyncratic elements of the house price, which might be very significant indeed, as in the computations of Case and Shiller reported in chapter 4.

What about the value of the systematic common components of real estate returns? Here the key fact is that Partnership Markets would open up a massive set of new diversification opportunities for the financial community. The return properties of large portfolios of Limited Partnerships would be closely correlated with the behavior of residential real estate prices. It is important to understand that currently it is very difficult to invest in the U.S. residential property market. The closest substitutes available for portfolio investors are the various recently launched real estate investment trusts (REITs). Many REITs are based on commercial real estate, and those based on residential focus primarily on rental properties in large apartment groupings.

The financial community would view the new diversification opportunities in a very positive light. Large institutions continuously search for new types of assets in which they can prudently invest. Broadly speaking, there are only a few classes of massive assets in the United States: stocks and a variety of bonds and fixed-interest instruments. Asset managers are always looking for new types of investment, particularly those with return patterns that differ from those on stocks and bonds. In the recent past, this led to the large wave of investment in foreign stock exchanges, even with the potentially high risks these markets involve. The U.S. property market is a natural place to look for a potentially massive new U.S.-based set of asset returns.

The Greater Impatience of the Home Owner

Many potential Managing Partners are relatively young first-time home buyers, who are at a life stage when they would like to consume, face many cash needs, and are therefore among the consumption-squeezed house poor. For these households, the current cash equivalent of a 50% share of the house's sale price is even further depressed because of their pressing need for current funds. In contrast, the institutions that would provide funds for Limited Partnerships generally have long investment horizons, investing on behalf of ultimate asset holders saving for future consumption.

The relevant discount factor would vary from household to household. It would likely be higher for younger and less wealthy first-time home buyers, and for this reason these households might be more powerfully attracted to Partnership finance.

6.3   The Managing Partner's Portfolio

The key reason for the gains from trade is the constraint that in the current market forces home owners to invest in the housing asset in order to consume housing services. This constraint leads many owners to hold a very large proportion of their asset portfolios in housing, and also distorts their consumption of housing and of other goods. These effects can be illustrated in a simple two-period model due to Jan Brueckner (1994). Brueckner considers a household that earns income in the first period of life, and retires in the second period. In the retirement period, the household sells all assets purchased in the first period, including the house, and spends the entire amount on nonhousing consumption. In the first period, the household chooses what size house to buy, how much to spend on nonhousing consumption, and the composition of its asset portfolio. The goal of the household is to maximize discounted expected utility subject not only to the standard budget constraint, but also to the housing investment–housing consumption constraint that limits the amount of first-period housing consumption to no higher than the level of investment in the housing asset. To further simplify matters, Brueckner assumes that the household cares only about the mean and the variance of the asset portfolio. Figures 6.1 and 6.2 illustrate the workings of this model.

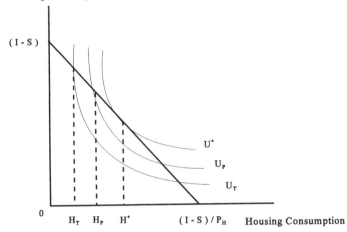

Figure 6.1
Binding housing investment-consumption constraint: impact on current housing consumption
Note: I = income, S = savings, P_H = unit price of housing.

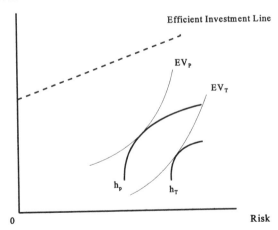

Figure 6.2
Binding housing investment-consumption constraint: impact on portfolio returns

With no housing investment-consumption constraint, the household's optimal current housing consumption would be given by H^* in figure 6.1. A binding investment-consumption constraint under traditional housing finance forces the household to a lower level of current housing consumption, $H_T < H^*$. By relaxing the investment-consumption constraint, Partnership finance would allow the household to increase their current housing consumption from H_T to H_P, which results in the utility increase from U_T (current household utility under traditional housing finance) to U_P (current household utility under Partnership finance). In addition, households could reduce their investment in housing, which would improve their investment portfolio. This leads to a gain in future expected utility illustrated in figure 6.2 by the increase from EV_T (expected household indirect utility under traditional finance) to EV_P (expected household indirect utility under Partnership finance). The overall benefit to the household from Partnership finance is the sum of the direct utility increase in the first period (U_T to U_P) and the indirect utility increase in the second period (EV_T to EV_P).

Quantifying the potential gain to the household is easier if we focus exclusively on the gain from the improved investment portfolio. We can illustrate the enhancement to the household's investment position by constructing efficient investment frontiers for the household using data on housing and nonhousing asset returns. The objective is to empirically estimate the magnitude of the separation between the h_P (the risk-return combinations possible with Partnership finance) and the h_T (the risk-return combinations possible with traditional finance and a binding investment-consumption constraint) investment frontiers illustrated in figure 6.2. We list the assumptions we use to carry out this calculation below.

First, households do not typically hold a diversified portfolio of real estate. Thus it is important to include the idiosyncratic variance to the housing returns used in the analysis. We defer to chapter 10 a detailed discussion of measuring housing returns. We make the conservative assumption that the individual house risk is four times the risk measured by average returns in the national market.

In addition, households are not completely free in setting the share of their portfolio invested in real estate. We assume that Partnership Agreements would require a minimum 50% ownership share, and that the 50% share would be sold at a par price. We will use an 85% investment share in housing for the traditional finance analysis, considerably below the estimates for most households we analyzed in the CES.

While the future need not always mirror the past, we follow the traditional approach of evaluating the potential attractiveness of Partnership

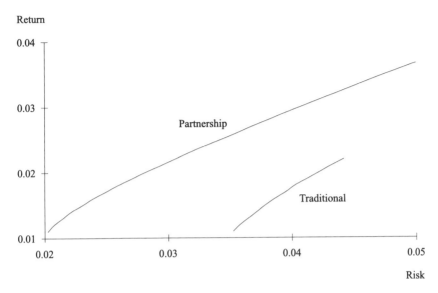

Figure 6.3
Efficient porfolio frontier, real annual returns, 1951–94, with manager partner's idiosyncratic risk

Contracts using historical asset returns. Nonhousing asset returns are published by Ibbotson and Associates (1996), who report returns for common stocks, long-term government bonds, and U.S. Treasury bills. Housing returns are derived from the FHA/Freddie Mac national price index.

Without Partnership Contracts, the household can optimally invest 15% of their assets across the three asset groups listed above. With Partnership Contracts, we assume the household can sell half of its house and shift the money into other investments. At par pricing, this would leave the household with the same total assets but a much smaller share invested in housing.

Figure 6.3 illustrates the shift in the investment frontier for the Managing Partner based on annual real national housing returns with the addition of idiosyncratic risk, over the period 1951–1994. The risk-return frontier for Managing Partners with par pricing would be significantly expanded, which would provide the household with a much greater range of financial options.

6.4 The Managing Partner's Valuation of the Second Half of the House

With par pricing, Managing Partners would clearly be better off than under the current method of housing finance, which suggests that potential

Managing Partners would be willing to sell shares of their houses at a *discount*. Measuring the potential magnitude of this discount requires that we place additional structure on the problem.

Consider the following example of a potential Managing Partner who owns outright a house worth $85,000. Again, assume that this house represents 85% of total assets. Currently, then, the household has $15,000 in nonhousing financial assets. Assume the owner is fifty-five years old and is planning on retirement at age sixty-five, when the house will be sold. The financial objective is to attain the most favorable total wealth distribution at the end of the ten-year period.

Our potential Managing Partner has two options: first, retain ownership of 100% of the house and optimally invest the remaining nonhousing assets over the investment horizon, or second, sell off 50% of the house and reinvest the proceeds optimally in nonhousing assets over the investment horizon. To compare these options, we adopt a specific utility function for the household and convert the wealth distributions into their certainty equivalent dollar amounts. We follow the equity premium literature and use a constant relative risk-aversion formulation.[1]

$$u(y) = \frac{y^{(1-\alpha)}}{1 - \alpha},$$

where α is the measure of the household's risk aversion (with higher values representing more risk-averse households). We consider values of α from 0.5 to 10.

To compute the value of the second half of the house to the Managing Partner, we first use the Ibbotson data and the combined FHA/Freddie Mac index for U.S. house prices to compute annual real returns on all assets. These real returns are assumed to be jointly normal, and the parameters of this distribution are estimated from data covering the entire period 1951–1994. We adjust the annual housing return series to account for the higher level of risk at the individual home level rather than at the national average level. We make a very conservative adjustment in which the individual house price is assumed to have a variance that is only four times as high as that of the national price index. We then take a sequence of draws from this joint distribution and compound up to get the ten-year pattern of real joint asset returns. We repeat the sampling procedure 10,000 times to generate the distribution of joint returns.

With this return distribution in place, we then determine the household's choice among all possible initial asset portfolios, under the assumption that they make no subsequent adjustments to the portfolio. For each possible allocation of initial wealth among the assets, we calculate the actual level of final wealth that would result for each of the 10,000 simulated profiles of asset returns. To derive the level of expected utility, we substitute the final wealth level in the utility function and compute the average utility level across all simulations. In this manner we generate an expected utility for all possible portfolios that the household could choose.

The actual choice that the household makes depends on the set of feasible portfolios, and it is here that the housing finance market enters the picture. In the traditional market, the household has to invest $85,000 of its $100,000 in owner-occupied housing, leaving only $15,000 to be divided optimally among the remaining assets. In the Partnership market, the household sells the second half of the house, so that they have reduced their holding of the house to $42,500. This leaves them with at least $15,000 to split among the remaining three assets, plus an additional amount that depends on the price they receive for the second half of the house. At a par price the household receives $42,500 from the Limited Partner, and therefore has a total of $57,500 to invest in nonhousing assets. At a 10% discount, the household receives $38,500 from the Limited Partner, leaving $53,250 for them to invest in nonhousing assets. For each possible price of the Limited Partnership, we compute the expected utility available to the household by appropriately changing their total amount of funds available to invest in nonhousing assets, and analyzing the corresponding optimal portfolio. Finally we estimate the household's valuation of the second half of the house by identifying the price that makes them indifferent between selling to a Limited Partner at that price, and operating in the traditional market.

The valuations produced by our procedure are shown in table 6.1. One striking feature of the numbers is that that the Managing Partner never places a value of higher than 81 cents per dollar on the second half of their house, and the value is far lower than this unless they are highly risk averse. This reinforces our point that the second half of the house is not highly valued for its asset-return properties, but rather because the household must buy it in order to move into the home. Another interesting feature of the table is that the relationship between risk aversion and valuation is not monotonic. When the household is close to risk neutral, the value placed on the second half of the house is very low due to the relatively low expected return on housing in comparison with stocks. As the household becomes more risk averse, the diversification properties of real

Table 6.1
Managing Partner valuation of second half of the house

Risk aversion parameter	Value of house (¢ per $)
1	53
2	59
3	65
4	71
5	77
6	80
7	81
8	81
9	80
10	79

Note: Uses real returns, assumes that housing represents 85% of initial total assets and a ten-year investment horizon.

estate come to be more highly valued. At very high levels of risk aversion, the variability of housing returns and the high share of the portfolio invested in real estate result in a reduction in the asset's value relative to that of safer assets, such as treasury bills.

6.5 The Limited Partner's Valuation of the Second Half of the House

Turning now to Limited Partners, we again want to calculate investment opportunities with and without residential real estate. We assume that the contract design and market structure eliminate all significant concerns by Limited Partners over such issues as moral hazard, taxes, and holding-period risk. In this case, we can treat residential housing as a new investment asset no different from existing equities or bonds. The value of residential housing as an investment asset will depend on its expected return, risk, and covariance with existing assets.

Two things change from the case of the Managing Partner. First, for Limited Partners we place no restriction on housing's portfolio share. Limited Partners would be free to purchase as much or as little residential real estate as they liked. Second, we assume that Limited Partners would hold a diversified portfolio of residential real estate. This is in sharp contrast to Managing Partners, who would own part of a single house.

We can carry out an analysis similar to the earlier one to determine the maximum premium a Limited Partner would pay for the second half of the

Table 6.2
Limited Partner valuation of a 20% portfolio share in housing

Risk aversion	Value of house (¢ per $)
1	63
2	82
3	97
4	97
5	98
6	98
7	99
8	99
9	99
10	100

Note: Uses real returns and a ten-year investment horizon.

house. We use the same utility function as above and start the Limited Partner with $100,000 in investment capital. For each level of risk aversion, we let the Limited Partner optimally invest this money among the three nonhousing asset groups in the current market structure and among the three asset groups and residential housing in the Partnership Market structure. In each scenario, we again simulate real asset returns for a ten year investment horizon.

Table 6.2 records the price that makes the Limited Partner indifferent between operating in the Partnership Market with 20% of their assets held in Partnerships purchased at that price, and operating in the traditional market with no housing. It is clear that the Limited Partner places a far higher value on housing returns than does the Managing Partner. The comparison is clarified in figure 6.4 which plots both Partners' valuations as a function of their levels of risk aversion. The gap between the two valuation lines provides a simple first approximation to the gains from trade in the Partnership Market. If both parties have a risk aversion parameter of $\alpha = 3$, then the gains from trade are 32 cents on the dollar, while at a risk aversion parameter of $\alpha = 5$, the gains from trade are 21 cents on the dollar.

A surprising feature of the computations is that the Limited Partner is willing to pay very close to a par price for a wide range of risk aversion parameters. There is a discount of no more than 3 cents on the dollar for risk aversion parameters of $\alpha = 3$ and above. These simple exercises lend no empirical support to the idea that Partnership Contracts would have to

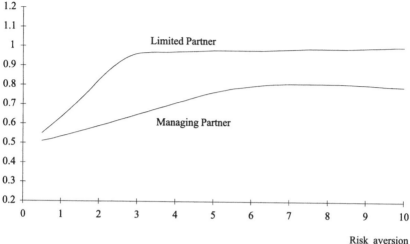

Figure 6.4
The gains from trade

sell for a price significantly below par, an issue that we take up again in chapter 13.

The computations also show that the gains from trade are very significant even when we assume that the Managing Partner and the Limited Partner have the same discount factor. These gains from trade would be even more significant for the house-poor home owners who are under great consumption pressure when they buy their homes, and for whom the relevant discount factor would be far higher than that of the Limited Partner. Overall, there are deep economic motives for the development of Partnership Markets, and the introduction of these markets would open up many new options both for individual home owners and for portfolio investors.

7   New Options for Home
       Ownership

In this chapter we provide examples to illustrate the many new options Partnership Markets would afford home owners, concentrating on opportunities for increased housing and nonhousing consumption. The numerical illustrations of the points we develop below are built on a number of assumptions.

• We concentrate on Partnerships that sell at par, with side illustrations to cover the impact of any possible discount to par.

• We focus on a home owner who wishes to sell a 50% share of the house to a Limited Partner and seeks additional funds from the mortgage market.

• We assume that the borrowing household has an A credit history and that they desire a thirty-year fixed-rate mortgage: either a conventional conforming mortgage with or without PMI or an FHA mortgage.

We also assume that the mortgage market operates in all essentials as described in chapter 3, with one minor difference concerning the treatment of maintenance costs that we outline below in the analysis of trade-up possibilities, and a one percentage point increase in closing costs to cover additional costs in the Partnership Market (4% of the appraised full value with Partnership Contracts).

7.1 Partnerships and the Costs of a $100,000 Home

Just how much less would it cost to buy a $100,000 house with a Partnership than it does in the current market? Figure 3.1 provides an example to illustrate the costs of buying a $100,000 home in the current mortgage market. The figure shows all the different combinations of cash at closing and annual carrying costs that would allow such a house to be purchased in the existing mortgage market.[1]

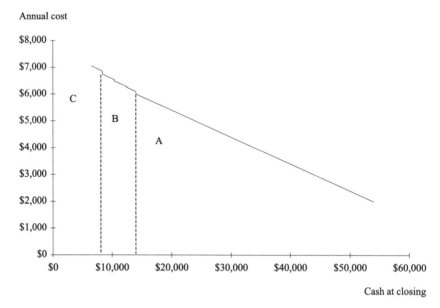

Annual cost

Figure 7.1
The costs of housing ($100,000 house), using Partnership financing (pricing at par)

Figure 7.1 provides a comparable illustration for the Partnership Market. It shows the combinations of up-front costs and annual carrying costs that would allow a household to move into a $100,000 home if they found a partner willing to take a 50% Limited Partnership stake at a par price.

Figure 7.1 consists of three distinct regions. Region *A* corresponds to the use of a conventional conforming mortgage without PMI, region *B* to the use of such a mortgage with PMI and an LTV between 80% and 95%, and region *C* to the use of an FHA mortgage with LTV above 95%.

The figure shows that if the household were to pay $54,000 up front, they would not need a mortgage and would be left with $2,000 in annual taxes and insurance as the only ongoing cost. On the other hand, if they took out a conventional conforming mortgage with an 80% LTV, they would need only $14,000 up front, consisting of closing costs of $4,000 and a down payment of $10,000. The remaining $90,000 necessary to purchase the house consists of $50,000 supplied by the Limited Partner and the Managing Partner's $40,000 mortgage. Note that this mortgage amount would represent an 80% LTV ratio, since the Managing Partner would have $50,000 equity in the home. Corresponding to this minimum

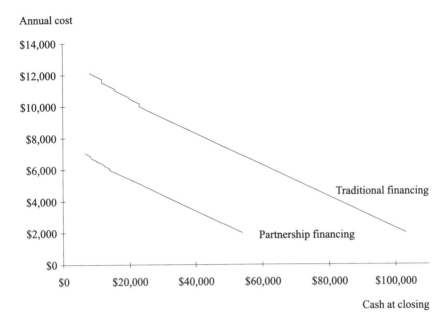

Annual cost

Figure 7.2
The costs of housing ($100,000 house), using traditional financing and Partnership financing (pricing at par)

up-front cost of $14,000, the household would be left with annual carrying costs of $6,000 excluding maintenance expenses, consisting of $2,000 in taxes and insurance and $4,000 in combined principal and interest.

The household would also have such intermediate options as paying $34,000 up front and $4,000 annually ($2,000 in taxes and insurance and $2,000 in principal and interest). The computations are similar for the 80%–95% LTV and the FHA regions of the figure, regions B and C.

Figure 7.2 superimposes figures 3.1 and 7.1. We use the label "traditional" to identify the costs of buying in the existing mortgage market as opposed to the Partnership Market. The figure makes evident the dramatic cost savings that would become available with a Partnership Agreement. The minimum up-front cost involved in buying the house using a conventional conforming mortgage without PMI would be some 40% lower in the Partnership Market: $14,000 as opposed to $23,000 in the traditional market. In general, the cost saving for a particular property (reduction in up-front cost for a given annual cost or in annual cost for a given up-front cost) would be around 40% to 50%.

The computations used in these figures are based on the numerical assumptions used in figure 3.1:

- Taxes and insurance amount to 2% of the house value annually.
- Principal and interest amount to 10% of the loan amount annually.
- PMI costs are an additional 2.25%, 3.0%, and 4.0% up front as the three LTV triggers of 80%, 85%, and 90% are passed.
- FHA costs are 2.25% up front with a 0.5 percentage point interest rate premium for the life of the loan.
- Closing costs amount to 3% of the house value in the traditional market, with an additional 1% in the Partnership Market to pay for the extra layer of transactions.

In our opinion, the incremental closing cost that we assume in the Partnership Market is on the high side of the likely range of additional transactions costs associated with the Partnership finance. One can even make a strong case for the possibility that transactions costs would be lower for Partnerships than for traditional mortgage financing, as we discuss in chapter 14.

7.2   Partnerships and Trading Up

The presence of a Limited Partner that supplies additional funds would clearly enable potential home owners to afford larger homes than is possible in the current market. In this section, we illustrate the extent of the trade-up possibilities in the Partnership Market. We base our analysis on the chapter 3 examples detailing the housing possibility function for households in the traditional mortgage market. As in chapter 3, we assume the household has no debts other than the mortgage, so that the front-end PITI ratio of 28% is the relevant test, and that the Limited Partner supplies 50% of the equity at a par price.

Adjusting the PITI Ratio for Incremental Maintenance Expenditures
Before quantifying the trade-up possibilities, it is important to consider one small but significant change that would likely arise when a Managing Partner applied for a mortgage. The presence of a Limited Partner, who would introduce additional funds for the house purchase, would clearly increase the maximum affordable house value. Mortgage originators would likely take steps to ensure that households remained in a position to afford adequate maintenance expenditures on the house and would therefore amend the existing PITI ratios.

Under the current PITI tests, the only expenses added to the principal and interest expenses on the mortgage are regular tax expenses and interest payments on other outstanding debts. But with Partnership Agreements, households would retain responsibility for 100% of maintenance expenses, even though their principal and interest payments would involve owning only 50% of the house's equity.

This means that as Managing Partners, households would be responsible for greater maintenance expenses than they would as sole owners paying the same principal and interest and might not be able to maintain the property in accordance with the terms of their Partnership Agreement unless the credit-granting process made explicit allowance for the increased maintenance expenses. Both lenders and Limited Partners would benefit were the lenders to adjust their lending ratios, and hereafter we assume that this adjustment would indeed take place. We make the simple assumption that the lender adjusts the PITI ratios by taking account of maintenance expenses stated as 1% of the appraised value for a 50–50 Partnership Agreement (this percentage could be adjusted to reflect different equity shares). We refer to the adjusted income ratio test as the PITIM test, adding maintenance (M) to the other forms of expense.

Computations

As pointed out in chapter 3, the two major economic factors that limit a household's ability to buy an expensive home are their level of cash available at closing to split between closing costs and down payment, and their level of adjusted annual income. We now recalculate the maximum affordable house value for the household with the resource range used in figure 3.3: $25,000 cash at closing, and gross adjusted income ranging from $10,000 to $100,000. Figure 7.3 illustrates the new housing possibility function.

Note that at low income levels, the PITIM constraint would restrict the maximum house value the household could afford. A household with income of $30,000 could afford a house with a maximum value of approximately $130,000 in the Partnership Market, as opposed to $90,000 in the traditional market. To see why, note that the household's maximum payments would be $8,400 and annual taxes and insurance on the house would amount to 2% of the purchase price, which would be $2,600. The additional maintenance expenditures would amount to $1,300, or 1% of the house price. Thus the household could afford principal and interest payments of $4,500, which translates to a loan amount of $45,000.

Maximum house value

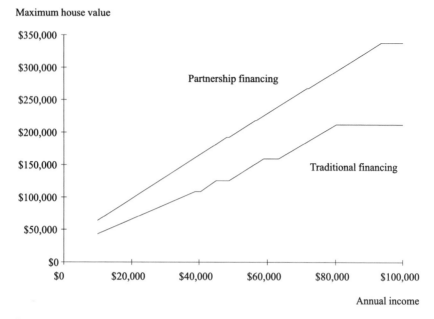

Figure 7.3
The housing possibility function ($25,000 available up front) using Partnership financing (pricing at par)

Maximum payments (0.28 · income)	$8,400
Less annual taxes and insurance	($2,600)
Less incremental maintenance	($1,300)
Maximum principal and interest	$4,500
Equivalent loan amount	$45,000

The 4% closing costs on a $130,000 house total $5,200, so that $19,800 would be available for the down payment:

Cash for closing	$25,000
Less closing costs	($5,200)
Cash for down payment	$19,800

With the maximum loan of $45,000 in addition to $65,000 from the Limited Partner to buy the house, the household could afford a $130,000 house:

Cash for downpayment	$19,800
Mortgage	$45,000
Equity from limited partner	$65,000
House value	$129,800

The derivation of the entire figure is detailed in the Appendix to this chapter.

For different levels of cash available at closing, the housing possibility function of figure 7.3 remains valid with some rescaling of the axes: with $12,500 up front, the figure remains valid if the numbers on both axes are divided by two, and with $50,000 up front, the figure remains valid if the numbers on both axes are multiplied by two.

7.3 Mixed Motives

Trading up and reducing costs could also be combined in various proportions. For example, a household could move into the same house with a 30% reduction in both up-front and annual costs or move into a home 30% more expensive than is possible under traditional financing. There would also be all the intermediate options. Figure 7.4 provides the trade-off between house value and annual costs for a given $25,000 in up-front costs. For a particular house value–annual cost mix under traditional financing such as point T, the borrower could choose, using Partnership finance, to increase the house value or reduce annual costs in any combination represented by the shaded triangle. The Partnership curve represents the upper bound of cost reductions and increasing house values. For a given house value, annual costs could be reduced by 30%–50% (50% at smaller house values, 30% at higher house values because the up-front PMI costs result in a proportionately higher loan balance).

We implicitly assume the household does not face a debt-to-income constraint. If such a constraint were binding in either market, the curve would become vertical where the maximum annual payment constraint binds.

We can draw a similar figure for the trade-off between house value and up-front cost for a given $15,000 in annual costs. This is shown in figure 7.5. Again, the shaded triangle under point T represents the possibilities for trade up and reduction in up-front cost attainable under Partnership financing for a particular up-front cost–house value combination under traditional financing.

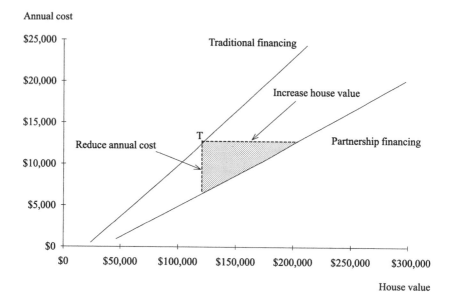

Figure 7.4a
Mixed motives: trade-off between house value and annual costs ($25,000 available up front), under traditional and Partnership financing (pricing at par)

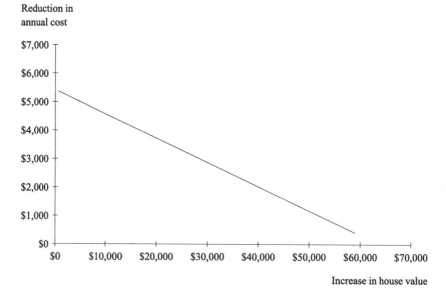

Figure 7.4b
Possibilities for point T under Partnership financing

Up-front cost

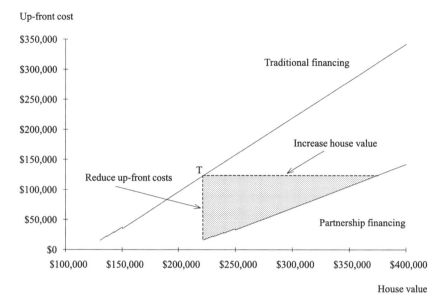

Figure 7.5a
Mixed motives: trade-off between house value and up-front costs ($15,000 annual costs), under traditional and Partnership financing (10% discount)

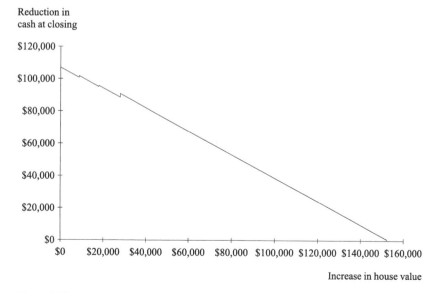

Figure 7.5b
Possibilities for point T under Partnership financing

Table 7.1
Mixed motives: Possibilities for increasing house value and reducing ownership costs

	Traditional financing	Partnership financing	Percentage change
House value	180,000	220,000	+22
Up-front cost	30,000	24,000	−20
Annual cost	19,800	16,900	−15
House value	150,000	180,000	+20
Up-front cost	27,500	25,000	−10
Annual cost	16,200	13,000	−20
House value	100,000	130,000	+30
Up-front cost	25,000	20,000	−25
Annual cost	9,900	8,200	−17

Figure 7.2 has already presented the trade-off between annual cost and up-front cost for a given house value. Analogously, an upper right triangle can be drawn for every point on the traditional financing curve that shows the possibilities for reducing annual costs and up-front costs with a Partnership.

It is also possible that improvements might occur on all three fronts: increases in house value and reductions in annual and up-front costs. Table 7.1 presents three examples to illustrate these possibilities.

7.4 The Impact of Price

It is important to see how the cost advantages and housing possibilities opened by Partnerships would be influenced by any discount or premiums to par. For simplicity, we limit attention to the case of a 10% discount.

Figure 7.6 reproduces figure 7.2 but shows the costs of housing with a 10% discount in the price of Partnerships. Although pricing at a discount would clearly not be as advantageous to the borrower as pricing at par, both annual and upfront costs would still be reduced dramatically compared with traditional financing. The results are similar for the housing possibility function, which is shown in figure 7.7.

7.5 Appendix

In this appendix we report the calculations underlying figure 7.3. To find the maximum house value H given annual income Y and cash for closing

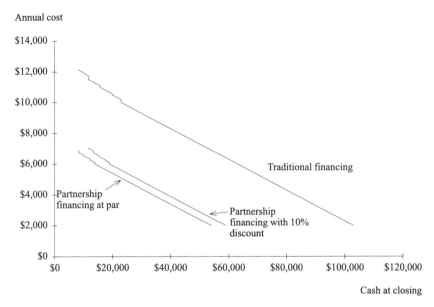

Figure 7.6
The costs of housing ($100,000 house), under traditional financing and Partnership financing
(10% discount)

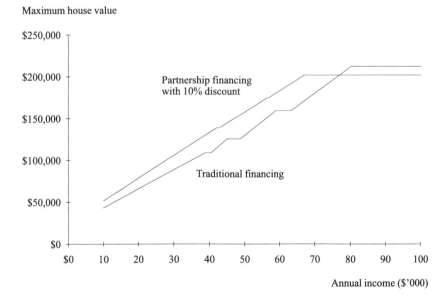

Figure 7.7
The housing possibility function ($25,000 available up front) under traditional financing and
Partnership financing (10% discount)

C, within the income range in which the PITIM constraint binds and the LTV constraint on a conventional conforming mortgage without PMI does not bind, we must solve the following equations:

$$M = 0.28Y - H(0.02 + 0.01) \tag{7.1}$$

$$C = D + 0.04H \tag{7.2}$$

$$H = 0.5H + L + D, \tag{7.3}$$

where M is the principal and interest payment. Equation (7.1) says mortgage payments must equal 28% of annual income less the 2% taxes and insurance and the 1% incremental maintenance. Equation 7.2 says that cash would be used up between the down payment D and the 4% Partnership closing costs. Equation 7.3 says the maximum house value would equal the Limited Partner's half share plus the loan balance and the down payment. Under our interest rate assumptions, the loan amount L equals ten times the principal and interest payments ($L = 10 \cdot M$). With a small amount of rearrangement and substitution, equations 7.1 to 7.3 reduces to the equation 7.4:

$$H = 3.33Y + 1.19C. \tag{7.4}$$

As in the traditional market, equation (7.4) would be valid provided the income constraint rather than the LTV constraint were binding. Once income exceeded a certain level, the LTV constraint rather than the PITIM constraint would become binding. When the LTV constraint was binding (e.g., at 80%), the down payment (cash less closing costs) would amount to one-fifth of the Managing Partner's 50%. The Limited Partner would again put up half the house value:

$$H = 5(C - 0.04H) + 0.5H$$
$$H = 7.135C. \tag{7.5}$$

With cash of $25,000, the maximum house value would be $178,500. Of the $25,000, roughly $7,100 would go to closing costs and $17,900 would be left for the down payment, so that the mortgage would be $71,350. Given these data, the PITIM test would be passed provided the annual mortgage payments of $7,135, the annual taxes of roughly $3,600, and the 1% incremental maintenance of $1,800 could be afforded under the PITIM test. This would be true provided the following inequality were satisfied,

$$Y > (7{,}140 + 3{,}600 + 1{,}800)/0.28$$

$$Y > 44{,}768.$$

(7.6)

For income levels between \$10,000 and the critical level of \$44,700, the maximum affordable value would rise as in equation (7.4). Then it would follow equation (7.5), that is, the maximum house value would be constant.

The use of conventional mortgages with PMI or FHA mortgages would allow the LTV to exceed 80%, and the equations must be modified to reflect this.

8   Partnerships and the Life Cycle

The existence of Partnership Markets would likely result in profound changes in households' consumption profiles, the behavior of their portfolio of assets and liabilities over time, and their behavior in the housing market itself. In this chapter, we expand on the many different ways households could use Partnership Agreements depending on their economic situation. To get the clearest view of Partnership Agreements' total value, we explore their potential impact on household behavior over the course of the life cycle along the lines suggested in chapter 4.

8.1   Easing the Transition to Ownership: Illustrative Examples

We begin at the younger stage of the life cycle, when the vast majority of households are renters, and explore how different households might use the Partnership Agreement to help them make the transition from renting to ownership. A key issue for renters is the possibility of waiting many years before having sufficient down payment to buy, or before earning enough to afford to pay the installments on a home of reasonable size and quality. We use the two examples from chapter 4 of young households without and with significant education debt to show how much more quickly these households could make the transition to ownership using partnerships.

NED and the Transition to Ownership
In chapter 4 we discussed an example of a young household with no education debt saving to buy a first home. Here we repeat this example, showing how access to Partnership Contracts would accelerate this household's transition to ownership. Below we review this example.

- The household has no assets and no liabilities.
- They wish to buy a starter house worth at least $60,000.

- Their annual income is $24,000.
- They seek a 90% LTV loan with PMI.
- The mortgage involves closing costs of 3% of the appraised house value under traditional financing, taxes and insurance of 2%, principal and interest amounting to 10% of the loan amount, and three additional up-front points for PMI.
- They face a combined federal and state average income tax rate of 25%.
- Their minimum consumption expenditure while renting is $16,000 per annum.

These assumptions imply that the household will have to wait five years to purchase its first house. Now consider the time to save for the same property under the same financial assumptions if the household were to buy using a Partnership Contract. Specifically, we assume that the household would sell a 50% ownership stake to the Limited Partner at par. A 90% LTV loan would imply borrowing 90% of $30,000 instead of 90% of $60,000, thus the loan would be $27,000. This would create principal and interest payments of $2,700 per annum. Combined with the $1,200 of taxes and insurance (2% of $60,000) and incremental maintenance of $600 (1% of $60,000) the PITIM ratio would be 18.75%, which passes the front-end PITIM test by a wide margin. The household would have to save around $6,200 in up-front costs consisting of the following:

A 10% down payment	$3,000
Three up-front PMI points on the $27,000 mortgage	$ 810
Closing costs of 4% of $60,000	$2,400
	$6,210

Thus the up-front costs would be reduced by 32% and the time to save reduced accordingly, to just under three-and-a-half years.

The above example can readily be generalized. Figure 8.1 illustrates the connection between household income and the time it would take the household to move into the $60,000 home under both traditional and Partnership financing. A low-income household's period of renting would be reduced by around two-and-a-half years. A high-income household's period of renting would be reduced by around one year.

Partnerships could ease the transition to ownership not only by shortening the time a household would have to remain in the rental sector, but also by improving their consumption prospects during this period of savings. Figure 8.2 illustrates, for a household with an annual income of

Time to save, years

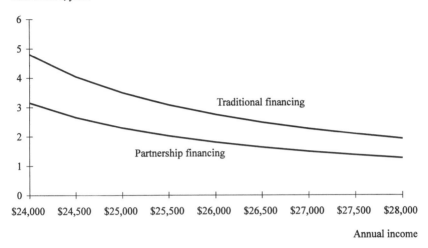

Figure 8.1
Time to save for a down payment (household with no education debt)
Note: Calculations are based on these assumptions: house price = $60,000, minimum consumption = $16,000 per annum, front-end payment ratio = 32%, interest rate = 9.6%.

Time to save, years

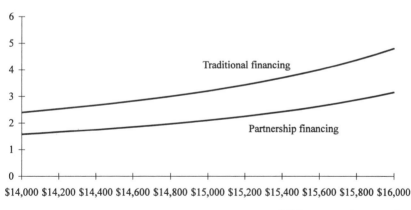

Figure 8.2
Consumption and time to save trade-off (household with no education debt)
Note: Calculations are based on these assumptions: house price = $60,000, minimum consumption = $16,000 per annum, front-end payment ratio = 32%, interest rate = 9.6%.

$28,000, the combinations of annual consumption and time to save under the traditional and Partnership forms of finance. For example, a household might decide that waiting five years to own a house is too long. Under traditional finance, they could reduce this waiting time to slightly over three years by lowering their annual consumption from $16,000 to around $15,000. With Partnerships, the household could maintain their annual consumption at $16,000 and still make the transition to ownership in just over three years.

Partnerships would also increase post-purchase consumption. Under traditional financing, the disposable income left over for consumption expenditures when the household has moved in can be computed as follows:

Gross income	$24,000
Less tax payments[1] (24,000 − 5,400) · 0.25	($4,650)
Annual after-tax income	$19,350
Less annual mortgage payments	($5,400)
Less annual taxes and insurance	($1,200)
Less annual house maintenance (1% of house value)	($600)
Net income available for nonhousing consumption	$12,150

In this example, the household has an income of $24,000 and spends $16,000 on rent and nonhousing consumption for five years, after which the household purchases a $60,000 home, leaving it with a net income of $12,150 available for nonhousing consumption.

Under Partnership financing, the household would spend $16,000 for three-and-a-half years, after which they would purchase a 50% share in a $60,000 home, leaving them with post-purchase nonhousing consumption of $14,175:

Gross income	$24,000
Less tax payments[1] (24,000 − 2,700) · 0.25	($5,325)
Annual after-tax income	$18,675
Less annual mortgage payments	($2,700)
Less annual taxes and insurance	($1,200)
Less incremental maintenance	($600)
Net income available for nonhousing consumption	$14,175

Thus Partnerships would have the benefit of reducing the time to save as well as increasing consumption before and after purchase.

ED and the Transition to Ownership

Now consider the potential benefit of Partnerships to a young household attempting to buy a first house while also paying off education debt. Specifically, we assume that:

• They have no assets and education debt of $40,000. The annual payment of principal and interest on the education debt is $6,000.

• They wish to buy a starter house worth at least $100,000.

• Their annual income is $40,000.

• The mortgage involves closing costs of 3% of the house value under traditional financing, taxes and insurance of 2%, principal and interest amounting to 10% of the loan amount, and three additional up-front points for PMI costs.

• They face a combined federal and state average income tax rate of 25%.

• Their minimum consumption expenditure while renting is $18,000 per annum.

As we saw in chapter 4, it will take this household more than five-and-a-half years to reach its savings target. With the possibility of Partnership financing, the household's situation would be very different. Again, we assume that the household would sell a 50% ownership at par. The household would now have a maximum of $6,000 in mortgage principal and interest, which would translate into a $60,000 loan.

Maximum annual payments (37.5% of income)	$15,000
Less annual student loan payments	($6,000)
Less annual taxes and insurance	($2,000)
Less incremental maintenance	($1,000)
Annual principal and interest	$6,000
Equivalent to loan amount	$60,000

However, since the 50% stake in the house would be worth only $50,000, the PITIM constraint would not bind; rather, the LTV constraint would be relevant. Assuming that the household did not want the LTV to exceed 90%, they would take a $45,000 mortgage, which necessitates saving $5,000 for the down payment plus $4,000 in closing costs (4% of the

Time to save, years

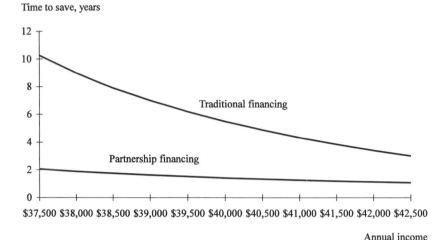

Figure 8.3
Time to save for a down payment (household with no education debt)
Note: Calculations are based on these assumptions: house price = $100,000, minimum consumption = $18,000 per annum, student loan balance = $40,000, student loan payments = $6,000 per annum, back-end payment ratio = 37.5%, interest rate = 9.6%.

house value) and $1,350 in up-front PMI points (3% of the loan amount), for a total of $10,350. The household would still be able to save $6,000 per annum so that they would take less than two years to save the necessary amount.

Thus, for households with significant education debt, Partnership Contracts would reduce waiting time until ownership even more. Figure 8.3 shows this relationship. Overall, access to Partnership Contracts would cut the transition time by at least 50%, because Partnerships would relax the PITI constraint, which is very binding for households with other forms of debt. For a low-income household, the period of renting would be reduced by around eight years, for a high-income household by around two years.

Overall, Partnerships would offer many young households chances to move to ownership and therefore to better housing and a better neighborhood more quickly. The reduction in financial strain from reduced interest and down payment obligations would open up the possibility of increased levels of consumption, which we believe would be very important for many households. The availability of Partnerships might also increase the level of savings in nonhousing assets.

8.2 Partnerships and the Middle Years

Households in the middle years of the life cycle have typically made the transition to ownership and are saving for a trade-up house, college for their children, and retirement. We consider households that have made the transition to home ownership and are now financing a trade-up home and estimate the investment risk facing the household as they make this purchase using the traditional and Partnership finance.

We assume that the trade-up house is valued at $100,000. Under traditional finance the home owner retains full ownership in the new house. We assume that the household invests 85% of their initial assets to serve as the downpayment on the new house. To minimize the household's level of risk, we assume that their nonhousing assets are initially allocated to minimize the total portfolio variance of the asset portfolio (which is achieved by investing the nonhousing assets in various classes of government bonds). We consider a range of initial LTVs from 80% to 95%.

Over a thirty-year investment horizon, we simulate housing and other asset returns based on their mean and variance-covariance properties. For each year, we update the house value and nonhousing asset portfolio value using the simulated returns. We calculate the household's home equity position as their current house value minus the outstanding mortgage debt (based on a thirty-year amortization schedule). We calculate their overall equity position as the sum of their housing equity plus the current value of their nonhousing assets. We stop a simulation if a household enters a negative overall equity position. A total of 1,000 simulations are carried out for each initial LTV position.

The purpose of this exercise is to explore the portfolio risks facing households making such a trade-up decision. We use SMSA-specific housing returns for this simulation, rather than the national housing returns that we use in the other simulations. Problems of housing lock-in and negative shocks to a household's wealth arise primarily as a result of sharp downturns in particular housing markets, rather than secular downturns in housing at the national level. We report results based on Freddie Mac housing returns for Los Angeles, where we have adjusted the variance to reflect the level of risk facing the individual homeowner. Although the specific results depend on the choice of an SMSA, the qualitative results are quite similar across a wide range of SMSAs.

The simulations are repeated for Partnerships. Here we again assume that the household is purchasing a $100,000 house, this time selling a 50% equity stake at par. We assume that the household has the same initial

Table 8.1
Comparison of equity positions for traditional and Partnership contracts Los Angeles housing returns

	Traditonal		Partnership	
Initial LTV (%)	% Negative house equity	% Negative overall equity	% Negative house equity	% Negative overall equity
80	10.7	6.7	10.7	0.1
85	16.3	11.8	16.3	1.2
90	23.2	19.6	23.2	4.7
95	32.2	29.8	32.2	17.5

Note: Households start with 85% of their net assets invested in housing. Nonhousing assets are initially allocated to place the household on the constrained efficient-investment frontier. Based on 1,000 simulations.

total assets as in our traditional household. For example, with a 90% LTV the traditional household has total assets of $11,765. This is divided into $10,000 in house equity (85%) and $1,765 in nonhousing assets (15%). Using Partnerships, the household puts $5,000 in home equity down on the house, leaving $6,765 to be invested in nonhousing assets. Again, their nonfinancial assets are initially allocated to minimize the home owner's total portfolio risk, and 1,000 simulations are done for each initial LTV level.

Table 8.1 reports the percentage of simulations in which the household experienced a negative housing equity position and a negative overall equity position. We can see from the table that the fraction of households that experience a negative housing equity position is the same with both methods of housing finance, and increases rapidly with the LTV level. Significantly different results occur, though, for the percent of households that experience a negative overall equity position. For traditional finance, this ranged from a low of 6.7% for 80% LTV mortgages to a high of 29.8% for 95% LTV mortgages. In sharp contrast, for Partnership finance this ranged from a low of 0.1% for 80% LTV mortgages to a high of 17.5% for 95% LTV mortgages.

While we would not expect that every household that experiences a negative overall equity position would default, this indicates a serious financial circumstance for the household. If the household's income prospects remain good, then they may be able to ride out the downturn in the housing market. However, this does not offset two important facts. First, the household has lost all their housing and nonhousing equity, a considerable financial setback. Second, in riding out the bad housing market, the household becomes locked into its current house. That is, the household may be blocked at various points from taking advantage of better income prospects in other labor markets because of their current negative equity position. This compounds the difficulty the household faces in rebuilding their financial prospects.

8.3 Partnerships and the Later Years

During the later years, older households often find the family home too large and thus want to move to a smaller home, perhaps located in a more temperate climate. The quality of life for a household in the later years will depend significantly on their physical and financial health. The latter will reflect the history of savings and asset allocations decisions made by the household and the vagaries of the market.

Households in the later years of the life cycle would like to enjoy the fruits of their lifelong labor. However, as we saw in chapter 4, for many elderly households the later years are difficult because of a very low level of income. The largest nonpension asset for many elderly households is their house. Many financial products have been developed over the years to enable elderly households to convert this asset into current income, including second and reverse mortgages. In addition, an elderly household can sell their house and buy a smaller house or rent as another alternative. There is considerable debate as to why so few elderly choose these options. The first two mortgage alternatives may not be attractive to some senior citizens because they involve new debt, and the third alternative requires that the household move from a house that they have most likely lived in for many years. For some households, this move may represent a long-awaited change in lifestyle, while for others it represents a substantial roadblock to a higher level of consumption.

Partnership Contracts would offer an alternative for elderly households. The simplest way for an older household to use the Partnership Market would be for them to apply as preexisting owners. With a Partnership, a household could sell off part of their existing house, converting the proceeds into an annuity. However, they would not be forced to move as they would if they sold their home, and unlike with second and reverse mortgages, they would assume no additional debt.

However, we realize that the behavior of home owners in their later years is not yet well understood and that Partnership Contracts might meet the same fate as reverse mortgages. One possible explanation is the broad inertia that appears to characterize the life choices of many elderly. Since all these transactions are stressful, the elderly may avoid them in all except the most dire of circumstances.

With this in mind, Partnership Contracts might benefit the elderly primarily to the extent they were adopted when the household was younger. By providing an ounce of prevention in the middle years, Partnerships might alleviate the need for a pound of difficult cure in the later years. As we saw earlier, Partnership Contracts would significantly improve the household's investment portfolio options. By allowing the household to build more wealth (and in more liquid forms), Partnerships could greatly enhance a household's retirement prospects.

To illustrate the point, we return to the computations from chapter 6 in which we identify optimal asset portfolios for households in the traditional housing finance market and in the Partnership Market. We again consider the situation of households at age fifty-five who are picking their portfolios to maximize the expected utility of wealth when they retire at age sixty-five. We continue to use the constant relative risk aversion utility function and to limit the set of nonhousing assets to stocks, treasury bills, and long-term government bonds. The procedure of chapter 6 is used both to generate the pattern of expected real asset returns and to simulate the resulting distribution of final wealth levels and the level of expected utility. The only difference is that we focus on the distribution of retirement wealth and its division between housing and nonhousing assets rather than on the valuation of the housing asset.

To illustrate the value of the Partnership in improving the wealth position at retirement, we consider the special case of a household with total assets of $100,000 and with a fixed risk aversion parameter $\alpha = 4$. The household is buying a home worth $85,000. They can either buy their home outright, as in the existing market, or can buy their home with a Limited Partner who pays a par price for a 50% share of the final sale price of the house. As in chapter 6, we assume that the household will choose an optimal asset portfolio subject to the constraints that are set by the way in which the home is purchased. In the traditional market, the household has $15,000 to divide among the nonhousing assets, while in the Partnership market they have $57,500 to divide among these assets.

Figure 8.4 gives the resulting smoothed empirical distribution of the household's retirement portfolio in the traditional market and in the Partnership Market. It is clear that the Partnership Market results in a significant improvement in the wealth distribution, largely because it frees up more resources that can be invested in stocks, which offer a higher expected return than does residential real estate. Table 8.2 produces sum-

Percentage

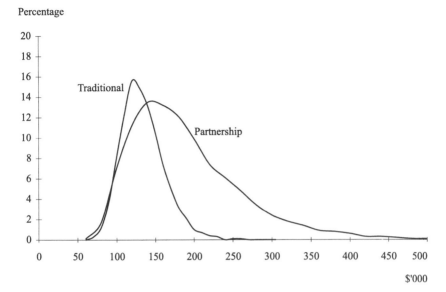

Figure 8.4
Managing partner's wealth distribution after ten years
Note: $100,000 invested, risk aversion parameter 4.

mary statistics for the wealth distributions, and shows that the Partnership Market results an increase of more than 40% in the expected level of retirement wealth.

The difference between the retirement portfolios is even more dramatic if we focus only on nonhousing wealth. As we have seen in chapter 6, it is common for older households to stay in their homes without taking a reverse mortgage, treating their housing wealth as completely illiquid. Table 8.2 shows that the level of nonhousing wealth for the household in the Partnership Market is more than three times as high as it is in the traditional market, averaging more than $130,000 as opposed to $35,000. While it is clear that the example above is special in many ways, the point that it makes is simple and robust. A household that buys a home with a Limited Partner is likely to retire with a far higher wealth level and a far superior set of consumption possibilities than a household that buys in the traditional market.

8.4   Dynamics and Adjustment in the Partnership Market

A household would be able to adjust their use of the Partnership Market in an appropriate manner at many different points in their life cycle, rather

Table 8.2
Comparison of retirement portfolios for traditional and Partnership housing returns

	Traditional		Partnership	
Percentile	Total	Nonhousing	Total	Nonhousing
90	$165,525	$59,037	$275,515	$225,783
75	145,001	43,832	216,480	167,701
50	125,744	30,603	164,892	117,152
25	109,529	21,139	127,159	80,977
10	96,338	15,082	102,114	57,817
Mean	129,000	34,718	180,000	132,859
Standard deviation	27,810	19,081	74,661	72,909

Note: Based on 10,000 simulations of ten-year real asset returns.

than in strict accordance with the three life stages outlined above. One of the critical margins of adjustment for the household would be adjusting their owned portion of the equity in the house. A young owner may want to own very little, but may be restricted to beginning with, say, the 50% share that we have been using in our illustrative examples. However, as the household gained a track record in the Partnership market, they may be able to lower this share by engaging in a sale of equity. The procedures for selling additional equity are outlined in the next chapter.

The issue of what would determine the optimal ownership pattern for the household in the Partnership Market is an intriguing one. As indicated above, this would interact in important ways with the optimal life cycle profile of consumption expenditures and asset holding. A household with pressing consumption needs would be likely to desire a lower equity share in their house than would a household without such needs. A household wishing to trade up to a new house in the same neighborhood would have very different portfolio diversification needs than a household seeking to move to another part of the country.

The actual choices that would be made by households as their circumstances evolved would be determined not only by their preferences, but also by the ease of adjustment and the pattern of asset availability in the Partnership Market. If the Partnership Contract is written in the flexible manner that we propose in the next chapter, it would allow the household to adjust its ownership share in a relatively frictionless fashion according to its preferences. The Secondary Partnership Markets outlined in chapter 10 would also provide the household with important additional flexibility over the life cycle. Our proposal is that there be secondary markets in Partnership Agreements originated in specific geographic and economic areas. As such markets developed, they would allow the household to buy and sell assets that would correlate very highly with any particular region of interest to the household. Thus a household anticipating a move from, say, New York to Chicago, would be able to sell off some equity in their home and buy funds to insure themselves against an increase in the price of real estate in Chicago.

There may be other adjustment margins for households beyond those relating to consumption needs and portfolio issues. In chapter 12 we outline some of the many different products that we would expect to develop as the Partnership Market evolved. To give one simple example, there is scope for variation in the contract clauses that relate to adjustments to the property. On the one end would be contracts that required careful consent procedures in the case of even moderate alterations to the house. On the other end would be procedures that involved no need for notification, with a simple final appraisal to account for all changes to the property during the life of the Partnership Agreement. A household buying an old "fixer-upper" home would be likely to choose the Partnership Agreement that minimized the need for notification and consultation. On the other hand, a first-time home buyer purchasing a highly standardized house may view themselves as most unlikely to make major alterations to the home, and therefore use the more restrictive product, which would presumably increase the price that the Limited Partner would pay for the product.

Overall, the nature of the choices that the household would make in the Partnership Market would be profoundly influenced by the nature of the supply side of the market, to which we now turn.

III

The Supply Side

In this section we provide proposals for the supply side of the Partnership Market to address the following questions:

- What are the key clauses in the Partnership Contract?
- Who would supply funds to the Partnership Market?
- How and why would they supply funds?
- What steps would the household have to take to obtain the funds?

9   The Partnership Contract

9.1   Guide to the Contract

While we view the Limited Partnership as the natural contractual format for the residential property market, agreement clauses and bylaws of residential property Limited Partnerships should be written differently from those structured for other limited partnerships. In this chapter we describe the key clauses that cover house purchase, house maintenance, alterations to the house and to the Partnership Agreement, sale of the house, and breach of the Partnership Contract.

The clauses we outline for the Partnership Agreement are not quite as unfamiliar as they may seem. Many have analogs in the existing Mortgage Agreement, and the Mortgage Agreement, so widely accepted and standardized, is itself every bit as intricate as the Partnership Agreement.

The contract would be guided in large part by a desire to keep owning a home as simple as possible for the Managing Partner. We believe that the Partnership clauses would ultimately not be perceived as profoundly onerous, especially in light of the many restrictions routinely accepted in the current housing market:

• Neighborhood associations and local regulation already provide various (and sometimes severe) limitations on the home owner's freedom of action.

• The implicit restrictions on a Partnership would be less severe than those that already exist for "fee simple" common property.[1]

• Co-ops can be even more restrictive, with boards that impose restrictions on who may purchase a property and whether one can use the property as collateral for a mortgage.

Therefore, we see no reason to view the additional issues of control and notification in the Managing Partnership as being of critical importance to potential home owners. In fact, certain potential home owners would be very happy to have a Limited Partner join them in the purchase of their home because of the dramatic improvement in incentives, as described in chapter 14. But whether Partnerships would be perceived as restrictive is an open question and might depend more on how the market is introduced than on the precise details of a written contract.

As a practical matter, the wording of the clauses in the Partnership Agreement would both give control to and restrict the control of both Partners. To deepen understanding of the agreement's meaning, we now discuss more extensively some of the major agreement clauses. It is worth bearing in mind that there is room for a wide variety of residential Limited Partnerships, as outlined in chapter 12. The major limitation on the proliferation of agreement forms would be the desire to standardize the market, in large part to make secondary marketing easier.

9.2   Clauses Covering the Purchase

Two major issues arise at the point of entering into the Partnership Agreement: fraud prevention and ensuring adequate appraisal.

The potential Managing Partner must supply a basic set of information to the Limited Partner upon application, and it would be criminally fraudulent to supply incorrect information. The required information would be quite similar to that requested for a traditional mortgage and would include the applicant's credit history, information on any past performance as a Managing Partner, and a list of past addresses and contacts. The application would also include legal releases granting the Limited Partner permission to gather various data.

Clauses would also be needed to formalize the process for appraising the house's value. The appraisal process would also have to be somewhat more detailed, because the Limited Partner would be receiving a partial interest and would want to specify just what is and is not included in the "property."[2] An approach for this more detailed appraisal might be taken from the site plans used by condos or Planned Urban Developments (PUDs) with common property. These site plans map in detail the location of each shrub, plant, tree, and the like because the association must track its assets and investments.

In the typical case in which a house purchase triggered the application for the Partnership, all the information on the purchase price of the house would have to be supplied in full detail,[3] in part because of its considerable and direct impact on appraised value. The Partnership Agreement might also contain the outline of a formalized appeal process should the Limited and Managing Partners' appraisals differ substantially. This process clause would also set out a specific time period considered reasonable for each party to take each contractually specified step.

9.3   Clauses That Ensure Adequate Maintenance

To mitigate any maintenance problems, the Limited Partnership Agreement would contain several clauses concerning the "Doctrine of Waste," owner occupation, and insurance.

The Doctrine of Waste and the As-Is Clause

The existing Mortgage Agreement already contains a form of as-is clause. In real property law, a principle known as the Doctrine of Waste makes it quite clear that the mortgagor is obliged to maintain the property being mortgaged and not allow it to waste. Upon ascertaining that the property is in a state of disrepair, the mortgagee can petition the courts to accelerate the debt and then make a motion to foreclose. As a matter of legal principle, then, the Partnership Agreement would require nothing new or substantially different than what already exists for a standard Mortgage Agreement.

However, a practical issue remains, since we regard it as important for the Limited Partner to be able to efficiently and effectively bond the Managing Partner to the maintenance of the property and have a course for legal remedy in the event of Managing Partner nonperformance. The first part of the remedy is an as-is clause that formally states that the Managing Partner must return the property at sale in a condition similar to or better than its condition when purchased. Such a clause is quite common in the leasing industry. In a Partnership Agreement it would clearly establish the legal precedent of who is responsible for the property's maintenance.

The effectiveness of such a clause would vary somewhat according to how strictly it was written and enforced. The courts or the Partnership Agreement itself would have a range of choices to specify for each Partnership how rigorous a standard to apply to the as-is clause:

• The minimum standard would obligate the Managing Partner to maintain the property only to the level of the local building code.

• A stricter standard would obligate the Managing Partner to maintain everything in or around the property in the original condition, as in many commercial-property and auto leases.

For this stricter standard to be applied, it would be important to agree on the appraisals involved in establishing damage to the property. A high standard of appraisal would be needed, with full data on a prospective Limited Partner's performance and record of partitions. This would require those who wished to be Limited Partners to divulge information on their past performance along a variety of different dimensions. Parallel records of potential Managing Partners' performance in past as-is clauses would also be required on the application form for new Partnerships.

The agreement would also specify a set of penalties to arise at discovery of either type of failure to maintain:[4]

• Failure to maintain to the minimum building code standard would constitute a breach of the Partnership Agreement, with the remedy being the right for the Limited Partner to file for partition (the separation and liquidation of the Partners' shares in the property).

• Failure to maintain to a stricter contractually specified level would impose a monetary penalty.

The court would set the amount of the penalty at the estimated repair cost plus expenses. That penalty would then become the Managing Partner's obligation enforced by a lien on the Managing Partner's interest in the Partnership,[5] junior in priority to any preexisting mortgage, that would be deducted from the proceeds of the sale of the home.

Owner Occupation and Insurance

The stipulation that the Managing Partner must reside in the property would provide another important incentive for proper maintenance. Although traditionally recognized as important in the standard Mortgage Agreement,[6] this aspect would be even more important in a Partnership Agreement, because an important compensation to the Managing Partner is the right to consume the housing services, and the value of this consumption depends in part on the property being maintained. Allowing the Managing Partner to rent the property would introduce an additional agency problem between the Limited Partner and the renters, since renters would have no equity interest in the property.

We would strongly recommend that Partnership Agreements be restricted to owner-occupied houses and not be made available to investor properties. The agreement should stipulate that the Managing Partner's failure to occupy the house could trigger partition under an event of breach of the Partnership Agreement and that unpaid rent to the Limited Partner would survive as a priority claim in the partition. However, as in the current mortgage market, in cases where the renter adequately maintains the property, we would not expect the Limited Partner to have any incentive to exercise this clause. Thus we would expect to find in the Partnership Market the same pattern of short-term sublets that exist in the mortgage market. We would also expect the Limited Partner to formally recognize subletting in states of breach by the Managing Partner.

The Limited Partner would be interested in ensuring that the house was adequately insured. The basic contract would specify that it was the responsibility of the Managing Partner to purchase adequate insurance to cover damage to the entire house, at replacement cost, with the proceeds to be paid to the owners pro rata. This would retain a feature that we see as valuable to the Limited Partner, which is the lack of expenses for them during the period in which the Managing Partner remains in occupation of the house. The Managing Partner would pay the premium directly to the servicer of the Partnership agreement, who would use escrow to ensure that the insurance was in force. To cover the unlikely event of a Managing Partner canceling their insurance policy in the hope of ultimately claiming the funds in escrow, the Limited Partner could authorize the servicer to maintain additional "forced place" insurance on their Partnerships. Forced place insurance is common in auto loans, and covers any losses from a consumer dropping insurance coverage without notifying the servicer. The cost would represent a small addition to the basic homeowners' insurance fee, because only a few customers ever cancel coverage.

9.4   Alterations

Alterations to the Property

A traditional owner considering a value-enhancing alteration to property receives 100% of any increase in value resulting from the improvements. But since a Managing Partner would in the same circumstances receive only a pro-rata share of any increase in the house value, it would be important to take contractual steps to restore the proper incentives for undertaking value-enhancing improvements. Thus we propose that the Partnership Agreement provide for an increase in the Managing Partner's equity share as reward for major improvements to the property.

This could be accomplished by developing a list of all potential types of improvements and providing an agreed-upon increase in the Managing Partner's ownership interest for each improvement.[7] The original Partnership Agreement would include a list of the standard types of home improvements, the expected percentage increase in home price from each type of improvement, and the formula for calculating the change in the pro-rata Partnership interests. Prior to any work, the Limited Partner would receive a detailed listing of all improvement work to be done and the estimated cost. The cost estimates would be verified ex post with copies of all payments.[8] The price and quality would be agreed upon in advance, and the Limited Partner would independently inspect the final repair. After the improvement was completed and inspected, the Limited Partner would forward to the Managing Partner or mortgagee an addendum to the Agreement and new certificates.

Although it might at first appear rather ungainly, this system is quite similar to the way insurance companies handle auto repairs. In fact, as auto insurance companies have done for auto body shops, we would expect Limited Partners to develop over time a list of "approved" home improvement contractors, which would be bonded and insured, with documented work records (see Colden 1996). This would also help reduce the temptation to overpay the contractor and get a kickback, which would, of course, be an act of criminal fraud.

One could also reduce fraud or overpaying by verifying the home improvements against the home's carrying value as filed after sale with the IRS on Schedule 1099B, which is used to calculate the home's carrying cost for capital gains tax (see Clements 1995). The Limited Partner would eventually want to have access to all such filings.

Another procedure that would be available in the agreement would be for the Managing Partner to negotiate directly with the Limited Partner the appropriate adjustment in equity position before undertaking an improvement. One method of carrying out this negotiation would be to appraise the property before and after the improvement was undertaken and adjust the Managing Partner's share accordingly upward. This method would be less attractive for projects that required a significant time to complete and in property markets experiencing rapid price declines.

Over time, as experience in designing and executing Partnership Agreements accumulated, we would expect standards to develop over which improvements could be adjusted using a schedule and which would require negotiation. As in the property and casualty insurance industry, smaller adjustments to the property would likely become standardized, so that only the larger, nonstandard adjustments would require negotiation. The Managing Partner would probably choose simply to expense the costs of very small improvements.

Alterations to the Partnership Agreement

We now discuss the mechanisms that would be put in place for the Managing Partner to buy from or sell to the Limited Partner portions of their ownership interest before the final sale of the property.[9] Consider first a case in which the Managing Partner wished to buy additional equity from the Limited Partner. This could be accomplished only through a negotiated deal with the Limited Partner:

• The Managing Partner would pay for an appraisal and also possibly a refundable fee set out in the original Partnership Agreement.

• After appraisal, the Managing Partner would submit a bid to the Limited Partner.

• The Limited Partner would have thirty days to independently appraise and respond with a counteroffer.

• The Managing Partner could then either accept, reject or make their own counteroffer; however, the number of Managing Partner counteroffers within a certain time period would be limited under the original Partnership Agreement.

Procedures for the Managing Partner to sell off equity in their house at a time other than the point of purchase are likely to be particularly important, especially in the early days of the market. We expect that there would be many existing home owners who have no desire to move into a new home, but who would nevertheless appreciate the opportunity to lower their levels of mortgage expense and asset risk by selling off equity in their home. The procedures for such "midterm" equity sales would differ little from those for new home owners, but there would be even greater emphasis placed on developing accurate appraisals, and it may therefore be especially important to develop lists of trusted appraisers who could be seen as beholden to neither the Managing Partner or the Limited Partner.

Although there would be nothing contractually tricky about sales of equity by existing home owners, several additional complications would arise if an existing Managing Partner decided that they wished to sell additional equity at a later date. The first issue would be the need to write into the initial contract a prohibition against equity sales that resulted in the Managing Partner's equity dropping below a specified minimum level, such as 25%. The Limited Partner would wish to limit the Managing Partner's freedom to sell off additional equity in their home to outside investors, since any such sales would reduce the Managing Partner's equity stake in the property, and thereby weaken the incentives in the original Partnership Agreement. One way to enforce maintenance of the specified minimum ownership level would be to have the Limited Partner retain or have escrowed the certificates evidencing the Managing Partner's ownership of the specified percentage of the property.

The Managing Partner would be able to sell off additional equity in the home, provided their level of ownership remained above the specified minimum level. The initial contract would specify procedures to be used for such equity sales, including details of the notification, appraisal, and negotiation procedures. It is important to understand that the Managing Partner would retain a significant margin of control of the terms of the sale, through their right to seek competitive bids from alternative Limited Partners. An interesting issue with respect to these sales of additional equity by the Managing Partner is whether the contract would provide any special incentives for such additional sales to be offered first to the Limited Partner involved in the initial Partnership Agreement.

9.5   The Sales Process

Another concern introduced by Partnership Agreements would be the need to prevent the Managing Partner from selling the house at substantially below its market price, either from the need for a quick sale or in case of fraud by sale to an affiliated party. Either event would impose sizable losses on the Limited Partner. Several clauses aimed at preventing this possibility would concern adequate and timely information, Limited Partner appraisal and right of first refusal, and prohibiting sales to affiliated third parties.

Adequate and Timely Information

The Managing Partner would be obligated to provide complete and timely information on the sales process to the Limited Partner. To sell with the help of a real estate broker, the Managing Partner would list the property and inform the broker that the property was co-owned. Third-party buyers would inspect the property, and in the event any such buyer submitted a bid that the Managing Partner wanted to accept, the following process would apply:

• The bid would be an offer to buy at a particular price subject to the standard conditions.[11] It would be received by the Managing Partner with no accompanying down payment. The Managing Partner would forward the bid and inform the Limited Partner of their intent to accept the offer.

• The Limited Partner would have a short, contractually set time[12] in which to appraise the property and respond to the bid, either accepting the offer or responding according to their right of first refusal.[13]

• The Managing Partner would pay a fixed fee for the Limited Partner's appraisal that would be pro-rata refunded at the closing. This fee would discourage frivolous use of the application by a Managing Partner to get a sense of their house's value.

In fact, the sales process would require a disclosure clause stating that even if there were multiple bidders, all bid information would have to go to the Managing Partner, the buyer, and the Limited Partner. Fraud would likely be very limited since it would be in the potential buyer's interest to forward their offers to the Limited Partner, and any withholding of information would result in a loss of the real estate agents' licenses.

Limited-Partner Appraisal and the Right of First Refusal
After receiving the intent-to-accept notification and the appraisal fee from the Managing Partner, the Limited Partner would have a contractually fixed time to make one of two possible responses: agree with the Managing Partner and concur with the intent-to-accept form, or exercise the right of first refusal. Exercising the right of first refusal would consist of making a bid to buy the property from the Managing Partner for a fixed premium above the proposed sale price.

By requiring a premium to be paid, this clause should not create added uncertainty for the prospective buyer if a bid at fair market price has been made, especially since the Limited Partner would not want to own 100% of any property and lose the maintenance benefit of having a Managing Partner. Only if the bid price were lower than the Limited Partner's estimate of market value by more than the value of the maintenance over the expected time to resale, plus the fixed premium, would the Limited Partner have an incentive to exercise the right of first refusal.

Upon receiving any bid from the Limited Partner, the Managing Partner would have some fixed period to search again, say thirty days. At this point, the Managing Partner could conduct a renewed search for additional offers, submit a new intent-to-accept form, and re-initiate the process. This process could be expedited and the cost reduced by having the Managing Partner pay for the appraisal at the time of listing instead of waiting for a buyer to bid.

Note that the Limited Partner would have an advantage over almost any third-party buyer in that the Limited Partner would always be a "qualified" (credit worthy) borrower, and the third-party buyer would often not be as credit worthy. Therefore a sale to a third party would have a higher probability of not closing, but this problem exists today when a seller chooses from among multiple buyers.

One way real estate brokers might respond would be by prequalifying more buyers and divulging more of that information to the Managing Partner and Limited Partner. They would have plenty of incentive to do so, as the listing real estate broker would work for both co-owners but would get paid only if a third-party buyer won the bid. Also, the buyers' real estate brokers would get no commission unless the buyers that they represented won the bid, which is the same risk faced today with multiple buyers.

Prohibiting Sales to Affiliated Third Parties
We propose that third-party affiliated sales be prohibited, as sales to a related party would create so many potential conflicts of interest between the Managing Partner and Limited Partner. The most obvious cases would involve false sales between spouses that involved no change of residence but rather an attempt to reduce the value of the Limited Partner's equity. The closing attorney for the Limited Partner would ultimately be responsible for checking adherence to this clause. Sales to parties whose affiliation was not disclosed to the Limited Partner would be criminally fraudulent.

In addition to the direct monitoring of the sales process provided for in the agreement, an additional disincentive to third-party affiliated sales would arise as the informational structure of the market developed. We expect methods of monitoring Managing Partners' sales performance in past agreements would develop and affect the terms offered to them in any future Partnership Agreements.[14]

The final set of issues in the sales process would concern death and estates. In the event of the Managing Partner's death, the Partnership interest would be part of the estate. Spouses might continue to reside in the property under the existing agreement, particularly if the Managing Partner's interest was itself held by spouses as joint tenants. However, we recommend a clause be inserted requiring descendants to sell the property or buy out the Limited Partner. Otherwise, upon any conveyance other than to a spouse, the Limited Partner could petition the courts for partition of the Partnership. The servicer would be obligated to inform the Limited Partner upon receipt of the notice of the Managing Partner's death.

9.6 Breach

We now discuss what would happen when the Managing Partner failed to fulfill their obligations under the Partnership Agreement (breach). The remedies available to the Limited Partner in such situations would be partition of the Partnership[15] or restructuring of the agreement. Several circumstances might give rise to a direct breach of the Partnership Agreement by the Managing Partner:

- fraud in the application (which would also be criminal behavior),
- failure to maintain the property (doctrine of waste),
- failure to maintain owner occupation of the property,
- breaking the ban on outside sales of equity,
- sales to affiliated third parties as well as hiding sales information.

Note that in all cases of liquidation, the property would have to be auctioned in accordance with established case law in the state, using auction procedures similar to those lenders undertake in a foreclosure on a mortgage obligation.

The Managing Partner would have powerful incentives to avoid direct breach of the Agreement, so this would not be a large-scale issue for Limited Partners. Direct breach would only arise when the household had already paid off the mortgage and let the house deteriorate substantially. This would be uncommon but might occur in catastrophic circumstances, especially for senior citizens. However, in such cases, one would expect the Limited Partner to contain their losses by hiring a firm specifically to step in and offer a third-party maintenance contract.

Far more important than direct breach would be the cross-breach clause on the mortgage. In formal contractual terms, it would be advantageous if the right of first refusal were to survive in bankruptcy, although this would be largely at the bankruptcy court's discretion.

Cross Breach and Cross Default

Managing Partners would be obliged to keep current on their property taxes, insurance, and any other escrows, as the Limited Partner would rather not be superseded by other claims in bankruptcy or liquidation of the Partnership. Therefore, we propose that records of all these transactions be maintained by institutions that would service Limited Partnerships.

In addition, any default on a loan secured by the Managing Partner's equity interest in the Partnership, such as a first mortgage, would place the Managing Partner in breach of the Partnership Agreement, allowing the Limited Partner to file for partition of the Partnership. The Managing Partner and the other creditors would also be obligated to give the Limited Partner notice of[16] the default itself and every default event requiring legal notification.[17]

Beyond the strict necessity of the Limited Partner's knowing who had been subrogated and when to exercise their rights of first refusal or to a pro-rata portion of the equity of redemption, the Limited Partner would also need this information because such defaults occur at points of financial stringency. At these times the Managing Partner would be increasingly likely to fail in their obligation to keep the property in adequate condition.

If there were a default on the mortgage, the courts and the lenders would likely let the Limited Partner dispose of the property, since the Limited Partner would have the strongest incentive to maximize the value of the sale. This would also benefit the Managing Partner, who would receive the Limited Partner's assistance in liquidation knowing that their incentives were closely connected. The Limited Partner might even choose to advance money to the Managing Partner to get quicker access to the property and help reduce the property damage caused by delinquent occupants.

9.7   The Partnership Contract and the Mortgage Contract

We envision the traditional mortgage and the residential Limited Partnership as being quite symbiotic. Neither would completely fulfill the benefits of the other, and yet neither alone would likely be sufficient for all home owners. Therefore, it would be important that the incentives contained in the two agreements fit well together. Fortunately in the United States these two types of agreements are now quite well developed, so there would be little need to develop new parts of the law. Instead, one would merely need to fit the existing frameworks together and smooth a few rough edges.

As we have already mentioned, one of these rough edges would occur when a Managing Partner defaulted. The point would not be that the priorities in bankruptcy are not well understood or outlined in the law, because existing law already handles far more complex multiparty issues of subrogation and the priority of various claims. Rather, the issue would be that the roles of the parties in the default would shift slightly, as a new third party, the Limited Partner, would be present.

This would present the mortgagee with the trouble of having one more party with whom to negotiate but also with the benefit of having an institutional counterpart that would share an interest in maintaining the asset during its court-monitored sale. This might prove to significantly lower the cost of moral hazard in the foreclosure process.[18] The Managing Partner would also benefit significantly from having an institution that would share similar incentives and have the knowledge and financial resources to maximize their returns from their jointly held asset. Together these new roles would also provide the Limited Partner and mortgagee with a more powerful and efficient set of options for restructuring the original agreements, which also might benefit the Managing Partner.

10

Secondary Partnership
Market for Trading Real
Estate (SCEPTRE)

10.1 The Secondary Mortgage Market

One of the most important institutional developments in the postwar U.S. housing finance market has been the rapid development of secondary mortgage markets. As these markets have grown, so have the sources of funds for mortgage finance. In the current market, institutional investors own securities that are bundles of mortgages issued by any number of mortgage originators. In this fashion, mortgages have become widely marketable commodities available to the widest possible investment community.

In the United States before the 1970s, issuing institutions generally held mortgages to maturity, which meant that customers retained a strong financial interdependency with the institution that issued their mortgage. It also meant that the risks involved in issuing the mortgage stayed with the issuing institution.

In the United States today, the issuer of a typical standardized mortgage almost instantaneously sells the mortgage to one of a small set of large financial institutions that pool the mortgages and provide credit guarantees in the secondary mortgage market. The investors in the secondary market buy the mortgage-backed security (MBS) and receive the underlying cash flows on the mortgages. Although they have little or no default risk, the investor still has considerable uncertainty as to the timing of the cash flows because of the possibility that the mortgage holder will suddenly pay off the mortgage because they are either refinancing or selling the home.

The largest among these market-making financial institutions are the three governmental agencies, Freddie Mac, FNMA, and GNMA. In addition, some private companies perform these functions, mostly for non-conforming mortgages,[1] such as Citibank through its Citi Mae subsidiary.

The agencies have several goals as stated in their charters, but the major one is to promote the mortgage market's growth and liquidity by providing services that increase the orderly flow of funds to the housing market. The agencies (market makers) in the secondary mortgage market provide the following services to accomplish these goals:

• *Buying and holding mortgages.* The agencies are the largest U.S. holders of mortgages, which they fund by borrowing as a government agency at very close to Treasury rates (below-market-rate funding).

• *Pooling.* They buy large blocks of similar, standardized mortgages and bundle them into large mortgage pools. They then issue share certificates (MBSs) on the mortgage pools and sell them to the broader financial community.

• *Selling credit guarantees.* The institutions also offer insurance, effectively offering security against defaults on the underlying mortgages.[2]

• *Standardizing and regulating the industry.* The agencies regulate many aspects of the mortgage industry by promulgating guidelines for what originating and underwriting procedures qualify a mortgage as conforming (sellers' guides) and what procedures a servicer must follow to earn the servicing fee (servicer's guides). They are also active lobbyists and litigators.

The market for MBSs has grown extremely rapidly. The secondary markets are now massive capital markets with more than $2 trillion in securitized mortgage debt outstanding in the second quarter of 1996 (see Secondary Mortgage Markets, Nov. 1996, p. 25). The markets are also extremely liquid and competitive, with total trading volume in the several-trillion-dollar range each year. Among the major holders of MBSs are pension funds, mutual funds, and financial institutions.

Also in the market are several investment and commercial banks that trade in MBSs, buying and reselling the securities hoping to make a profit. These banks also create synthetic securities by "stripping" bundles of securities into discrete sets of cash flows, such as collaterialized mortgage obligations (see Lederman 1987). The cash flows in these more exotic products usually have even greater volatility than those of the ordinary MBS, but the products can be customized to provide better hedges against a particular firm's other interest rate exposures.

10.2   The Secondary Partnership Market

We envisage a practically identical set of basic institutional structures developing in the Partnership Market. At origination, the Limited Partner would own an investment with acceptable return properties but an uncertain maturity. One of the Limited Partner's first concerns would be to sell off the Partnership Agreement at a fair price without waiting for the uncertain termination. This would be quite analogous to the situation in the current secondary-mortgage market, where the uncertain maturity of the underlying mortgages primarily results from prepayment risk.

As in the secondary mortgage market, we would expect an institution to appear in the role of specialist or market maker for Partnership Agreements, standing ready to buy or sell the contracts at all times with a commensurate bid-ask spread. Also as in the mortgage market, Partnership Agreements would represent an interest in an idiosyncratic household living in an idiosyncratic property. Therefore the specialist would find it quite difficult to obtain sufficient trading volume without bundling the contracts. Again as in the mortgage market, the specialist would have to issue guidelines on what constituted an acceptable contract, so that while the contracts' individual terms would vary, Partnership Agreements could be composed of standardized covenants.

Therefore, we envision the specialist buying the Partnership Agreements, placing them in a mutual fund, and issuing shares on the underlying baskets (Partnership Real Estate Funds with Equity Fund Returns or PREFERS).[3] The specialist could choose to split the portfolio into geographic baskets (region, state, metropolitan statistical area, zip code) or along a variety of other dimensions depending on the desires of the institutional holders of PREFERS and any pertinent guidelines provided by government policy makers.

The specialist's precise role cannot be predicted at this point. One interesting issue is whether the specialist would add any form of credit enhancement to PREFERS. Another complex issue is how the underlying Limited Partnership Agreements could be optimally combined into pools. The methods used to bundle Partnerships Agreements into mutual funds would have a significant impact on the behavior of the market, and for this reason deserves careful attention. Given the proper degree of consideration, the pools could greatly improve the efficiency of the housing market by introducing valuable new hedging opportunities both for home owners, and for the broader financial community.

Once an institution stood ready as the specialist, it would have to find institutional or individual buyers of PREFERS. These would likely appeal to several types of institutions as buyers, with the most likely being large portfolio investors,[4] who would want the return properties of PREFERS. These return properties would be uniquely valuable because of their correlations with other assets and inflation, as explored in chapter 13.

In addition to large financial institutions, other potential investors would include

• individuals who as future first-time or trade-up home buyers might wish to incrementally hedge their future housing price purchase by buying a consistent amount of PREFERS over time;

• property and casualty firms that have underwritten replacement cost contracts as home owner insurance, for whom PREFERS would provide some hedging ability for future increases in policy payouts due to house price appreciation; and

• foreign investors, whose purchase of PREFERS could provide a new low-cost source of funds for the U.S. residential housing market.

10.3   SCEPTRE and New Investment Vehicles

If the massive secondary market in conforming mortgages is anything to go by, Partnerships would likely bring about very large-scale changes in asset markets that are especially intriguing in light of the new investment and hedging opportunities that would be presented as Partnership Markets develop. After the standardization and packaging discussed above, a great many new opportunities would arise for the trading and capital markets as "slicers of risk." The secondary markets in Partnerships would represent a novel and important set of investment vehicles, and we would expect a tremendous development of surrounding asset markets of even greater significance than the current derivatives markets in the secondary mortgage markets.

Once the market for buying PREFERS evolved, we would quickly expect to see the market develop for shorting the shares. Brokerage firms and other financial institutions would become market makers in PREFERS and begin to accumulate inventory in them. As they accumulated this inventory, they would find it profitable to lend out PREFERS to firms or individuals who wished to short the market. The availability of shorting would allow all investors with positive positions in housing, including individual home owners, to cheaply and efficiently hedge their exposure to general house price declines.

We would next expect development of markets for future delivery of the Partnership Agreement as forward contracts, future contracts, or both. Many parties in the housing market expect to change their exposure to the market at some point and would desire the opportunity to hedge that risk through either forwards or futures.

At the early stage of development of markets for future delivery, we would expect large institutions to be the main players, since they would have the capital to cover any counterparty risk. In many cases they might execute forward contracts, possibly with the specialist or the market makers. The specialist might have a natural incentive to hedge either future appreciation, geographic risk, or volume at any time. Forwards would be an inexpensive way for larger institutions to hedge larger, more discrete exposures such as a factory investment. However, the individual nature of the forwards (lack of standardization of terms such as amount, delivery date, underlying commodity definition, and so forth) would mean that trading or settling these contracts prior to settlement would probably mean trading in a somewhat illiquid, brokered market.

In time this illiquidity might give rise to a futures market. As the specialist, market makers, and participants gained experience in the performance of the pools of properties underlying the Limited Partnership shares, the market could begin to construct extremely accurate indices of their returns. At this point we could envision one of the futures exchanges setting down delivery terms, trading dates, and all the standards that would make for an orderly futures market. Smaller institutions could then enter the futures market by posting margin to cover counterparty risk (although this would still be a cost), and one could trade the future commitments easily and cheaply across a commodities exchange without actually accepting physical delivery or waiting for the settlement date.

At the same time the futures market developed, one would expect to see the beginnings of the markets for options and other derivatives using PREFERS as the underlying asset. The main advantage for the market participants from this evolution would be the ability to increase leverage and thereby lower the costs of hedging.

Another benefit might arise from the ability to dynamically hedge these contracts. The basic underlying asset has a rather long economic life, and many of the market participants would be investing with a long-term time horizon. With this long time frame, one could imagine various institutions lengthening the potential time frame for future delivery by engaging in dynamic hedging and arbitraging across the forward (future) market, the underlying asset market, and the debt market. These institutions could then offer insurance to mitigate long-term risks for a fee to smaller investors, who would not want to engage in the transactions costs and lack the technical knowledge to dynamically hedge for themselves.

Many institutions would have reason to take positions in these hedging markets:

• *Home builders*, which could be expected to engage in short selling from time to time to enable them to smooth their production schedules and hedge any losses in their inventory of homes.

• *Firms that make products primarily sold to home buyers or builders*, (carpeting, appliances, heating, bathroom fixtures and so on), which would be expected to short from time to time to hedge their fixed-cost investment in the production facilities or to balance their mix of financial and operating leverage.

• *Individual home owners*, who could short PREFERS to provide a partial hedge against losses in the value of their property, although there would be some basis risk since their individual home would not be perfectly correlated with specialist PREFERS.

• *Municipalities* that raise a significant share of their revenues in the form of property taxes would wish to hedge against a fall in home prices (and thereby a decrease in tax assessments). This would be particularly important in cases in which the municipality had long term obligations, such as school bonds, backed by the revenues.

Note that the precise nature of the hedging possibilities the market maker could offer would depend on how the specialist bundled the original Partnership Agreements.

11

The Primary Mortgage Market

11.1 The Household's Search-and-Application Process

Before presenting our picture of the primary Partnership Market, it is important to sketch the breadth of the primary mortgage market. To begin this sketch, we follow a household's journey through the housing finance market, starting from when they have identified a home they are interested in purchasing. At this stage the household must give serious attention to financing the purchase.

Given the wide range of options available in the mortgage market, the household looks for advice on where and for which type of mortgage they should apply. Frequently the real estate agent provides a referral, but a cottage industry of independent mortgage brokers also provides a similar referral service in guiding households among the many different mortgage originators. Sometimes the real estate agent refers the household to a mortgage broker who works for the parent company (in house).[1] In other instances, the originator is independent and part of the broader mortgage origination industry (out of house).

With this advice, the household identifies a particular institution that issues mortgages. The mortgage can be issued by a wide variety of institutions, such as commercial banks, savings and loans, and other mortgage originators. We refer to all institutions that issue mortgages as mortgage originators.

An important stage for the household is to take a first pass to see whether they can afford their dream house: after all, all parties lose if the household is looking at houses they cannot afford. The typical approach to approximating housing affordability is to prequalify the household for a "roughly appropriate mortgage." At the prequalification stage the realtor typically asks the household to answer some key questions concerning their financial situation. The realtor may also request the buyer's permission to pull a credit bureau report on the household.

If this prequalification stage indicates that the household can afford the house, they submit an offer to the seller that includes, among other things, the offer price, a description of what is being purchased, an estimate of when the closing would occur, and a clause that voids the offer if the buyer cannot obtain financing.[2]

If the offer is accepted, the household examines in more detail all the mortgage products available, makes a specific product selection, and then completes an application form and submits the materials requested. The application form includes information on the household's

- balance sheet,
- income statement,
- employment,
- other indebtedness,
- property being purchased,
- past addresses, and
- type of loan requested.

In addition, the application form includes a release that allows the bank to gather additional information it needs to assess whether to grant the loan, including

- credit bureau reports,
- employment verification,
- income verification (directly from the IRS),
- property appraisal,
- criminal record,
- judgments, and
- identity verification.

We now examine what the mortgage bank does with the application and how it determines the reply the household receives.

11.2 Screening by the Mortgage Originator

To keep this overview simple, we describe the review process for an application for a conforming mortgage product of the type analyzed in chapter 3. With the application in hand, the mortgage bank initiates four basic checks:

• verifications of material on the application form,
• credit history check,
• debt-to-income test, and
• loan-to-value test.

To verify the application materials, the mortgage originator makes contact with a variety of investigation and information providers:

• *Appraisers* make a formal estimate of the house's market value.

• *Lawyers* assure compliance with real property laws and identify the party who appears at closing as the buyer.

• *Structural engineers* assure the building's structural integrity.

• *Title companies* search the title record for past legal filings under the applicant's name, research the title history, and provide insurance against any title imperfections.

• *The IRS and employers* verify income and employment.[3]

The mortgage originator also runs a credit check through the credit bureaus. The three large credit bureaus are Transunion, TRW, and CBI/Equifax.[4] These firms collect individual consumer information on past payment performance through owned and affiliated offices that in turn obtain information from voluntary reporting by financial institutions, retailers, collection agencies, and others. In addition to the credit bureaus, another set of firms take the credit bureau information and the lender's loan experience file and develop statistical scores for evaluating a consumer's willingness to pay.

To carry out the LTV test, the mortgage originator must contact an appraiser. Appraisal is something of a cottage industry, consisting of a very large number of small local firms. The valuation involved in an appraisal is intended to indicate the price for which the house would sell assuming the average time on the market. The appraiser verifies or assesses the collateral value of the home using the "comp method."

In the comp method, the appraiser finds three trades of comparable houses that have taken place over the previous six months. Adjustments are then made for differences between the current property and the comparables and for perceived changes in market conditions. If comparable houses are not easy to find, then the definition is widened in terms of neighborhood and time and greater judgmental adjustments are needed.

At the end of the screening period, which typically lasts between one and two weeks, the household receives one of three possible replies from the financial institution: rejection, counteroffer, or acceptance. If rejected, the applicant is legally entitled to know why the rejection occurred and can appeal the decision.[5] The recourse to appeal is based on the judgmental components of the process, and issues can also arise in judging income, such as whether a big increase in income is the sign of a bright future or an element of instability that should be discounted when evaluating longer-run prospects. At all points of judgment, there is room for error, both systematic and unsystematic.

In a counteroffer, the original application is not granted, but the financial institution provides a set of adjustments that would make them willing to move forward with the credit-granting process. Typical adjustments (compensating factors) implicitly lower the risk to a level the financial institution is willing to take on, either by increasing the down payment[6] or by lending the requested amount on condition that the household obtain PMI.

Having failed in their appeal or counteroffer, the household may at this point apply elsewhere in the A market, adjust and resubmit, or give up entirely on the A market. The appropriate course depends on the reason given for the original rejection. One important point is that similar decision criteria are used by all A-market lenders, who underwrite the applications using ratios closely related to those set by the agencies, although the precise details vary from lender to lender.

Finally, if the application is accepted without additional comment, then the household has obtained the right, but not the obligation, to a mortgage contract for a particular house purchase.

11.3   The Variety of Mortgage Products

The Range of Conforming Mortgage Products

The concept of "the" mortgage market is something of an abstraction, since so many different products and institutions are involved in the market. Among the more obvious dimensions along which conforming mortgages vary are:

• *Mortgage program.* Mortgages are available through various programs (conventional, FHA, and VA, among others).

• *Size class.* Loans can be classified, according to amount borrowed, as conforming, jumbo, and super-jumbo.

• *Maturity.* One feature by which mortgages are commonly grouped is their original maturity. The most common are thirty year and fifteen year, and less common are seven year and twenty year.

• *Rate.* The main choice being between fixed and floating rates. If one chooses a floating rate, one must also consider the initial rate (often a teaser[7]), index, reset period, spread above the index, and any options to convert to a fixed-rate loan.[8]

• *Amortization.* Some mortgages are principally distinguished by their amortization features. Examples are negative amortization loans, in which the initial N years of payments may not be sufficient to fully pay off the contracted principal and interest payments, so the deficiency is added to the loan's remaining principal balance, which causes the loan amount outstanding to increase over time. Another example is balloon (or bullet) loans on which only interest payments are made over the loan's life, until the last payment, which is for the full principal balance and the last interest payment. Typically balloon loans have maturities of five or seven years, and the borrower refinances the remaining principal in the last year.

• *Assumability.* General real estate law allows a borrower to pass on the mortgage obligation to another borrower by having a third party (grantor) assume the obligation, unless the mortgage contains a Due on Sale clause. The Due on Sale clause requires the borrower to repay the loan in full on any transfer of title, and most standard mortgages today contain one. Even if the loan is assumed, the original borrower remains liable in most cases should the grantor fail to fulfill the mortgage obligation.

• *Property type.* Another set of differences relates not to the mortgage but to the type and ownership structure of the property. Structural differences include the differences between single family, multifamily, houseboats and manufactured housing. Different ownership structures include sole ownership (and joint tenancy), co-op, condo, PUD and time share.

• *Occupancy.* Occasionally mortgages are distinguished by the principal use or occupancy of the property, such as vacation homes, owner occupied, investor properties, or businesses.

• *Points.* Sometimes the distinguishing characteristic of a mortgage may be whether the borrower pays points.

Nonconforming Mortgages and the B through D Markets
The complexities of the conforming mortgage market are dwarfed by the complexities of the nonconforming market. The simplest of the

nonconforming mortgages are a variety of high-quality A-credit mortgages that are nonconforming. The most common are jumbo mortgages that conform in all ways except size and mortgages on certain idiosyncratic property types such as co-ops with fewer than ten units. Conforming mortgages offer the issuer the chief advantage that they can readily be sold into the secondary market. But today this is equally true for some, though not all, of the high-quality nonconforming mortgages. For instance there is now a ready market for high-quality jumbo mortgages.

In cases with easy access to the secondary market, the distinction between conforming mortgages and nonconforming is relatively trivial, but for other nonconforming loans, the issuer typically must hold the mortgage in inventory for some considerable time before a sale is possible ("seasoning").[9] Such loans are riskier for the issuer and will therefore typically be more expensive for the household.

The costs of obtaining a mortgage rise rapidly for households that must leave the A-paper market altogether because of a broad failure to pass the three screens, but they can find financing in the lower-quality loan market. The industry commonly grades loans that suffer from a deficiency in one of the three screens on a scale from B through D (B-D), as shown in Table 11.1.[10]

Not only are B-D loans far more expensive than A loans, but they are also far less standardized. Many aspects of the B-D markets involve indi-

Table 11.1
Credit classifications

	A Credit	B Credit	C Credit	D Credit
Bankruptcies or NOD[a]	None in the past 7 years	None in the past 2 years	None in the past 1–1.5 years	None in the past 1 year
Debt-Income Ratio	36% or less	50% or less	55% or less	60% or less
Maximum LTV	95% owner occupied; 80% investor	80% owner occupied; 75% investor	70% owner occupied; 70% investor	65% owner occupied; 65% investor
Delinquencies	None in last 12 months	Maximum of four 30-day derogs[b] and no 60-day derogs in last 12 months	Maximum of six 30-day derogs and one 60-day derog in last 12 months	Maximum of twelve 30-day derogs and two 60-day derogs in last 12 months

a. NOD is the industry term for "Notice of Default."
b. "Derogs" is the industry term for an unsatisfied line of credit with some lender.
Source: Groves and Prigal, Mortgage Finance Review (1995).

vidual negotiation rather than selection from a menu of contracts. In the past, originators typically held mortgages that did not conform because of credit quality in their portfolios until such time as they seasoned, paid off, or defaulted. Today even these loans are securitized. Table 11.2 gives an estimate of the spreads:[11]

11.4   The Structure of the Primary Mortgage Industry

The agencies with their federal charters sit at the heart of the conforming mortgage market. The conforming market maker's role is very profitable. It is by far the least competitive part of the mortgage market, as the major players all have implicit federal subsidies, ruling out effective purely private-sector competition for their roles. As market makers, they write books setting the standards mortgage originators must meet to sell their mortgages on the secondary market. They are prevented, however, by their charters from processing payments made by the household paying off the mortgage and resolving issues that arise when the household has trouble making payments. The mortgage servicer takes on the role of handling these payments and is sometimes the same party as the mortgage originator.

As mortgages must meet stringent requirements to conform to agency standards, the mortgage originator in the conforming mortgage market is really a transaction-making intermediary rather than a supplier of credit. If the originator follows the procedures the agencies specify, they can rest assured of selling the mortgage immediately. Originators that sell into the secondary market often derive their profit in large part from their continued role as servicers of the mortgage,[12] processing payments and handling the other ongoing operational requirements of the mortgage, including but not limited to escrow, investor tracking, pool accounting, and collections. All procedures and fees are specified by the investor agreement. A typical fee paid on a conforming loan is twenty-five to fifty bps annually, and the average annual cost of a large efficient servicer is $50–$70 per loan.

Table 11.2
Credit spreads by credit classifications

	A credit	B credit	C credit	D credit
Credit spread (bps)	35	60	85	135

Although the mortgage originator quite commonly also serves as mortgage servicer, there is a considerable trade in servicing contracts. The servicing role is itself more specialized, with the industry consolidating toward the more cost-effective servicers. In the end, origination and servicing of mortgages has become a fragmented and highly competitive industry offering participants a relatively low profit margin.

The securitization that the agencies offer on mortgages helps explain the many specialist suppliers of information and assessment that operate on the market's supply side. While some subtle differences exist between the securitizations offered by the different market makers, the basic idea is always that the market maker ensures timely payment of interest and principal, even in cases of default on the underlying loan. Securitizing their pools of MBSs means the market makers have a direct interest in ensuring that default is kept to a minimum. The cost of offering this insurance increases as the costs of default rise, and the desire to keep default risk down motivates many agency guidelines on conforming mortgages.

For this reason, the market makers carefully monitor the application process and the methods of screening. Not only do they provide precise guidelines on issuing mortgages, but they also keep a very close eye on the actual default performance of the loans they purchase, with the constant possibility of heavy scrutiny of those whose mortgages display unusually high default rates. Mortgage-granting institutions that fare especially badly in this respect may find themselves locked out of future sales to the market maker.

The need to monitor applications gives rise to a massive need for information on household credit-worthiness. In the old days, such information would reside with the manager of the bank with which the household did business. Nowadays, such close personal knowledge is rare. The loss of direct knowledge means these information services must be provided by new agencies that have developed, the credit agencies. A large number of firms have developed to gather impersonal credit information that enables the secondary market to operate.

The high degree of standardization that characterizes the primary mortgage market is closely connected to the development of ever more sophisticated information on household behavior. Our proposal for the primary Partnership Market is predicated on the continued development of such impersonal credit information.

12   The Primary Partnership
Market

Much of the proposed market structure in the primary Partnership Market is driven by the attempt to keep the procedures as close as possible to those that exist in the current primary mortgage market. We therefore mimic the analysis of chapter 11 and concentrate on describing the places where the Partnership Market would necessarily differ from the mortgage market. As in chapter 11 we focus our attention on its most standardized section, the issuers of Limited Partnerships who would sell their equity interests immediately onto the secondary Partnership Markets.

12.1   The Household's Search-and-Application Process

Consider a household that has just struck a tentative deal on the home they wish to buy and wishes to finance the home using the Partnership Market. As in the current market, the potential buyer would likely have to prequalify for the deal to confirm that they were not wasting their own and others' valuable time. While the idea of prequalification would be no different than in the mortgage market, the actual process would be slightly more complex. The key difference would be that the household applying for Partnership finance would typically also want to obtain a mortgage on their equity share in the home. This would mean that to prequalify, the household would have to fill out two forms, one applying for mortgage funds and the other for Partnership funds. The real estate broker would then have to verify these applications' acceptability to the mortgage originator and the Limited Partner respectively, at which point the buyer would be prequalified, and the buyer and seller could agree on terms. Provided the buyer had prequalified, the buyer and the seller could sign a contract on the house, with the normal financing contingency.

At this point the actual detailed search and application process would begin. The household would look for information on financing contingencies and products available from both Limited Partners and lenders. Based on this information, the household would then select the combination of Partnership finance and mortgage finance they desired and complete the relevant application forms. In applying, the household would have to specify the amount of ownership being offered to the Limited Partner and any other relevant contract choices from a standard menu. The household would also have to declare the type of mortgage for which they would apply should the Limited Partner supply the expected funding. Rather than submitting the Limited Partnership and the mortgage applications separately, it would be more natural to have the buyer send their entire combined Limited Partnership and mortgage application forms to the Limited Partner. Only once agreement was reached with the Limited Partner would the form be forwarded to the mortgage bank, as the terms of the mortgage might need some adjustment depending on exactly how the Limited Partner viewed the application.

The application form would include not only the standard package of information the household currently submits in a mortgage application, but also any conventionally agreed to information on the household concerning past performance as a Managing Partner. In addition to specifying the desired form of Partnership Agreement, an application fee would be paid to the potential Limited Partner. The release for additional information collection would also cover additional sources of information that would develop to help predict the behavior of Managing Partners, along the lines of the way credit bureaus supply information in the current mortgage market.

12.2   Screening by the Partnership Originator and the Mortgage Originator

The Partnership Originator

With the application in hand, the potential Limited Partner would conduct an appraisal, analyze comparable equity pricing, and check on the information provided by the Managing Partner. If the Managing Partner had a good record and the appraisal came in close to target, the Limited Partner would check the pricing on similar equity and come up with a price offer on their share. Just as the majority of the screens in the current mortgage market are designed to reduce default risk and default, so many of the screens in the Partnership Market would be designed to reduce breach costs.

One noteworthy feature of the Limited Partnership origination process would likely be the additional care that the Limited Partner would take in ensuring that the buyer was striking a fair deal in buying the house. The appraisal would therefore likely be performed to a higher standard than currently required. Even so, we see no reason that well-informed partners could not respond to the request for a Partnership within fifteen days, which would be five days after their independent appraisal arrived.

One possible concern might be the procedures should the house appraisal come in significantly below the bid price, in which case the applicant could either accept a disappointingly low price on their equity percentage, put additional equity into the purchase, renegotiate the bid price on the house, or withdraw their bid. In extreme cases, the Limited Partner might reject the deal altogether (in the standardized part of the market, the price on the equity probably not to be subject to significant individual negotiation) and would then likely have to specify some reason for the adverse action.[2]

If the Limited Partner made an offer, they would transmit it to the Managing Partner, who would have a few days to decide on conditional acceptance or rejection. In cases of conditional acceptance, the Managing Partner would then make any necessary revisions to their mortgage application, which the Limited Partner would then forward to the lender of choice together with a second application fee. The lender would be placed after the Limited Partner in the process mainly because the amount to be borrowed could only be confidently specified after the Limited Partner had made an offer on the equity share in the house.

The Mortgage Originator
With the completed application in hand and the financial terms of the Partnership Agreement settled, the lender would gather all the traditional information together with the terms of the Limited Partnership. The Partnership Agreement would change the lending institution's underwriting process little. The lending institution would obtain an appraisal on the property, conduct a credit review, and verify the information provided on the mortgage application. We expect the Limited Partner and the lender would often share appraisal and credit findings to avoid duplicating efforts.

The lender would process the application much as outlined in chapter 11 with the three options of acceptance, rejection, or asking for straightforward modifications such as PMI. Again, if PMI were required, the PMI company would do its own information gathering and make its own determination. At the end of the process, the decision would be sent back to the potential Managing Partner. If the application were accepted, the issue would be back in the Managing Partner's hands.

One important issue to address would concern the lender's attitude toward making a loan to a Managing Partner rather than a standard home owner. One simple change would be the likely addition of estimated incremental maintenance costs to the flow of expenditures.[3] But beyond this we see no first-order reason for the lender to change the nature of their loan-granting process when the purchaser is using a Limited Partnership rather than the traditional method of full ownership. If anything, we believe the presence of a Limited Partner who had already screened the application would encourage the lender also to accept, as default on a mortgage in the Partnership Market would be part and parcel of breach of the Partnership Agreement, and as the presence of a Limited Partner with an interest in maintaining the underlying property would be likely to make the mortgages better credit risks. As we argued in chapter 9, a borrower who defaulted on the mortgage would also breach the Partnership Agreement, and the lender would stand to benefit from the presence of a Limited Partner that would ensure the property sold for the highest possible price. In such cases, the lender would be happy to have the Limited Partner step in and help curtail the losses that would otherwise belong to the lender.

Lenders would be concerned about granting mortgages in cases where the Partnership Agreement sold at a significant discount to par and, at least on initial consideration, would not be willing to lend to cover the discount to par without some kind of rate penalty or a tightening of the payment-to-income ratios. Nevertheless we expect there would be some room for adjustment of terms along these lines, because we believe lenders would prefer lending to Managing Partners over lending to the classic 100% owner-occupant.

The Closing
Once the applicant received a commitment from the lending institution and the Limited Partner, their contract with the seller would be finalized at a closing. The title would indicate that the property was co-owned and would list each partner's equity ownership shares. If the Managing Partner also needed a mortgage loan, we would expect to see at closing all the

standard parties and an attorney representing the Limited Partner. All parties would come with the contractually stated amounts of funds:

- The Managing Partner would bring the down payment.
- The Limited Partner would bring payment for their equity investment.
- The lender would bring the mortgage funds.

In return, the Managing Partner and Limited Partner would each receive a title with certificates evidencing the ownership interests and the specific Partnership Agreement, and the lender would receive the mortgage contract and hold the Managing Partner's certificate as collateral.

12.3 The Range of Partnership Products

We would expect to see a very wide variety of products develop in the Partnership Market, differing along even more dimensions than do the products in the mortgage market. There would be a variety of "qualities" of Partnership, depending on the household's record, corresponding to the A-D papers of the mortgage market. Just as in the mortgage market, there would likely be more individual negotiation in the lower-quality markets and more standardization in the higher-quality markets. We also expect there would be conforming and nonconforming Partnerships, depending on whether they met the criteria for sale in some simple secondary market for standardization, and conventional and government Partnerships, depending on the role chosen by the federal government. To get a clearer picture of the dimensions of difference, we concentrate on the most standardized conforming conventional Partnerships. Even within this class, there would be products differing along several dimensions, including the nature of the Limited Partner's share of the sale price and the contract clauses.

The Limited Partner's Share of the Sale Price

The idea of a 50% share of the sale price for each partner is far from the only possibility for division of the ultimate sale price. We imagine contracts would vary not only the absolute percentage of the price going to each partner but also the path these shares would take over time and their dependence on the behavior of variables other than time.

To give a simple (albeit unrealistic) example of how this might work, consider the hypothetical case of a Limited Partner who wished to provide the Managing Partner with an incentive to sell the home within a certain time, such as twenty years. One way to encourage this would be to have the Partnership Contract specify that the Limited Partner's share of the sale price would gradually increase if the asset were held in excess of twenty years. To generalize from this example, flexibility in contract design would allow both parties to obtain additional insurance against various contingencies they wished to avoid.

Contract Clauses
The basic contract we have sketched would leave all rights with the Managing Partner and involve no monitoring. But we perceive households as having different preferences in the trade-off between Limited Partner advice and any perception that their rights would be limited. Demand for restrictive space as in many planned communities is indicative of the lack of absolute interest in control over all other things.

We would expect a wide range of contracts to develop, with more onerous contracts fetching a higher price from Limited Partners. We would also expect contracts to differ in the monitoring of maintenance and improvements, with an extreme possibility involving the Limited Partner's providing maintenance services for a fee.

We would expect the range of contracts to get ever broader as the market developed. One way in which this might happen would be the development of contracts tailored to specific target audiences. For example, a contract aimed at older home buyers might involve a shift in the maintenance expenses away from the Managing Partner and onto the Limited Partner, with a commensurate reduction in price. In fact, there are currently proposals for the development of markets in which older owners essentially sell off their homes, while retaining life-long residence rights and handing over maintenance to the new owners (see Rosenbaum, Goren, and Jacobs 1995). We regard the Partnership format as providing an altogether more comfortable set of options for older owners, since they would be able to retain their 50% share in the home, and thereby feel less like renters in their own home.

Other differences would likely involve changes in the flow of payments, with some contracts involving the Limited Partner's sharing in more of the Managing Partner's expenses. At the other end of this spectrum, we would not be surprised to see contracts develop in which the Limited Partner received some form of additional rental payments from the Managing Partner. All such clauses would change the price accordingly.

12.4 The Structure of the Primary Partnership Industry

Just as in the primary mortgage industry, we would expect the most profitable and least competitive role in the conforming Partnership industry to be that of the standard setter and securitizer in the secondary markets. We also believe the presence of such a strong and central player in the market would have ramifications for the entire structure of the supply side, along lines similar to those of the mortgage market. Thus the Partnership originator would be primarily a transaction-making intermediary carrying out a well-defined series of steps for a relatively small fee in a highly competitive industry.

We would expect new information services to develop to supply the needs of the Partnership Market relevant to the Managing Partnership issue. Separate scoring methods might develop to inform prospective Limited Partners of any potential problems in dealing with the Managing Partner, focusing on the likelihood the Managing Partner would properly maintain the property, and including information on prior property dealings, rent records, legal filings, and possibly personal references. Among the probable checks would be a matching of IRS Form 1099b filings against past house prices to check for fraud. We would expect the credit agencies to report on

- breaches of the Partnership Agreement,
- petitions filed to partition the Partnership assets,
- filings against the Managing Partner for failure to maintain the property, and
- filings against the Managing Partner for failure, as owner, to occupy the property.

These new information services might also benefit some groups currently difficult to serve in the traditional mortgage market, such as the "no-hits," who have an insufficient credit history for potential lenders to have a clear idea of their risk status. This group is especially likely to be young, first-time home buyers. At present, the standards set by the mortgage market make it unlikely they will be able to obtain an A mortgage, as they are likely to fail the credit screen unless there is some way to judgmentally overturn the lack of history and identify the applicant as having a reason for an exception to the credit policies. In the Partnership Market, however, the additional information provided by the no-hits experience with maintaining other assets might provide the necessary rationale for the exception. Examples of such other experiences with maintaining assets are car leases, apartment rentals, appliance leases, library records, and the like.

Other information services would be required to help the household approach the Partnership Market in a reasonably well-informed manner. Just as in the current mortgage market, we could expect various agents to provide advice and information to potential Managing Partners. We would also expect active competition among potential Limited Partners and the development of public information on Limited Partners' performance records. It would also be important that prospective Managing Partners have a clear idea of the terms Limited Partners were likely to demand of them and whether Limited Partners would pay a par price for the shares.

One obvious change called for would be that appraisers and others would need to operate at higher standards in the Partnership Market. More broadly, the development of the Partnership Market would also alter the roles a wide range of businesses currently play in the housing market, from real estate agents through structural engineers, builders, and so on. We discuss many of these altered roles in our discussion of the housing market (rather than the housing finance market) in chapters 14 and 15.

13 Pricing Partnerships

The asset purchased by the Limited Partner would be a share in the ultimate sale price of the house occupied by the Managing Partner, who would determine the time of sale. To a first approximation, the return pattern on packages of Limited Partnerships would mimic those on residential real estate, where the maturity would be uncertain because of the Managing Partner's right to select the date of sale. To open the chapter, we review and extend an existing literature on the housing asset. We then turn to the many adjustments relevant to the Partnership context.

13.1 Measuring House Prices

Any analysis of residential real estate's potential contribution to investment portfolios must begin with measuring the returns on residential real estate. We focus on measures that use transactions data to avoid the smoothing of returns inherent in using appraisals and residents' self-reported estimates of value. Two key issues in constructing an accurate index are how to construct a quality-constant index given housing's heterogeneity, and sample selection bias in transactions data. The problems arise because of the many dimensions of heterogeneity of residential real estate assets.

A preliminary point to note is that although the uncertain maturity of the Partnership Contract would have some effect on its value, this uncertainly would not in any way commit the Limited Partner to holding their share until the house is sold. In fact the entire structure of the secondary market in Partnerships would be designed to ensure a continuously operating market in which these Partnerships would be bought and sold, so that there would be the usual asset market separation between asset maturity and trading period. Most companies are also perpetual, but this does not mean that equity in them cannot be sold. Similarly, the underlying maturity of standard MBSs depends on when the underlying mortgages are refinanced or the house is sold. The existing and extremely liquid market in mortgage-backed securities fully handles this uncertain maturity.

Quality

The literature has used two methods to attempt to produce quality-constant price indices: hedonic and repeat sale. Hedonic methods attempt to standardize prices across houses by adjusting for differences in observed characteristics. Implicit prices for different characteristics are estimated using regression methods. A price index can then be estimated by adding time indicators to the regression. This method imposes tremendous data requirements because of the need to keep track of each house's characteristics. In addition, it is difficult to adequately control for quality even using an extensive list of housing characteristics.

Case and Shiller (1987) propose using repeat-sale methodology to address some of the hedonic approach's shortcomings. The repeat-sale approach matches transactions on the same house over time. The difference in log house price is regressed on time-of-purchase and time-of-sale indicators, and the coefficients on these indicators are used to construct the price index. The basic idea is that comparing prices on the same houses eliminates heterogeneity across houses. The only remaining heterogeneity is due to changes in a particular house's quality because of improvements or neglect. Case and Shiller attempt to delete from their sample houses on which significant improvements have been made. One difficulty with the repeat-sale approach is that there are only a few repeat sales in any given year for a housing market. Data on many years of repeat sales need to be collected to estimate the resulting housing price index with precision. Freddie Mac now produces repeat-sale price indices for many metropolitan areas based on their extensive data files.

Peek and Wilcox (1991) discuss adjustment methods that can be applied to either hedonic or repeat-sales price indices to further control for quality changes. They propose using data on the net investment in the existing stock of housing. The U.S. Department of Commerce publishes data in real terms on residential property maintenance, repair, and improvements. Generally, more than half these expenditures are listed as improvements. Peek and Wilcox construct a net investment series by subtracting physical depreciation from the census gross investment numbers and dividing this difference by the census estimate of the stock of residential housing. A further adjustment can be made to account for the fact that the census data reflects only improvements that generate market transactions—the home owner's "sweat equity" is missed. The sweat equity adjustment is more ad hoc and assumes that the value of the owner's labor is the same as the value of the materials purchased by the home owner.

Self-Selection in Transactions

Both the hedonic and repeat-sale methods are based on transactions data. However, the price indices are meant to reflect the change in underlying prices for all houses (or the average house) in the market. This raises the issue of selection bias in the estimation. The houses that sell in a period are unlikely to be a random sample of the available housing stock. Turnover of housing in part depends on a house's place in the price distribution and the state of the housing market. Starter homes in the lower part of the housing distribution tend to turn over more quickly and therefore generate more repeat-sale observations. Trading volume drops appreciably in declining markets. Houses that trade in down markets are on average better-quality houses, which would lead to underestimates of the price decline for the average house. Declining markets can also create lock-in effects where recent buyers may be reluctant to sell a house and realize a loss of equity.

Two methods have been used to address selection bias. Jud and Seaks (1994) use a statistical procedure to correct for nonrandomness. They obtained 1986 data on appraisals for all houses in Guilford County, North Carolina that also listed the last three sales transactions for the houses during the period 1980–91. The country tax office deleted from the sample houses with significant alterations. There were 23,095 sales over the period. These data allow the authors to estimate the likelihood that each property sells in each period based on house characteristics and prevailing economic conditions. The hedonic regression using the sales price data is augmented with a "mills ratio" term designed to control for the sales data's nonrandomness. The authors find statistical evidence of selection bias. Controlling for the selection bias results in a slight downward revision of the price index. However, the housing price returns (the slope of the price index) do not appear to be significantly affected by adjustment.

Goetzmann (1995) uses simulation techniques to investigate the potential impact of selection bias in housing sales. He generates initial prices on 100 assets so that these prices are uniformly distributed on the interval (0,1). He then revalues these assets over forty time periods. In each period, the price of all 100 assets is affected by a common market return drawn from a normal distribution with a mean of 0.05 (positive "drift") and a standard deviation of 0.1. Each individual asset is also affected by an idio-syncratic price adjustment drawn from a normal distribution with a zero mean and a standard deviation of 0.4.

Goetzmann uses several decision rules to generate different transactions data. Each rule involves comparing the asset's current price with some historical price for that asset (or past transactions prices for other assets). The asset is sold only if the current price exceeds the "target" price specified by the rule. Each simulation, then, generates a series of forty prices for each asset as well as transactions prices for the traded assets. A total of 100 simulations are carried out for each trading rule investigated. The simulated data allows Goetzmann to compute the true-price index (unconditional on a sale) as well as the observed-price index (conditional on a sale). The average difference between the true-price index and the repeat-sale price index is 4.7%, which is similar in magnitude to the average true-price appreciation, which is around 5%. These results are quite dramatic but reflect the choice of parameters for the simulation.

13.2 Real Estate in the Limited Partner's Asset Portfolio: The Literature

Given a residential real-estate price index, the next issue is how to evaluate real estate's potential role in an investment portfolio. A key issue here—the extent to which the investor can diversify the real-estate risk—would sharply divide the Managing Partners and Limited Partners. The Managing Partners by definition would live in the principal residence, and given their wealth constraints, would have little scope for diversification into other real estate. Managing Partners, then, would be exposed to individual price risk as well as the market risk captured in the house price index. Limited Partners, in contrast, would have a much greater scope for diversification both within a housing market and across housing markets. The house price indices discussed earlier would more accurately reflect the level of risk exposure for Limited Partners.

With this distinction between classes of investors in mind, Goetzmann and Ibbotson (1990) provide a basic characterization of real estate as an investment tool.

There is compelling evidence to recommend including a significant proportion of real estate in an investment portfolio. Not only does real estate provide returns comparable to those on bonds and stocks, but the low correlation of real estate with other assets makes it valuable for purposes of diversification. Because real estate returns fluctuate with changes in the Consumer Price Index, they also provide a hedge against inflation. (p. 65)

Table 13.1
Correlations of residential real estate with other assets—1970 to 1986

Farm real estate	S&P 500	20-year government	1-year government	Influenced
0.49	−0.20	−0.54	−0.56	0.56

Source: Goetzmann & Ibbotson (1990): Table 2.

Goetzmann and Ibbotson use repeat-sale data from Case and Shiller to construct an aggregate house price index for the period 1970–86. The geometric (arithmetic) mean return over this period is 8.5% (8.6%) with a standard deviation of 3.0%. This compares with a mean and standard deviation return for Treasuries of 7.6% and 1.4% and for the Standard & Poor 500 of 9.2% and 18.2%. The low standard deviation for the housing returns reflects neither individual house price risk nor leverage effects.

Residential real estate's diversification benefits come from its low correlation with other asset returns. Table 13.1 gives the correlations between the Case and Shiller composite index and the other assets in the Goetzmann and Ibbotson study.

> This low correlation means that real estate, both residential and commercial, is an effective hedge against fluctuations in the financial markets. Thus, even if real estate returns were expected to be relatively low, and the standard deviation were expected to be relatively high, it would still occupy a significant percentage of an optimal investor portfolio. (p. 74)

Goetzmann (1993) creates "efficient" investment frontiers for each of the four Case and Shiller housing markets and characterizes his results as follows.

> The four portfolio studies suggest that, at least over the sixteen years for which we have reliable data, many of the ex post efficient allocations contained a significant proportion of wealth in a single home, although the home investment was not the predominant asset class. Perhaps more significant is the fact that the home investment increases toward the risk-averse portion of the frontier. Indeed, the minimum risk portfolio ... typically allocates 50% to the home investment in each of the four cases. (pp. 210–11)

Goetzmann and Ibbotson (1990) also note the low correlations between Case and Shiller real estate returns across the four housing markets. They find the largest correlation, 0.25, between Atlanta and San Francisco. This low correlation between housing markets underscores the advantage of regionally balanced investment portfolios.

Grauer and Hakansson (1995) extend the analysis in two dimensions. First, they explore discrete-time investment portfolio models instead of simply looking at mean-variance models. Second, they use ex ante empirical approximations to the asset returns distributions rather than ex post estimates. That is, investors in period t use observed asset returns up to period $t-1$ in their investment decision. Assuming no leverage for real estate purchases, they find access to farm and residential real estate increases mean returns by around 300 basis points with little overall increase in risk. For relatively risk-averse investors, real estate largely substitutes for the risk-free asset (Treasuries) and corporate bonds (similar to our own findings).

Another important issue is the relevant holding period. The risk results above correspond to holding periods of a single year. The risk involved in longer holding periods depends importantly on the autocorrelation between annual residential real estate returns. Case and Shiller (1988) report positive annual autocorrelations ranging from 0.41 to 0.62 for their four housing markets. The positive autocorrelations mitigate the risk over longer holding periods. Goetzmann (1993) reports five-year holding-period risks roughly comparable to the one-year risks.

13.3   Simple Estimates of the Demand for Residential Real Estate Assets

We now provide our own simple estimates, in the spirit of the existing literature, of the potential demand for real estate in asset portfolios. In looking at the national market, using the FHA housing series has advantages. We apply the standard procedures used in much of the portfolio literature based on the capital asset pricing model and therefore the accompanying idea that assets find a place in the portfolio provided they reduce the risk associated with any given rate of return.

The first exercise we perform is to take the major categories of U.S. assets, primarily stocks and bonds, and add the possibility of a new asset, the purchase of the FHA/Freddie Mac price index, a fairly standard index of the value of U.S. residential real estate. Assuming that the index is sold at a par price (corresponding to a par price for the Limited Partnerships), how does the asset's availability affect the mean-variance efficient frontier, and what share does residential real estate have in the efficient portfolio? We answer these questions looking at these assets' historical variance-covariance structure as well as their correlation with inflation. Table 13.2 gives the correlations for the period 1951–94.

Table 13.2
Correlations of residential real estate with other assets and inflation, 1951 to 1994

	Residential real estate	Inflation	Standard & Poor 500	Long-term government bonds	Treasuries
Residential real estate	1.000				
Inflation	0.596	1.000			
Standard & Poor 500	−0.091	−0.278	1.000		
Long-term government bonds	−0.082	−0.149	0.166	1.000	
Treasuries	0.300	0.713	−0.161	0.255	1.000

Note that real estate has been a good hedge against inflation. The only other asset that has been such a good inflation hedge is the treasury bill. The pattern of correlations has been broadly similar over the more recent period 1976–1994, as shown in table 13.3. Real estate has continued to be a good hedge against inflation, and also has become an increasingly good hedge against stock exchange risk. Over the period 1976–1994, returns on real estate and returns on stocks have been almost entirely uncorrelated.

The potential demand for a residential-housing-based asset can be estimated from the impact it has on the efficient frontier. Although the pattern of correlations shifted considerably over the period of study, the potential value of residential real estate to a portfolio manager remained qualitatively similar—a significant reduction in risk for a given level of return. The impact of residential housing becomes small only for the high-risk end of the investment spectrum. Figures 13.1 and 13.2 give the efficient investment frontiers with and without access to residential real estate for both the entire period and for the most recent twenty years.

To gain additional insight into the pricing of Partnership contracts, we extend the valuation exercises of chapter 6. We again consider a Limited Partner with a constant relative risk aversion utility function who is selecting an optimal portfolio comprising four assets: treasury bills, long-term government bonds, stocks, and residential real estate. We base all computations on the Ibbotson real returns data as well as the FHA/Freddie Mac housing series for the entire period 1951–1994. However, we begin by using an annual investment horizon to reflect the fact that the Limited Partner need not hold a fixed portfolio for the entire ten-year horizon used in chapter 6. We also remove the restriction that the Limited Partner hold a predetermined share of their portfolio in real estate, and solve instead for the unconstrained optimal portfolio.

Figure 13.3 plots the optimal portfolio holdings for the Limited Partner as a function of the level of risk aversion, on the assumption that Limited Partnerships sell at a par price. The figure shows that at low levels of risk aversion, the household holds only stocks, since stocks have the highest expected return. As the level of risk aversion increases, the household diversifies first into treasury bills and then into housing assets. It turns out that long-term government bonds form no part of the optimal portfolio in this simple exercise.

Naturally, the demand for the housing asset increases if Partnership Contracts sell at a discount. Figure 13.4 illustrates the share of the port-

Table 13.3
Correlations of residential real estate with other assets and inflation, 1976 to 1994

	Residential real estate	Inflation	Standard & Poor 500	Long-term government bonds	Treasuries
Residential real estate	1.000				
Inflation	0.559	1.000			
Standard & Poor 500	0.006	−0.030	1.000		
Long-term government bonds	−0.418	−0.507	0.475	1.000	
Treasuries	0.018	0.588	0.100	−0.006	1.000

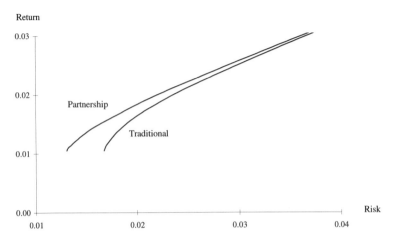

Figure 13.1
Efficient portfolio frontiers, annual real returns, 1951–1994

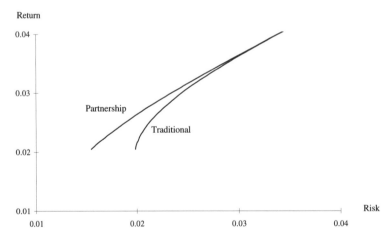

Figure 13.2
Efficient portfolio frontiers, annual real returns, 1976–1994

Portfolio share

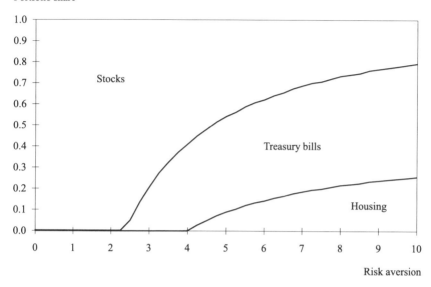

Figure 13.3
Portfolio shares under par pricing, annual real returns, 1951–1994

Portfolio share in
housing assets

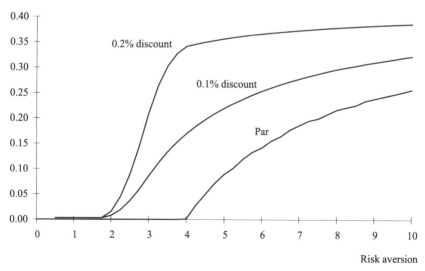

Figure 13.4
Demand for housing assets under various pricing schemes, annual real returns, 1951–1994

folio in housing for small discounts of 0.1% and 0.2%. It is striking how much real estate holdings increase at even very small discounts to par.

To gain further insight into the demand for Limited Partnerships and to relate the results to those produced in chapter 6, we redo the above exercises based on the ten-year holding period used in that chapter. For this longer holding period, figure 13.5 shows the proportionate holding of housing in the optimal portfolio of the Limited Partner at discounts ranging from 1% to 3%. Figure 13.6 plots demand for all three assets at the 2% discount. As in figure 13.3, note the overwhelming importance of stocks for low levels of risk aversion, with treasuries significant only at a risk aversion levels above $\alpha = 2$, and housing at risk aversion levels above $\alpha = 3$.

For a given level of risk aversion, our computations would allow us to illustrate the demand curve for housing assets as a function of the discount. Unfortunately, the economics profession has been unable to come to any consensus on the appropriate value of the risk aversion parameter. One reason for this lack of consensus is described in the literature on the "equity premium puzzle"; see Kotcherlakota 1996. The puzzle is how to explain the high holdings of fixed income assets given the very attractive-long-term return properties of stocks. To relate this puzzle to the exercises of this chapter, note that according to our calculations, there should be zero demand for long-term government bonds. More broadly, researchers have to assume "unrealistically" high levels of risk aversion to explain the actual pattern of asset holdings. There is a vast literature on this and other related asset return paradoxes, but there is as yet no answer. Calculations of asset values based on the assumption of a specific utility function remain more of an art than a science.

The analysis to date has used the combined FHA/Freddie Mac housing returns series. An important issue is the sensitivity of the results to the use of alternate housing returns series. Peek and Wilcox (1991) compare seven different housing returns series over the period 1970–89, examining only the average return and variability of the returns (in real terms). Table 13.4 summarizes their findings.

The major implications of table 13.4 are that the FHA/Freddie Mac returns series is roughly in the middle of the range of overall returns. The Census—average and MIRS—existing series give returns on the high end, and the Residential Investment series produces returns on the low end. The latter can be explained by the fact that the series only reflects returns to structures.

Portfolio share in
housing assets

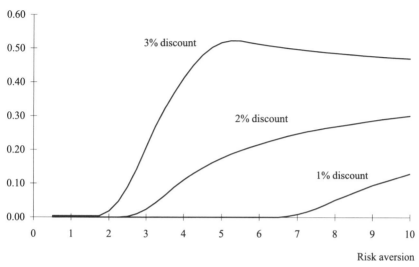

Figure 13.5
Demand for housing assets under various pricing schemes, ten year returns, 1951–1994

Portfolio share

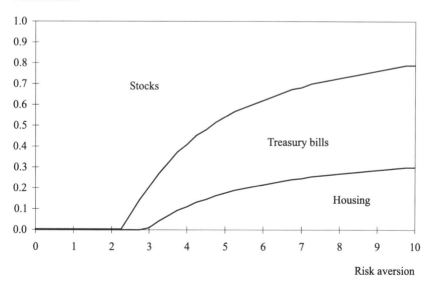

Figure 13.6
Portfolio shares under 2% discount pricing, ten year real returns, 1951–1994

Table 13.4
Measures of real house prices: 1970–1989

Series	Cumulative percentage change	Percentage standard deviation	
		Without regard to trend	Relative to trend
FHA	26%	12.4%	5.4%
NAR	34	9.5	4.3
Census—average	86	18.4	5.5
Census—hedonic	17	8.1	5.2
MIRS—existing	53	17.1	9.7
Residential investment	12	5.4	4.0
Freddie Mac	31	7.9	5.2

Source: Peek and Wilcox (1991), table 2.

All the aggregate series are built up from more disaggregate housing returns series. The FHA/Freddie Mac series is aggregated using portfolio weights that change from year to year, implying that the series does not strictly capture the returns from holding a fixed representative investment of national residential housing over a period of time. To accomplish this, one would want to hold fixed the weights used to aggregate the underlying housing series.

13.4 From Real Estate Price Indices to Partnership Funds

The estimates suggest that real estate has a potentially massive role in asset portfolios, primarily because of its low correlation with the other major asset classes. While the estimates above suggest a potential demand for Partnerships at a par price, we do not have enough information to make a precise prediction of the equilibrium price for Limited Partnerships.

One simple point is that current real estate price indices are not constructed to mimic the payoffs of Partnership fund shares. A Partnership fund share would comprise a set of houses from a single geographic area all of which were purchased within a short time of one another. The returns to this shareholding would be the stream of sales of these properties, which would be spread over time according to the properties' different holding periods. In contrast, a typical real estate price index concentrates on a set of house sales from a single geographic area all of which take place within a short time of one another.

Another set of complications arise from general equilibrium effects. Neither the price of housing nor its pattern of returns would remain unchanged if Partnership Markets were successful. In particular, the availability of capital on the price of housing and housing's value in an asset portfolio would increase. Most importantly, the increased demand for housing would likely change both the price of housing and the pattern of appreciation. In qualitative terms, the price would rise and the rate of return would fall. The extent of this effect is very hard to predict.

Some of the other major adjustments that we expand on below are

- new opportunities for diversification,
- self-selection effects, and
- transactions costs.

13.5   New Opportunities for Diversification

One problem with the estimates of value provided using the capital asset pricing methodology is that they are based on the idea of complete markets. In reality, markets are incomplete and present a wide variety of risks that are very hard to hedge against. Partnerships would add to the set of states spanned in a potentially significant way, and this might make them even more valuable than would be the case in the simulations that ignore such changes in the state space.

In this manner, the Partnership mutual funds that we envisage might open up profound investment opportunities that would go far beyond the simple notion referred to above of investing in U.S. residential real estate. The method of packaging the Partnerships would influence their value, as would the actions of the surrounding "slicers and dicers." While its quantitative would be hard to assess, this has significant potential to add value to Limited Partnerships.

The ease with one could hedge certain risks would depend greatly on how the basic Limited Partnership Contracts were pooled into PREFERS. Therefore one of the first and more interesting activities would be for the distributors of PREFERS to gather the institutional buyers into groups that have common risk-return or hedging demands. From this activity the distributors would begin to build order books for interested buyers of PREFERS. The first few issues would be experimental, but one should remember that all the participants would have a lot to gain from creating these new markets in an optimal fashion. One could imagine several potential dimensions for setting up PREFERS depending on final demand:

- Geographic: national, by region, by MSA, state, urban, suburban, rural, and so forth.
- Property type: single family, condo, co-op, vacation, large, small, contemporary, traditional, acreage, tax status, and so forth.
- Occupant status: income, occupation, marital status, and so forth.

Altogether one can envisage an endless set of new insurance markets being developed as the financial markets become ever more sophisticated in their methods of bundling partnerships, and developing derivative products.

13.6   Self-Selection Effects

The households that would use Partnerships could not be expected to be average households, nor could the holding period of Partnership properties be assumed to agree with the current average holding period. In both cases, it is important for the returns on Partnerships to consider how these choices would be made.

Customer Self-Selection at Purchase

The dangers of breach of contract and of poor maintenance of the property would depend to a certain extent on who became Managing Partners. The contracts might have greatest appeal to lower- and middle-income potential home owners, raising the possibility that the relevant rates of delinquency would be somewhat higher than those on the average mortgage. Offsetting this, those who became Managing Partners would not need such large loans, which would lower the delinquency risk. How these forces would balance is an empirical matter. Note also that to improve the treatment of this effect, and thereby price or hedge it more accurately, pools could be constructed based on the LTV on the underlying mortgage. However, much ignorance would remain on this score until the contracts were launched and the secondary markets developed.

Self-Selection in the Sale Process

The timing of sales is complex and would have to be factored into the return structure on the asset. One interesting interaction would occur in cases in which there is a non-par price, as Limited Partners would wish to estimate the return they could expect. The returns to a discounted security depend on sale time: The expected return is very high if turnover is immediate, but at a longer horizon, there is literally no difference from purchasing at no discount. The weight on the old and the very high shorter return would depend on turnover time, and so shorter turnover times would lower the need for a discount to attract funds.

The subtle issue here is the interdependence between the level of the discount and the mobility of the buyers of Partnerships. The larger the discount, the greater is the likelihood that those who intend to stay in an area for a longer than average time will be drawn into becoming Managing Partners. This self-selection would in turn lengthen the average turnover time, and in this fashion would increase the level of the discount. On the other hand, it is equally possible that younger home buyers would be most attracted to the Partnership Market, in which case the turnover time on house sales by Managing Partners would be shorter than the overall market average. Overall, it is hard to make predictions in this area given the massive uncertainty concerning the types of households that will make greatest use of the Partnership Market.

13.7 Transactions Costs

Several different forms of transactions costs in the Partnership Market would reduce their value. The servicer would require a fee for monitoring the contract, and certain residual issues of moral hazard might result in a less careful treatment of the property and fewer additions to the house than for a fully owned home. There is no reason to believe these issues would loom large provided the contract was well written and the servicer enforced the contract proficiently.

A more difficult issue to assess is the cost arising from breach of contract by the Managing Partner. However, a contract written according to the outline in chapter 9 would keep these issues to a minimum, and the problem would primarily arise when the Managing Partner breached their agreement by defaulting on the mortgage they had taken out on their portion of the equity. Even if default caused the breach, that would not necessarily imply a loss for the Limited Partner. The Limited Partner would lose only if the default event causes either the property to lose value specifically from the fact of default or the Limited Partner to bear some additional cost they otherwise would not have borne.

Default is well studied, and there is no reason to expect it to cause more of an issue in valuation of Limited Partnership contracts than it currently causes in the secondary mortgage market (see Quigley and Van Order 1991 for confirmation of the low default rates on high-quality mortgages). Indeed, the specialist might act as a securitizer by offering insurance against this form of breach similar to that currently offered on many mortgage pools.

Given the strong rationale for institutional investors to invest in the residential real estate market, Partnerships would offer a far better vehicle for such investing. A detailed contract aligning the Managing Partner's interests with the Limited Partner's financial interests would allow the Limited Partner to view the housing Partnership Market as primarily a financial market in which the Managing Partner is an agent whom the Limited Partner is paying to provide a set of value-enhancing and value-protecting measures with respect to the underlying property.

IV Partnerships and the Housing Experience

In this section we present a picture of how the Partnership Market would affect the broader experience of buying, selling, and living in a home. Key differences include:

- a new incentive structure,
- a new information structure, and
- a new balance of power in the market.

14   Partnerships and the Home Purchase

It is a commonplace that many households suffer panic and dismay after closing on their dream house. And there are very good reasons why a deal that looked good just a short while earlier can look decidedly more questionable upon further reflection. The root cause of buyer's remorse is the combination of the profoundly complex nature of the buyer's search problem and the extremely poor incentive structure in the housing and mortgage markets.

14.1   The Searcher's Problem and the Real Estate Agent

Consider the housing search problem for a young couple who are first-time buyers. They are looking to move into a new district within reasonable commuting distance of their workplaces. The couple is willing to commit the standard amount of time, money, and effort to the search process. They make several preliminary decisions to start the process, such as identifying the broad geographic area in which they can live in light of the locational constraints of their work and social activities, and choosing what type of house best suits their lifestyle and tastes.

With these two choices made, the couple still faces an extremely complex problem of searching and matching, with uncertainty about such varied and important issues as:

- which neighborhoods to look at,
- which houses to look at,
- how to judge house quality,
- which houses best match their needs,
- what price to offer for a chosen home,
- how to respond to counteroffers,

• whether to have a lawyer present at the closing, and

• how much to set aside for escrow accounts.

These questions and many additional ones are raised by Ilyce Glink in her book on the complexities of buying a house; see Glink 1994. But it goes even deeper than this, because for most households the key question is, "What are the important questions in this market?" Given this degree of ignorance, the couple is very poorly equipped to carry out any kind of sensible search process without seeking some advice from the professionals surrounding them. This is especially important for first-time buyers operating in a profoundly unfamiliar setting. The couple therefore selects a realtor to help with the multiple dimensions of uncertainty. Now the couple enters a new stage of the process in which the real estate agent guides them. The agent dominates their experience of the housing market during the home search. The agent guides the search process by discussing all aspects of the offer process, helping the buyer prequalify for mortgage finance, and taking their side in all visible interactions.

Seller Sub-Agent

Unfortunately, the real estate agent who takes this critical role can have financial and/or legal incentives that are strongly at variance with those of the buyer. The vast majority of real estate agents are paid as a percentage of the final sales price of the house, and both are commonly paid by the seller of the property. This means that the basic financial incentives point to the agent aiming to close deals no matter what happens, and maximizing the price that the buyer pays subject to this constraint. A profit-minded agent has little interest in helping the buyer minimize the price they pay for their home.

In addition to this basic incentive problem, there are often legal reasons that the agent does not operate in line with the buyer's interests. Some real estate agents acting on the buyer's side of the market operate with the legal status of seller sub-agent. This name itself indicates a source of the underlying tension between the buyer and their agent. In addition to the standard financial incentive problem, this gives rise to some very real legal constraints in terms of the agent's ability to represent the buyer's interests. For example, they are not allowed to tell the buyer what to offer for the home, which home to buy, what are the defects of the home (unless they are hidden and material), nor any relevant comparison prices and listings (unless they are specifically requested). These are very real constraints in the sense that the seller can sue the agent if they find out that they were violated.

There is a growing awareness that there is something unusual in a market structure in which both agents are responsible to the seller. Partly in response to this, there are now a number of states that are replacing the traditional seller sub-agent form of agreement with the so-called buyer's agent form of agreement. Mostly this is accomplished by changing the legal nature of the real estate agent's contractual obligations. The use of a buyer's agent, however, does nothing to change the financial incentive problem. The agent often receives a commission that is proportionate to the final sales price, so that their financial incentives still point in the direction of making the deal happen at as high a price as possible.

Given the depth of these incentive problems in the current market, a few brokers are now trying to change the incentive structure. One idea that has been tried is a search contract, with a fee paid for an exclusive period of search. But search contracts are very hard to write, and for this reason have not yet taken a significant share of the market. The key problem revolves around the exclusivity defined in the search contract (see Razzi (1996)).

In practice there are two conflicting approaches to defining the exclusivity, each of which has an incentive problem:

• If there is a period of exclusivity, the buyer has the incentive to delay purchase of a house until the period is over.

• If exclusivity derives from a list of properties the agent supplies, the agent has the incentive to hand over the telephone book, sit back, and relax.

More generally, why will the agent work hard if their pay is independent of their role in the sale process? Why will the buyer pay the agent if they can find a way to claim, either fair or foul, that they did not hear about a given house from the agent, but found it themselves through private search?

14.2   Incentive Problems and Networks

On top of the central incentive problem with the agent, there is a second source of danger for the unwary buyer. As the search progresses, the household often relies on referrals from the agent to other market professionals, and the agent guides them to a member of their network. Thus the original incentive problem permeates the entire transaction. The subdivisions in the market make the problem all the more severe, with little information available about the reputations of the various players with whom the buyer comes into contact. In most local housing markets, one or two networks of insiders dominate the market. While the agents are central figures, they are merely the most visible link in a chain of housing market professionals that includes appraisers, structural engineers, title companies, mortgage originators, and lawyers. Once the buyer chooses their real estate agent, they are also implicitly picking the specific network of that agent's connections.

In the next sections, we expand on some of the dangers buyers face as a result of these referrals. The story is old and familiar:

• An ignorant buyer shows up willing to spend a lot of money to buy a good they have minimal ability to assess.

• On their way through the market, they meet many parties who are happy to assist while they spend a large amount of money.

• Unlike the household, everyone else in the picture is extremely professional at what they are doing.

Guess who wins?

14.3   The Right Home?

The real estate agent can provide a valuable service for the potential buyer in the search phase by using his or her knowledge of the local property market to minimize the cost of search. As part of this search process, the agent performs several functions: prequalifying the buyer, assessing the buyer's housing needs, and locating the best homes. More than in any other market, however, the watchword remains "caveat emptor."

Prequalifying
Usually the real estate agent's first step is to investigate the buyer's financial condition. One of the key lessons a rookie real estate agent learns is that there is a tremendous financial incentive in screening potential buyers up front to make sure they will qualify for a mortgage. Despite the heavy precautions they take, even experienced real estate agents lose many deals after having the seller accept an offer.[1] Limiting this fallout is a major determinant of the agent's success.

In many cases the agent fills out a standardized mortgage application for the buyer, and using the information, can calculate the debt burden for the buyer.[2] If the agent remains uncertain whether the buyer will qualify, the agent may submit a mortgage application to a mortgage originator, who pulls the credit bureau report. Note that the real estate agent has the incentive in this case to choose not the mortgage originator with the lowest rate, but the one who provides the most assistance in ascertaining the buyer's credit standing by explaining in detail any reason for rejection.

Assessing the Buyer's Needs

With prequalification completed, the agent helps the household zero in on the appropriate types of property. Particularly for first-time home buyers, the real estate agent can provide invaluable assistance in determining what kind of house will meet the buyer's living needs. Issues arise at this stage such as the number of bedrooms the family needs, the nature of the local amenities, and how the neighborhood is changing. The chief incentive problem here is that the real estate agent has strong motivation to suggest houses that exceed the household's real needs.

Locating the Best Home

During the actual search for the home, the incentive problems really begin to show. The real estate agent can be of great value here by lowering the search cost using their intimate knowledge of the local property markets. However, the agent also has a clear incentive to show the potential buyer a location (and house) that is not necessarily the most affordable but that makes the most profit for the agent.

One strategy is for the agent to show the buyer four houses the first day. Each of the first three has one locational feature the buyer really does not want, and the last is perfect but a stretch on affordability. The last house also is preferably one where the buyer's agent has one of the following:

- *Dual representation.* The firm for which the buyer's real estate agent works also represents the seller (has the listing).

- *Increased commission.* Some rather shrewd sellers increase the commission to the buyer's agent.[3]

- *A friendly seller's agent.* If the buyer's agent cannot get either of the first two, the sale may be steered to an agent who is a close friend and can be trusted to return the favor in due course (see Razzi 1996).

Additional problems arise from the fact that so many of the agents receive commission from the seller. The agent has little financial incentive to volunteer information on bad features of the local environment and also faces a legal restriction against making any comments on defects that are not "hidden and material (see Hymer 1996)." The definition may go so far as to make it impossible to point out that the factory down the road is known to be a source of environmental contamination. This is usually not a hidden defect,[4] and so the seller would have a right to sue if the agent revealed it. What results is a case of buyer beware with a vengeance.

14.4 The Right Price?

Once a house has been selected, the buyer must decide on an offer strategy. The negotiation process is complex and multifaceted and extends from the initial offer through possibly numerous counteroffers. The process can also cover negotiating several contract contingencies as well as defining exactly what is to be sold. In this process the buyer and seller interact, with their respective agents' advice.

Some buyers use the tactic of being fully open with their agent and submitting a low bid but giving the agent indications they would be willing to go higher. Given the agent's incentives, this is a little like saying: "I am going to offer you a low commission, but I am ultimately willing to pay you a higher commission." It would be no great surprise that the seller did not accept the initial offer but instead held out for more. In fact, unscrupulous agents have dreamed up some complex stratagems for achieving these goals. Less scrupulous agents in some cases attempt to drive up the price in the course of negotiation by using phantom bidders, selective release of seller information, and the creation of phony seller reserve prices.

To keep these problems to a minimum, a wall of silence is supposed to be erected between agents on either side of the market. This is not a profoundly meaningful barrier to communication, since the agents are usually very well acquainted with one another. In fact, the agents on both sides of the deal, who have very similar financial incentives, often communicate a great deal. These incentives involve finding the deal that best furthers their interests, a far cry from the deal in the buyer's best interests.

Given these problems, many buyers begin with relatively low bids, often against their agent's advice. Having received a relatively low bid for the property, the seller and the agents may choose among several responses to try to increase the price:

- use the bid to try to flush out other bids
- tell the buyer there is another interested buyer even if there are no other bidders
- drop the asking price of the property but remove any free perks so the price appears to drop more than it really has[5]
- exclude some of the physical items normally considered to be attached to the property, such as appliances, from the offer

The agent has an incentive to help the buyer see through seller stratagems only if they are seen as potential deal-breakers.

Few buyers realize that the entire negotiation process and the agent's advice to them can be profoundly influenced by the payment scheme the seller has selected. The seller has a variety of tools at their disposal to help them both boost traffic and pull the buyer's agent even further into their corner. The simplest tool is to depart from the standard commission rate.

In most states the standard commission is 6%, with 3% to the selling agent and 3% to the buying agent. A shrewd seller may offer 4% to the agent on the buyer's side of the deal. The extra commission motivates the agent to steer customers to the house and increase walk-through traffic and keeps the agent firmly on the seller's side through the transaction.

In an even more blatant attempt to influence the transaction, some sellers offer the agents additional commissions for a high sale price. The seller can offer a bonus to the buying and/or selling agent if the offer price is above a certain level (e.g., 20% of the amount over $120,000 in final price). It is hard to strike a good bargain when the agent in your corner will lose $200 for every $1,000 you save!

14.5   From Contract to Closing: More Players, More Games

Assuming that the two parties can arrive at a mutual understanding, they then draw up a contract. At this point the buyer will put down a deposit on the deal that is said to be nonrefundable except for the exclusions the contract specifically mentions,[6] mostly relating to both parties' performance of various obligations. The next phase involves fulfilling the terms spelled out in the contract for these obligations, such as obtaining financing, having the property appraised by the lender, and having a structural engineer look at the building. While these stages provide some safeguards to the buyer, there is still plenty of scope for gaming.

The Housing Financing Market and the Appraisal

The buyer hopes the issuer of their mortgage has an incentive to ensure the property is priced fairly to reduce the risk of default loss. Unfortunately, although lenders have a strong interest in ensuring the deal they are financing is not sufficiently bad to impair their collateral, the buyer can still lose a lot of money before the price paid is sufficiently over market value to affect the lender's collateral interest, particularly if the deal involves a large down payment. The key issue here is that the appraisal process lenders use to certify whether the deal is at market price has its own very profound problems.

An appraiser typically enters the scene when the mortgage originator is assessing the value of the collateral to see whether the loan is worth making. At this point, the price has been set, and they are literally determining whether the amount applied for in the mortgage application is worth lending.

Two outcomes typically are possible:

• If the appraiser values the house for near enough its offer price, the application goes through (subject to other checks' and verifications' being passed).

• If the appraisal is significantly different from the offer price, the applicant who is near the minimum down payment may be turned down or told to get PMI.

As one might guess, an easy way to become an unpopular appraiser is to value a property at significantly under the purchase price and thereby break a deal and take a commission away from the agent. It is therefore tremendously important for the appraiser to "hit the number" by appraising at or above the purchase price.

The pressure to hit the number is intensified by the fact that although the mortgage originator pays the appraiser, the real estate agent typically controls the appraiser's livelihood both by supplying recommendations and using their power to request that particular appraisers not be used. Originators typically follow agent recommendations concerning which appraisers to use, because agents are notorious for shopping their mortgages around to other lenders if unhappy with the appraisals requested by a particular mortgage originator. Overall, an appraiser must have an extremely strong reason for not hitting the number, or they will soon find themselves out of business.

To make matters worse, appraisal is not an exact science. The heart of the matter involves comparing the unit to three recent comparable sales (or comps), and carrying out "appropriate adjustments" to price the unit at hand. But this leaves many gray areas:

- Which units are considered most comparable?
- What are the appropriate adjustments?
- How far back should one look for comps?
- If more than three comps are available, which ones should be used?

Given this inevitably cloudy definition, that the same house can have widely differing appraisals is no surprise. In particular, relatively few transactions cannot be justified in this manner by the choice of comparisons and adjustments. The appraisal process contains massive room for error or individual judgment.

One might wonder why standard appraisals' unreliability does not put lenders ultimately at risk. After all, if households are overpaying for their homes, default losses will be more severe. In this respect the originators' two different business strategies cause a significant difference in incentives:

- *Mortgage originators*[7] quickly sell their loans into the secondary markets, so that guarantors such as FNMA, Freddie Mac, and GNMA hold the credit risk.
- *Portfolio lenders* hold loans in portfolio.

For mortgages sold to secondary markets, the issuer is protected if the package conforms to the guarantor's standards.[8] This standardization takes into account the appraisers' incentives to hit the number to preserve their stream of referrals. The bias itself has become standardized and would be corrected only if a particular appraisal were biased in excess of the typical amount. The fact that any particular appraisal is biased is very hard to track down in the current process.

The bias would have a bigger effect on the extent of default loss than on the probability of default. If the loan defaults after a few years, it is always possible to blame an unusually low resale price on a later collapse in that property market, poor management of real estate owned (REO) by the creditor, or buyer negligence of the property. These cases exert little obvious pressure for the appraisal to be extremely accurate. And if the general bias itself should increase over time, the only evidence of that would be a big wave of unusually costly defaults, which could probably be attributed to some adverse shock to the economy, given our limited knowledge concerning default's true determinants.

The case is somewhat different for mortgages that will be held in portfolio. Here the originator has a more direct interest in the underlying collateral's value, as they may actually own the collateral if the owner defaults. Not surprisingly, when their own interest in the quality of the loans is heightened, mortgage originators will apply stricter appraisal standards, challenge the appraisers, remove appraisers from the recommended list, or use in-house appraisers.

Appraisals are scrutinized more carefully not only when the loan will be held in portfolio rather than sold into the secondary market, but also when there is additional scrutiny on the performance of the loans mortgage originators are selling onto the secondary market, or when the loans they have recently sold to the secondary market have a suspiciously poor performance record. For this reason even mortgage originators often have both in-house appraisers and lists of outside appraisers with whom they maintain a close relationship. For both types of appraisers the incentive is to more accurately value the house.

The mortgage bank also raises appraisal standards by insisting the buyer take out PMI. The PMI business may be run separately from the mortgage origination industry in part because of the industry's low opinion of the current appraisal process. When the PMI company receives an application for a high-LTV loan, the company does their own checks on the loan. Not surprisingly, they often insist on a new appraisal. More over, they actually keep their own list of trusted appraisers, who face entirely different incentives, since their flow of business depends on maintaining a record of providing accurate appraisals.

The Structural Engineer
Often the agent advises the buyer to have a structural engineer assure the building's structural integrity, and the sale is contingent on the building's passing such an inspection. The structural engineering industry is again something of a cottage industry, with a typical fee that varies between $350 and $500 per inspection. Structural engineers' professional responsibility is to make the buyer aware of any structural problems or building code violations.[9]

However, they work for the real estate agent and are dependent on home purchase referrals. If their report breaks a deal, they have some explaining to do to get any more business from the agent from whom they have just taken away a commission. Besides losing future referrals, they can be held liable for any disparaging remarks they might make about items that need repair or maintenance if the remarks do not strictly address code violations or structural defects. They are therefore good only for protection against out-and-out disasters, rather than for warning against the entire list of problems which the buyer will shortly own.

Games at Closing

Should the buyer have a lawyer and an agent at the closing? Buyers and sellers commonly practice brinkmanship and debate the quality of the property at closing. Usually the attorneys resolve such issues by providing escrow to cover any repairs that are felt to be necessary. Of course the key items to negotiate here are how much escrow is needed, and the standard to which the repairs must be completed before the funds are released.

A lawyer may help the buyer at closing by insisting that funds be set aside in escrow to cover problems unnoticed until closing. Unfortunately, many slips in the current purchase process leave room for error. As we have mentioned, the buyer's agent, as a seller's sub-agent, has a legal incentive not to mention any defects in the house that could be seen. However, because their commissions are paid on the amount before escrow, even if the buyer notices such a defect, the buyer's agent still has a financial incentive to underprice the cost of renovations or improvements implicit in a bid and to underreserve escrow for performance at closing. This means that if there are hidden dangers and some mutual recognition that major repair is likely to be needed after the house is occupied, the agent has no incentive to raise these issues to the level that they threaten either to be deal breakers or to reduce the house's price.

14.6   Partnerships and the Buying Experience

In the Partnership Market the Managing Partner's interests would align powerfully with those of the Limited Partner. Both would share an interest in keeping the price paid by the Managing Partner as low as possible. Both would:

- suffer if some defect with the building became evident, or some problem with the neighborhood;
- want to keep the payment on mortgage debt as low as possible;
- be interested in maintaining adequate insurance on the house;
- want to ensure that the escrow accounts are adequate; and
- have lawyers at closing who would likely cooperate on various issues.

But it is not just alignment of interests that would improve in the Partnership Market. There would also be the matter of experience in the housing market. The Limited Partner would be a financial institution extremely experienced in the housing market and know all the twists and turns in the purchase process. The Limited Partner would also be suitably skeptical of the standard of the appraisal carried out in the existing market structure. This means they would insist on the appraisal's being conducted to a higher standard. Their record of experience with the various real estate agents and appraisers would also inform their willingness to offer a high price for their share of the housing equity. By specializing in properties in a given neighborhood, they would reduce the current informational imbalance in which the buyer is generally overmatched with the seller and those whose interests are aligned with the seller's.

This evening of the balance of information and power in the purchase transaction would affect the behavior of all agents even before the Limited Partner appeared on the scene. A buyer who intended to use Partnership finance would so inform the agent at introduction, and this knowledge would influence the agent's behavior. A Limited Partner's impending presence would add great discipline to the entire purchase process. As part of helping the buyer find the home, the agent would have to prequalify with a Limited Partner. This means they would have to provide information to the buying household on the average price on Limited Partnerships in the neighborhood, and also that they would have to strike the sort of deal that would make the Limited Partner willing to offer the required amount of money. In particular, a key issue in determining whether the deal went through would be the price the Limited Partner was willing to pay for their share of the housing equity, which would depend on whether the Limited Partner's detailed appraisal came in at or around the transaction price.

Knowing that a knowledgeable Limited Partner would have to approve the deal would provide the real estate agent with a far stronger incentive to prevent the price of the property from becoming inflated. Since the agent would know that a high-standard appraisal was coming, they would have good reason to fear a poor deal would fall through, resulting in loss of both commission and reputation for the agent. This additional level of scrutiny would protect the buyer against various defects in their home. The seller just would not get away with grossly misleading the buyer, because the Limited Partner would carry out a high-standard appraisal.

Furthermore, the price the Limited Partner put on the Managing Partner's interest in the Partnership would communicate to the buyer the result of that appraisal. And at issue would be the real estate agent's reputation not only with the buyer and the seller as individuals, but also with the financial institution exploring whether to be Limited Partner. The Limited Partner would interact with real estate agents continuously and would undoubtedly have a good memory of which performed poorly. More generally, the need to face the financially powerful and well-informed Limited Partner's scrutiny might greatly discipline the other market participants' behavior.

The presence of a Limited Partner would have additional effects beyond disciplining agents. The mere fact that a Limited Partner was averse to a given deal or offered a low price on the equity would warn the buyer they might not be getting a good deal, even if the real estate agent believed otherwise.

Against this, a low offer from a Limited Partner might in some cases signal simply that particular Limited Partner's feelings or even an attempt to take advantage of the household's ignorance. To keep this to a minimum, we would definitely want a very competitive market with many Limited Partners competing for deals.

We basically view the Partnership as a positive step toward a more cooperative form of agreement between households and financial institutions than exists in either the current mortgage or housing markets. This cooperative agreement would be important for both parties. As detailed above, the Managing Partner would want to take advantage of the Limited Partner's superior information and market position; in exchange, the Limited Partner would want the Managing Partner to provide optimal upkeep on the property.

15

Partnerships and the Ownership Experience

Having bought the home with a Partnership, the home owner would need to be aware of other changes that would result. At all stages, Partnership finance would involve a trade-off, with additional transactions costs counterbalanced by an improved incentive structure. But the details of the trade-off would vary in interesting and sometimes important ways depending on the stage of the household's tenure in the home.

15.1 Partnerships and Life at Home

The Partnership Agreement would affect the household's living experience little during phases of routine behavior. Specifically, a household would find their behavior little or no different with a Partnership than without, if they followed the normal routine of living in the house, maintaining the house in decent shape, and paying off their mortgage and other financial obligations. The only issue during routine occupation would be a slight change in the incentives in maintaining the house, with the Partnership Agreement mandating perhaps a level of maintenance slightly higher than the household would otherwise have chosen. But during nonroutine behavior, the Partnership experience would differ most significantly from the classical experience of home ownership.

Home Improvement and Partnerships

According to the Partnership Agreement, if the Managing Partner wanted to substantially improve the property, the Limited Partner would need to adjust the pro-rata shares of the Partnership to compensate for improvements. The Partnership Agreement would include a list of the standard home improvements, the expected percentage increase in home price from each improvement, and the formula for calculating the change in the pro rata Partnership interests.

As in the auto insurance industry, Limited Partners would also keep a list of approved home improvement contractors. These contractors would be bonded and insured, with documented work records. The price and quality would be agreed in advance, and the Limited Partner would independently inspect the final repair. After the improvement was completed, the Limited Partner would inspect the work, then forward the Managing Partner an addendum for the Agreement and new certificates.[1]

If the Managing Partner wanted to make a nonstandard improvement, the Managing Partner would have to independently negotiate for the prorata increase with the Limited Partner. In this case the Managing Partner would have to pay a small fee for the Limited Partner's appraisal, and negotiating time. The Managing Partner would merely treat small improvements as a repair.[2]

The procedure we have suggested for improvements is imperfect. But it is not appropriate to hold it to a standard of perfection, since the home improvement area today is not without its own incentive problems. In fact, cases of fraud and shoddy workmanship are so common that Disney can make a movie about them (*Tin Men*). The common thread is that we have individual consumers with little experience hiring home improvement contractors without strong methods of certification, bonding, or monitoring. This is a classic agency problem. Problems also exist in getting trustworthy advice on the marketability of changes to the house. Just how much added value does a swimming pool provide in the resale market?

The Managing Partner could suggest and ultimately carry out almost any form of alteration they desired but would not be entitled to compensation from the Limited Partner if an alteration did not enhance value. Thus the Partnership Market would help clarify for the home owner those improvements that must be regarded as pure matters of personal taste and those that add value to the market price.

The method we have outlined might at times be cumbersome, but it would probably be better than the existing market in the dimensions of fraud and quality of repair, and it would be similar to two existing insurance markets (auto and medical) in the operating methods used to adjust the pro rata ownership interests. But we would not be at all surprised if someone told us of a household that chose not to take a Partnership for their property because they either planned to buy an old house with a lot of work needed or were avid gardeners who planned to invest vast sums in landscaping.

Partnerships and Major Shocks

Some important shocks to households would be covered in relatively straightforward fashion under the Partnership Agreement but bear mention because of their importance to the Managing Partner:

• *Natural disasters.* Insurance payments would be escrowed each month by the Partnership servicer so that when a disaster occurred, the Managing Partner and the Limited Partner would split the compensation pro rata. In any event, the Managing Partner would gain a formidable negotiator to assist in dealing with the insurance company to prevent artificially low settlements, another major worry of consumer groups.

• *Condemnations and easements.* Any proceeds or losses incurred by a condemnation or easement would be shared pro rata. Again the Managing Partner would get the support of a tough negotiator to make sure the price was fair even if the government were exercising eminent domain.

• *Death of a spouse.* The Partnership would automatically pass to the spouse without any change. If both spouses passed away, the Limited Partner might file for partition of the Partnership. The heirs would be free to negotiate with the Limited Partner to prevent partition.

• *Divorce.* As long as one party occupied the property and maintained all other obligations, the Partnership could remain in force. If not, the Limited Partner might file for partition.

15.2   Partnerships, Breach, and Default

Financial distress in the current mortgage market restricts the home owner's consumption levels and in worst cases may cause default on the mortgage and a bankruptcy filing. In the Partnership Market such extreme levels of financial distress would give rise to breach of the Partnership Agreement in addition to, or in place of, default on the mortgage. How would breach of the Partnership Agreement differ from defaulting on a mortgage?

One significant difference would be that the Limited Partner would in many ways add a layer of protection for the Managing Partner at times of severe financial distress and could help in several respects:

• *Rentals.* Even though rental would be prohibited under the Partnership Agreement, the Limited Partner would have an incentive to allow it (by not enforcing the non-rental clause) in situations of financial strain for the Managing Partner. In fact, the Limited Partner would have an incentive to assist the Managing Partner in finding a good tenant, managing the rental, and collecting the rent. The Limited Partner would share pro rata in the rent unless they waived that right. In effect this rental income would convert the economic opportunity cost of rent lost during the foreclosure and eviction process to the cash market value of that rent.

• *Relocations.* The Limited Partner would also have an incentive to help the Managing Partner find a less expensive property for relocating during times of financial stress while renting out the co-owned property. This would allow the Managing Partner to quickly reduce living expenses while securing the maximum financial gain from renting out the property. This would also convert the bankruptcy court's benefit of exercising the borrower's automatic stay into a market value cash payment.[3] (These periods of automatic stay are notorious for creating a prime opportunity for property damage.)

• *Foreclosure sale price.* Much has been written by lawyers who worry that the incentives in the foreclosure auction do not work when there is a "chilled" bid.[4] In fact this concern has caused some states to enact a "right of statutory redemption," which grants the borrower the right to repurchase the property within a specified time after the foreclosure sale at the foreclosure sale price.[5] With a Limited Partner bringing capital, experience, and the correct incentive to the foreclosure auction, incidences of chilled bidding would virtually disappear.

• *Property swaps.* The Limited Partner would have an incentive to allow the Managing Partner to "swap out of" the property for either cash or a much smaller property with reduced payments. This would avoid the direct expenses of foreclosure costs[6] as well as the indirect expense of property price depreciation from foreclosure. This process would be similar in effect to a "deed in lieu of foreclosure" in the traditional mortgage market, but the Limited Partner would have a much better incentive to make this happen than any mortgagee. Typically the borrower has few reasons to trust the mortgagee in the traditional mortgage "deed in lieu" process.

• *Foreclosure fees.* The Limited Partner would have a strong incentive to make sure all foreclosure costs were kept to a minimum. Also the Limited Partner could ensure quality standards for the services provided. In fact the Limited Partner might be able to assist by arranging volume discounts.

• *Reducing the foreclosure "knockdown price" effect.* The Limited Partner would act to counteract any knockdown of price due to labeling a property as a foreclosure. The Limited Partner might temporarily manage the property and find good tenants for it.

• *Work-out alternatives*. The Limited Partner would also have the incentive to ensure that all the potential work-out alternatives to foreclosure were vigorously pursued.

• *Joint investment in repair*. The Limited Partner would have both the incentive and the capital to invest in the repair of the property if it would improve the sale price.

15.3 Partnerships and the Sales Process

There would be a complex interaction with the Limited Partner when the Managing Partner decided to sell.

Preparations for the Sale and the As-Is Clause
In the current market, owners are advised to prepare their homes carefully to help the home sell (see *Home Buyer's Guide*, Better Homes and Gardens 1995, p. 42). This process of house preparation would be even more important in the Partnership Market, especially in light of the as-is clause. As time passed, we would expect a new service to develop in which an agent familiar with the as-is clause helped the owner identify any problems of inadequate maintenance. This would also help prevent the wastage caused by sellers who "overimprove" their house before sale under the illusion that the market places a high value on idiosyncratic improvements (see *Home Buyer's Guide*, Better Homes and Gardens 1995, p. 47).

The Sales Process
There would be a certain similarity between selling a Partnership home and deciding to purchase using a Partnership, because in both cases the owner-occupant would trade some additional transactional inconvenience and costs against improved incentives in the form of:

• protection for the unaware seller,

• protection for the seller under time pressure,

• protection against a reduction in their negotiating power at the closing table,

• performance standards for the seller's real estate agent (lawyer, title, and so forth), and

• downward pressure on selling costs.

In the current market, the majority of sellers pick a sales strategy in the face of tremendous underlying uncertainty (see Glink 1995 for an outline of the seller's problems in the current market). The seller's sales strategy is extremely complex, running the entire gamut of factors:

- listing price,
- choice of agent,
- flow of customers brought round by the agent because of the commission,
- back-and-forth with the bidder,
- selection of lawyers,
- closing of the deal.

The seller's agent has the job of ensuring the sales strategy chosen is optimal. This provides the seller a certain amount of protection, as the payment to the agent is proportional to the sales price of the house. There is also the increasingly complex decision on just how much information the seller must pass on to the buyer in order to avoid possible later legal action (see Romano (1996)).

Despite the broad alignment of incentives, there are many horror stories about poorly informed sellers who accept too little for their house. Given the agent's incentive to get a high price, whether the home is undersold may depend on the nature of the relationships between the buyer and the seller's agent and sub-agent. Being involved in the occasional bargain sale may be a very good idea for the agent in terms of long-run relationships. But there is more to it than this. Agents differ widely in their levels of competence and in their commitment to each seller. Some of this may be for simple incentive reasons, as when one seller gets favored treatment by setting a high commission rate and therefore getting an unusually favorable flow of traffic. But other parts are simply matters of differences in knowledge and in ability that may result in a poor selling experience, and in particular, a low selling price.

The presence of a Limited Partner would increase the seller's protection against bad experiences selling the house. The key protection for the seller would arise from the Limited Partner's right of first refusal. The Limited Partner would be an experienced financial institution that would review each step of the sales process independently and have every incentive to maximize the price for both partners.

In the actual mechanics of the right of first refusal, once the private agreement was reached, there would be a mandatory process of communicating the offer to the Limited Partner who would have a stipulated (and short) time available to make a counteroffer at a predetermined fixed amount above the original offer. The Managing Partner would then have a choice of either accepting the counteroffer (Limited Partner right of first refusal) or restarting the entire negotiation process. The Managing Partner would pay a fee for the Limited Partner's appraisal if the offer process were restarted, to discourage Managing Partners from using the bidding process as a cheap valuation service.

The fact that the Limited Partner was standing ready to buy would protect even the most ignorant of sellers from accepting an unduly low offer. The most direct protection would be the fact that a very poor deal, even if struck, would not be consummated, because the Limited Partner would instead exercise their right of first refusal to buy the house themselves.

But this would probably not be the main source of additional protection for the buyer. Those who negotiated with Partnership owners would more likely understand that there was a bound on how significantly they could underbid for the home to take advantage of the fire sale, as they would have to bid within a range that would prevent the Limited Partner from buying the property. Indeed, the agent would likely be even less willing to consider low-ball offers, simply because the Limited Partner would instead buy the property, and the agent would lose their commission. On the other side, the fact that a house was owned by partners might result in fewer bargain hunters' coming to visit the property, a factor which might reduce the flow of offers and the flow of customers.

This would mean agents might wish to familiarize themselves with the behavior of Limited Partners. One could also imagine a world in which Limited Partners could use their experience to make available lists of recommended selling agents to their Managing Partners. At a minimum such performance records could consist of how many rights of first refusal were exercised against each agent.

Low offers are commonly seen when the seller is in a profound hurry. In such situations, the owner is in a very weak bargaining position. In the current market, such sellers are well worth identifying, since they have lower reserve prices for their houses. The most knowledgeable buyers will find out they are in a rush and use this to their advantage to buy for very little.

The industry is very aware of the connection between speed of sale and the price that can be expected on a home. Some of this of course represents the cost of carry for the home, but in down markets the uncertainties of time to sell can make prices diverge substantially. One formalization of this is in the variety of different bases used for appraising homes:

- *Appraisal*: the price a house will get using the current average time on the market
- *Broker purchase opinion* (BPO): the price the house will get in three months given current conditions[7]
- *Quick sale price*: the price for an immediate sale to an institution as part of a "bulk sale"

One can even use divergences between these prices as an indicator of a poorly performing housing market. In the New York area it has not been uncommon during the past four years to see BPOs at 15% less than appraisals and bulk sales at another 15%–20% discount.

Additional seller protection would arise from the presence of a Limited Partner, as it would be more difficult for the buyer to play brinkmanship by bringing up quality issues at the closing table. This would reduce the need to argue over escrow. The buyer would still have the incentive to try, but the Limited Partner would likely be a formidable negotiator with a lot of experience concerning what and how much should be escrowed.

The Limited Partner would also likely be of sufficient scale to provide downward pressure on commission rates for sales. This might operate as it did in the stock market, with institutional investors getting very low trading commission rates and ultimately pressuring them down for everyone through the advent of the discount brokerage firm. In addition, sharing of certain selling costs might be written into the contract. On the other side of this, additional transactions costs would be involved in providing timely information to the Limited Partner. The net effect these factors would have on the actual costs of sale are unclear.

V

Partnerships, Policy, and
the Big Picture

16

Partnerships and the
Federal Government

16.1   Federal Housing Policy: The Status Quo

There is currently a bewildering array of costly and ill-coordinated federal housing policies. One idea that underlies federal housing policy is that home ownership involves a large number of benefits that accrue to the broader society, not just to the owning household. Included among these are the household's greater involvement in the upkeep of their property and their greater economic and political interest in neighborhood dynamics. At the even broader familial and social level, ownership is believed to be an indirect aid in various aspects of parenting, so that housing policy interacts with policies aimed at helping children. Unfortunately, existing policies are poorly designed to meet these goals.

Preferential tax treatment of homeowners is a central component of federal housing policy. The most significant of the federal tax benefits for ownership is mortgage interest deductibility, which has been basically unchanged since 1913. The cap imposed on the maximum loan principal currently stands at $1 million. About 28 million home owners benefit from the mortgage deduction, and the estimated annual cost to the government is about $60 billion; see Rosen 1995.

Not only is the mortgage interest deduction very expensive, it is also highly regressive. Poterba (1992), using the National Bureau of Economic Research TAXSIM model (micro tax returns data), finds that in 1988, more than half the tax savings from the deduction accrued to the 8.5% of tax returns with the highest incomes. For comparison, these top 8.5% of taxpayers received 35% of total income. The reasons for the regressiveness are: higher-income taxpayers have higher marginal-tax rates so they receive a larger proportion of the benefits, higher-income taxpayers buy bigger houses, and lower-income households are less likely to itemize, especially since the Tax Reform Act of 1986.

The direct impact of this tax deductibility is also geographically concentrated. One estimate is that lowering the cap to $250,000 would annually raise $10–15 billion in additional federal tax revenues and would affect about two million home owners. Those who would be affected are concentrated in the eleven wealthiest states. California alone would provide almost half the estimated additional tax revenues.

The most direct question with respect to the mortgage interest deduction and the Partnership Market would be whether to extend deductibility to the Limited Partner. Doing so would act as an additional subsidy to ownership. Otherwise, opening these markets would offer significant potential savings to taxpayers. There are also many intermediate options.

A second important component of federal housing policy is support for various public housing programs. Currently, HUD provides financial assistance to local authorities for acquiring and operating properties for public housing programs. This aid consists of loans to finance new developments, annual contributions for properties that charge affordable rents for eligible tenants, and funds for cooperative housing for low-income and other groups.

Much has been written on the rather obvious problems with HUD housing projects. Lack of proper incentives has created awful conditions and widespread crime problems in many projects. In many cases people now believe these projects serve as magnets for many social ills, concentrating them in one location. This in turn has led to profound local resistance to the projects. And in addition to all this, recent years have revealed much evidence of fraud and corruption in issuing HUD funds. The Partnership Market would offer a number of extremely innovative possibilities for public housing, as discussed in the next section.

A third major set of policy tools in the current federal arsenal are the subsidies to low-down-payment FHA and VA mortgages. Many of these programs are focused on first-time home buyers.

Because of their lower down-payments, higher up-front costs, and more-relaxed credit standards, FHA and VA loans have a higher probability of default than conventional loans. The government guarantee costs are in effect another government subsidy to promote home ownership. Cunningham and Hendershott (1984), Hendershott and Schultz (1993), and Hendershott and Wadell (1992) analyze the default performance of these loans. Partnership Agreements have the potential to reduce the total amount of the FHA and VA losses.

At first sight, the first-time buyers who currently choose FHA programs seem like ideal customers for Partnership Agreements, since they would very likely be attracted to owner-occupied housing's increased affordability. On the other side of this, given the higher risk of default on FHA loans, Limited Partners at first glance might not be willing to pay as much on the dollar for equity Partnerships with FHA borrowers because of the substantial transactions costs for Partnership dissolution and costs of subrogating the interest of the FHA lender. However, the issue is more complex, because ability to interest Limited Partners in investing in properties with FHA borrowers would depend on the policies the federal government set through HUD and through the government's influence on the agencies. Furthermore, using a Partnership might enable the buyer to borrow less money, and interest payments and default losses would then be lower.

Therefore, predicting Limited Partners' ultimate willingness to supply these Partnership Agreements on FHA and VA loans is quite difficult because of the offsetting impact of lowering the FHA default subsidy versus any increased cost from promoting Limited Partnerships. What seems certain is that with a wise response by the various government agencies, these Partnerships would open possibilities to expand the opportunities for first-time home buyers without increasing the underlying subsidies.

The final aspect of federal housing policy is the subsidy to the agencies in the form of lower borrowing costs. These are currently under debate (see Stevenson, *New York Times*, May 30, 1996).

16.2   Targeted Partnership Subsidies and Community Reinvestment

One measure of federal housing policies' recent performance is that despite their great expense, the ownership rate has stagnated in the past decade. Recently, the Clinton administration and HUD reaffirmed the importance of increasing home ownership in a joint statement with the United Homeowners Association (see United Homeowners Association, 1995). The claim of renewed federal commitment to home ownership comes at a most challenging time, as another federal goal is even more firmly in the spotlight: that of spending less money. We believe that the federal government might use Partnership Markets through several intriguing routes to achieve the simultaneous goals of reducing federal spending on the housing market and increasing home ownership.

The simplest idea is to use *targeted partnership subsidies* (*TAPS*) to expand ownership opportunities for selected communities. These subsidies could be delivered in many different forms. One simple idea would be for the

federal government to stand in as the Limited Partner in cases in which
the private sector would be willing to buy Limited Partnerships only at a
steep discount and the federal government believed there were especially
significant externalities associated with either maintaining or increasing
the amount of privately owned property in the community in question.

In this fashion TAPS could become the model for a new style of federal
housing policy that would focus on creating and building incentives on an
individual level to maintain property. This might be of particular value for
neighborhoods regarded as underserved by the current housing finance
market and where it was believed that the judicious application of subsidies might either help turn the neighborhood around or safeguard the
neighborhood from decline. If a subsidy were offered to Limited Partners
to operate in particular areas, some neighborhoods might resuscitate that
otherwise would fall into deterioration.

This is a far from trivial concern, since untended properties can decline
rapidly. And if a significant amount of housing in a neighborhood is
becoming dilapidated, there are real dangers of a broader decline. In fact,
one contributor to a declining neighborhood may be the classic problem
of "beggar thy neighbor," whereby the first few residents who fail to
maintain their properties can cause losses for all the neighbors.

In such neighborhoods, a further investment in maintenance by the
other residents may be money down the drain. Neighbors who have the
resources may leave the neighborhood for one where the implicit contract
remains in force and they can invest in maintenance without fear of wasting money. In this case the issue is not one simply of building housing
but of encouraging or ensuring that home owners' investments will likely
be worthwhile. How effective would a policy of increasing insurance
against neighborhood decline by offering subsidies to Limited Partnerships be in a community identified as at risk?

Essentially, we are suggesting that Partnerships offer the potential for
vast improvement over traditional methods of providing subsidies to specific groups of renters. They might also help resurrect an acceptable format
for support for public housing, which has become increasingly unpopular
in the United States and in many other countries because of the terrible
economic and social problems housing projects create.

16.3   Precedents for TAPS

The idea that the Partnership format might provide a new direction for
public housing subsidies has several interesting precedents in other coun-

tries. One has been developed by the state government in Victoria, Australia (see Yates 1992). In the Victoria scheme, the government itself takes a role somewhat analogous to that of the Limited Partner. The program is primarily a method of offering a different form of subsidy to low-income borrowers in the stock of public housing. In effect, its primary goal is to move some public housing stock into a form of partial private ownership.

A somewhat broader approach to Partnership Agreements in which the government takes the role of the Limited Partner has also been developed and implemented by housing associations in the United Kingdom since 1980. The U.K. shared-ownership schemes largely target current and prospective public-sector tenants who cannot quite afford to buy a home outright because of a lack of income, savings or credit history. The idea is that as well as being a cheaper form of subsidy than public housing, shared ownership can release some much-needed public housing stock for those in greater need. In the U.K. shared-ownership model, a role somewhat analogous to that of the Limited Partner is taken by a housing association[1] or a local authority,[2] hence known collectively as "providers." Some of the most important aspects of the U.K. shared-ownership market are

• *Maintenance.* As in the Partnership Agreement, the household buys a share of the property (50% is the most common) and is responsible for all repairs and maintenance.

• *Rental payments.* One significant difference from Partnerships is that rent is paid by the household on the portion they do not own. This rent is subsidized so that the rental costs less than would a mortgage on this remaining part of the property.

• *Mortgage.* As in our Partnership Markets, the home buyer obtains a mortgage on their half of the house.

• *Mortgagee protection clause.* This important clause in the shared-ownership contract gives the lender a call on the whole value of the property even though their loan may only have been for 50% of its value.

• *Increasing the share of ownership.* From the outset, the aim of the British schemes has been to promote home ownership. Shared ownership is seen as a transitory phase that can help households meet this goal. Purchasers have the option to buy more shares, known as "staircasing," and eventually become a full owner. At any time after the purchase, the shared owner can buy more shares. An appraisal is performed at that time to determine the value of these additional shares.

• *Sale of the property.* A partial owner is subject to some additional rules on resale. An owner who wishes to move must first notify the provider and arrange for an appraisal of the property. The provider then has a period of time (generally twenty-eight days) to find another buyer who will purchase the property at the appraised price. Once the time is up, if the provider has not found a buyer, the owner can sell the property to any other third party for the appraised price or above and pay back the provider a pro rata share of the proceeds. The household can sell for below the appraised price but still must pay back a pro-rata share of at least the appraised value to the housing authority.

• *Improvements.* At the point of sale, if any improvements or alterations have been made, valuations of the property with and without the alteration are made and the provider receives only a pro rata share of the property's appraised value without the improvements.

• *No secondary market.* There is no secondary market. In fact, secondary mortgage markets are relatively limited in the United Kingdom, let alone a secondary market in the shared-ownership holdings of the providers.

• *Standardization of the contract.* The National Federation of Housing Associations issues guidelines for a standard contract, although individual providers can modify them according to their needs. Providers use a variety of eligibility criteria in allocating shared ownership. Applicants are heavily screened according to income and ability to obtain a mortgage. Many providers have minimum- and maximum-income criteria, and some restrict the type of dwelling depending on family size and composition.

• *New development or old.* There are two main forms of shared ownership: conventional shared ownership (CSO) and do-it-yourself shared ownership (DIYSO). Under CSO, the provider builds a new development partially funded by government grants, then sells the properties under shared-ownership terms. Under DIYSO, the household looks for a property themselves on the private market and coordinates with a provider to buy it under shared-ownership terms. Contractually the two schemes are very similar.

A preliminary evaluation of shared ownership was conducted by the Department of the Environment (1995). One finding was that about 40% of shared owners had previously been living as part of another household, another 40% had been renting, and 14% had previously been owner-occupiers but needed to move because of a change in personal circumstances such as separation or divorce. Not surprisingly, shared owners generally had lower incomes than other first-time buyers, and shared own-ership has been more popular where 100% purchase is highly expensive.

Shared ownership is perceived as the fastest and perhaps the only route to full home ownership. Two-fifths of shared owners said they would still be living in their previous accommodation but for shared ownership. Only one-fifth said they would have become full owners anyway. The staircasing rate (both partial and full) was 5% per year on average, with more than 90% of households staircasing to 100% ownership in one step. Almost all the staircasers financed their additional share by increasing their current mortgage or obtaining a new one. The report concludes that shared ownership is clearly an extremely popular tenure. It finds that a very high proportion of shared owners were satisfied with shared owner-ship, and fully staircased owners were even more satisfied. However, the report did identify a number of problems, primarily related to public and professional awareness of shared ownership and the big issue of public funding. Awareness will naturally increase over time as more homes are bought under shared-ownership agreements. The extent of transactions costs can then be expected to diminish.

Two serious proposals have been advanced in the United Kingdom for the evolution of shared ownership: they are known as "flexible tenure" and the "equity loan scheme" (ELS). Flexible tenure was motivated by the recent collapse in property markets in the United Kingdom coupled with an economic recession. It is a shared ownership scheme which would allow households to staircase both downward and upward according to their needs, so that if hardship arose the shared owner could sell some of their equity and increase the rental component of housing, thus lowering costs, since housing benefit is only available for rent and not for mortgage payments (see Terry 1996).

The ELS would be an extension of a program introduced in Wales known as the home buy option. Unlike as in shared ownership, no rental payment would be involved. Instead, the buyer would be given an "interest-free loan" on part of the property (in Wales, this is 30% of the cost, so that the household must finance the remaining 70% from other sources). Upon sale of the property, the housing association would receive 30% of the proceeds. Thus, what would be called an interest-free loan would really be an equity share, and in this sense the program resembles the Limited Partnerships discussed in this book. Proponents of the ELS suggest that the amount of the interest-free loan be means tested, and they argue that it would involve no additional cost to either the home owner or the government compared to shared ownership with the rental component (see Terry 1995).

Since shared ownership accounts for only about 1% to 2% of the entire market for mortgages, lenders have been slow to become acquainted with this new form of tenure, and so it is usually more time consuming for a potential shared owner to obtain financing. There has as yet been no talk of commercialization of shared ownership in any form for the United Kingdom. The tenure is seen as purely a means of public subsidy for home ownership.

Limited Equity Housing cooperatives are perhaps the closest scheme to shared ownership in the public housing sector in the United States. Certain multifamily public housing developments have been converted into private cooperative ownership (similar to the co-ops found in New York City). The residents are shareholders in the corporation that owns the development, and they have the right to occupy their particular unit. The co-ops are limited equity in that both the purchase and sale price of the shares are restricted to keep them affordable for low-income families. Case studies have produced mixed results with respect to the success of these co-ops (see Rohe 1995).

16.4   The Agencies and the Evolution of the Housing Finance Market

We believe the federal government might have an important opportunity to guide the development of Partnership Markets using its influence with the agencies. To understand how this influence works, we look briefly at the history of federal intervention in the housing market in the period following the financial disasters that occurred during the depression of the 1930s.

Prior to the depression, the vast majority of mortgages were balloon loans.[3] Given their relatively short term, the borrower counted on qualifying for credit when time came to take out a new loan to repay the principal at the maturity of the original mortgage. Therefore, with this type of mortgage the ability to refinance was crucial.

But with the massive fall in property values during the depression, many home owners were unable to obtain new loans to pay off their balloon mortgages when they became due. The result was disastrous for both the owners, who now stood at great risk of becoming homeless, and the financial institutions, which could not hope to salvage much from taking possession of the property. These circumstances produced a real reduction in the supply of private funds to the residential mortgage market, which ultimately led the government to take unprecedented steps to change the nature of the housing finance market.

The first key step was the introduction of the FHA mortgage program. In this program, the government provided default insurance on mortgage applications that met its underwriting standards. To qualify for the default insurance, the FHA insisted that the mortgage be of a novel kind. Rather than having the short seven-year term of the previous privately issued mortgages, the FHA program applied only to thirty-year fixed-rate mortgages that were amortizing. The hope was that the default insurance would rekindle private interest in supplying funds to the residential real estate market. The federal government also offered financial incentives to the private sector to issue FHA mortgages.

By 1938, the government felt the process had taken too long in the private sector, and this led to FNMA's establishment. At its inception FNMA was authorized to purchase from originating financial institutions all qualifying FHA mortgages on newly constructed homes. In this manner, it became a market maker in the FHA mortgage, allowing originators to find a buyer willing to buy and sell at all times. One consequence of FNMA operations was that trading of mortgages became more commonplace, and in this manner their operations prepared the way for the subsequent development of the broader secondary markets.

In 1954 the goal of promoting the development of the secondary market was explicitly written into FNMA's charter. In its earliest phase, FNMA did not have a great deal of success in establishing a broad and deep market in FHA mortgages and instead continued to operate largely as a stockpiler and source of funds for the market. In their assessment of the development of secondary markets, Jones and Grebler (1961) looked for explanations for the slow pace of secondary-market development. (Indeed at that point it was altogether uncertain that the market would take off.)

The takeoff of the secondary market occurred only following a major change in federal government policy. In 1968, FNMA was reconstituted as a private GSE.[4] At the same time GNMA was set up as part of HUD to handle policy-related tasks.

Interestingly, GNMA issued the first MBSs. The GNMA MBSs were comprised of pools of federally insured FHA and VA loans, with all payments of principal and interest (net of fees) passed through to the ultimate investors. In addition, GNMA guaranteed timely payment of interest and principal even if the borrower defaulted on the mortgage. Since GNMA deals only in federally insured mortgages, its securitization of the mortgage consists only of an additional guarantee that the payment will be timely.

Freddie Mac was then created in 1970 as a GSE, and its main business was the same as FNMA's only focused on serving the thrift industry. Both began to create pools of conventional mortgages.[5] Today the MBSs offered by Freddie Mac and FNMA differ little. Both offer similar securitization features by guaranteeing payments even in the event of borrower default. With all three federal agencies taking market-making roles and providing securitization on pools of securities, the secondary mortgage market really took off, and has never looked back. Issuing MBSs is a hugely profitable business for FNMA and Freddie Mac, with combined profits well in excess of $3 billion in 1995. This makes them among the most profitable corporations in the United States.

It is hard for private corporations to compete with the agencies in their market, since they have access to lower interest rates as a benefit of their government sponsorship. But the federal government has also constrained its creations and in that way has indirectly opened up some parts of the market for private competition. For example, the agencies are not allowed to issue MBSs on jumbo mortgages.[6] Consequently this has allowed private conduits to enter the business of forming MBSs based on pools of jumbo mortgages, which is now a rapidly growing market.

The growth of secondary mortgage markets has changed fundamentally the nature of the primary mortgage market, as detailed in chapter 11. The adoption of Partnership Agreements would require even more far-reaching changes in the behavior of almost all participants in the housing market. To bring about such changes in a timely fashion would require an impressive feat of coordination, and we believe a large institution would need to take a lead role in market development. This role could ultimately be taken either by a public agency or private consortium assured of federal sympathy, or by several independent institutions. We take this issue up again in chapter 18.

Partnership Markets and the Broader Economy

In this chapter we explore some economic consequences of widespread acceptance and use of Partnership finance. The reader would do well to bear in mind the extraordinary level of uncertainty concerning many of the broader impacts of these markets.

17.1 Housing Market Equilibrium and Housing Finance Markets

Direct Impact on Short- and Long-Run Housing Market Equilibrium
Some of the most direct and important impacts of Partnership Markets would be felt in the prices and quantities of various types of residential housing. Among the most likely impacts would be:

• *Short-run price increase.* In the standard Marshallian short run, Partnership finance would increase the demand for housing, which would affect prices more than quantities. There would also likely be important shifts in the relative prices of different types of housing, depending on the types of buyers who made heaviest use of Partnership finance. In the short run, the quantity impacts of the increased price of residential housing would likely be limited to increased conversions from rentals to owner-occupied homes.

• *Long-run supply increase.* In the long run, the demand increase would cause supply to respond. As the price of houses rose, so the demand for land that could be used for the construction of buildings would increase, leading to some conversion of land from other uses, such as agriculture, into land for home construction. It would then be a straightforward matter for a home builder to contract with construction companies and other building-related activities to build houses on the converted land, leading to an additional supply of housing.

• *Increase in quality*. Another major change in the housing market would be a general tendency to trade up houses, resulting in a greater demand for higher-quality houses. This in turn would open the base end of the housing stock for those who are currently poor and also possibly indirectly benefit those currently without homes.

• *Increased home ownership*. The home ownership rate would increase. Altering the mix of owner-occupied and rental housing would have other important indirect effects. A smaller rental market segment might work against mobility. But since equity losses would be partly diversified, value collapse might affect such things as mobility less.[1] Any reduction in down payments would mean fewer liquid wealth constraints on mobility.

• *Changes in the returns on the housing asset*. The change in the ownership structure of housing will affect the return on the housing asset, as indicated in chapter 13. It is likely that the expected returns on housing would fall in a new long-run equilibrium with a fully developed Partnership Market, since the degree of portfolio risk involved in owning the home would be reduced. However, the transition path to the new equilibrium is particularly hard to predict, since one way for the expected return to fall would be through an increase in the current price of housing. Changes in the correlation between housing and other assets are even harder to predict.

The short-run increase in the housing prices might be quite significant if Partnership Markets became highly successful. In this case, the markets would to some extent become victims of their own success, especially in the short run. To the extent the price of housing increased, this would temporarily offset the increased affordability of housing at given prices. Of course, this would occur only if the markets were profoundly needed, and price increases would moderate as time passed. For a large group of existing home owners, the resulting wealth increase might be more than a little attractive. At any rate, we regard as more likely the idea of a relatively gradual market take-off, in which case the price impact would be more moderate.

Indirect Impacts of the New Housing Market Equilibrium
The changes in housing market equilibrium outlined above would have some important indirect effects on other markets:

• *Improved local public goods*. The increase in overall ownership would be associated with improvements in neighborhood quality along the standard lines of improving the quality of local public goods by increasing the residents' commitment to the neighborhood. For example, the increase in ownership might have a positive impact on the quality of schooling. The local political situation might also change significantly as Limited Partners became advocates for neighborhoods in which they were heavily invested.

• *Changes in rental markets.* The likely direct impact of the Partnership Markets would be to make owner occupation more attractive than rental housing and thereby shift property from rental to owner-occupied status. But it might not be accurate to view the rental markets as static institutions incapable of responding to the introduction of Partnerships. We conjecture that there might be a significant response in the form of new types of rental contracts designed to compete better with the Partnership Market. One simple possibility would be somewhat more-detailed and longer-term rental contracts designed to remove some issues of uncertainty and moral hazard that appear to plague the current market. Of course, to understand how the rental markets might respond would require a study every bit as complex as the current book. In the meantime, we can only raise the issue.

• *Labor market spillovers.* A recent study of the Italian housing market and labor market has addressed the connection between labor market status and the level of household mortgage payments. Del Boca and Lusardi (1996) analyze the labor force participation of young married women who own homes. When there is a mortgage outstanding, 61.2% of these women participate in the labor force, while the corresponding proportion is 48.5% when there is no mortgage. Del Boca and Lusardi carry out a variety of econometric exercises to understand the reasons for this difference in behavior, and conclude that the effect of the mortgage market remains strong and statistically significant even when other causal factors are taken into account. This is but one of many intriguing connections between the labor market and the housing finance market.

• *Complementary market reforms.* The introduction of Partnership Markets would provoke other changes in the institutional structure of the housing finance market. For example, suggestions are being floated in many areas for other changes in the housing finance market, and some of these reforms would be more likely to occur in the presence of Partnership Contracts. One such area of reform is in the arena of innovations in housing finance designed for older households. In addition to the burst of attention being given to reverse mortgages, there is also the intriguing idea of deferred sale and maintenance contracts as described in chapter 9. We believe that Partnership finance might go hand in hand with increased attention to housing finance for the elderly, among other issues.

17.2   Macroeconomic Effects of Partnership Markets

Partnership Markets and the Volatility of the Housing Market
One important macroeconomic issue for housing analysts is that historically, housing markets have been highly volatile. On several occasions
large waves of defaults on mortgages have coincided with a property
market crash, the most extreme case being the Great Depression. Connected to this are the boom-bust nature of housing construction and the
radical changes in the turnover rate in the housing market. The fluctuations in house prices have been much analyzed,[2] as has the connection
between price, volume, and the housing market's general liquidity.[3]

We feel that the introduction of Partnership Agreements would be
likely to change and possibly moderate these extreme fluctuations. The
most direct reason for this is that Partnerships would improve risk sharing
across the economy and might lower default risks inherent in housing and
affect the depth of the cycle itself. A more intriguing channel of change
might arise from the new information provided by the trading in pools of
Limited Partnership Agreements on secondary markets.

To understand how Partnership Markets would affect the informational
structure of the housing market, consider the potential impact of a liquid
secondary markets in PREFERS for a wide variety of types of property in
many different locations. Suppose also that the prices for trading in PRE-
FERS were widely quoted, so that all households could readily observe the
value that the investment community placed on different types of Limited
Partnerships. In this case, there would be a tremendous source of information on the value that investors place on different residential property
markets. If investors were optimistic about housing in a particular area,
this would be reflected in an increase in the price of PREFERS for that
location. It is unlikely that this information would be ignored by house
buyers or house sellers in the existing market, and it would therefore
influence the current prices of homes in the area, and their appraised
values. Indeed it is likely that the appraisal procedure would be updated
to take account of this new information source.

The important point of comparison is that in the traditional mortgage
market, very little information is available on how the investment community views residential property, since it is so hard to invest in it in the
current market. Given this paucity of information, there is room for tremendous uncertainty and disagreement between different market participants on the valuation of residential property. It would be interesting to
see whether the reduction in the level of uncertainty in the Partnership

Market would reduce the fragility and volatility of the market and so moderate the housing cycle itself.

Partnership Markets and Insurance Against House Price Fluctuations

The potential for reduced housing market volatility with Partnership Markets would result in part from their role in providing increased insurance against house price decreases at the level of the individual household. In this regard, it is important to mention another innovative suggestion for reforming the housing finance market, the price index futures market suggested by Shiller and Weiss (1994) based on the repeat sales indices pioneered by Case and Shiller (1987). Conceptually, the idea is to have the household that buys the home take one side of a futures contract on a related house price index. The contract would specify that the household would be compensated if the value fell below the contractually set index level, and otherwise they would pay the excess over this contractually set price, which would typically be set so that the price of the futures contract was zero at origination.

Although these price index futures would not be substitutes for the Partnership Markets, they might turn out to be very valuable complements. In fact it would be of great value to design the Partnership fund shares in such a way that their properties could be compared as closely as possible with the behavior of local house price indices. We do not view these markets as substitutes for the Partnership Market for several reasons. In the absence of Partnership Markets, the use of price index futures would involve:

- *High expense.* The home buyer would buy the home and have to put up additional cash to cover and maintain the appropriate level of margin. In contrast to the Partnership Market, this would be a cash-in method of diversification.

- *Basis risk.* The value of the home and the index need not be perfectly correlated. If the index were based on a highly localized index of prices, it could be manipulated. If based on a broader index, it would be far less likely to correlate highly with the price of any individual's house.

- *Liquidity problems.* When futures were marked to market, the home owner would face a margin call as the futures position went deep out of the money. One could therefore imagine the household's being forced to take out a second mortgage to pay the margin call, with all kinds of possible difficulties ensuing if their own house was not appraised as having risen in value to the same extent as the general index. There would also be a major tax and liquidity problem in a situation where futures gains were subject to current taxes while the corresponding capital loss was still unrealized.

• *Short horizon.* The fixed and typically short time horizon in futures contracts may not match the owner's tenure, and this would raise a number of difficult issues. A household that wished to sell their house before the contract became due would face an additional risk concerning house price movements after they moved out. A household that wished to remain in their house after the contract became due would face "rollover risk." Dynamic hedging strategies would be necessary to offset the rollover risk. Since the majority of households would be unfamiliar with these techniques, they would hand the responsibility over to professionals, who would receive a fee. In addition, some quite sharp changes in house prices might make it especially hard to apply classical dynamic hedging techniques.

Even though price index futures markets would not substitute for Partnership Markets, they could provide valuable complementary services. To envision this, consider the life-cycle pattern of Managing Partnership shares alluded to in chapter 8, and in particular the likelihood that households would wish to change their exposure to various different housing markets as they considered relocating, and as their preferences changed over the course of the life cycle. One method for doing this would be by negotiating a direct purchase or sale of equity with a Limited Partner, as outlined in chapter 9. Another method would be by investing in the appropriate PREFER funds and their derivative securities. A third method would be by using an appropriate price index futures. This third option would have advantages for those who have sufficient funds to handle the additional risks outlined above, and who also seek to invest more directly in a given local property market, rather than in the indirect fashion offered by the PREFERs.

Partnerships, Asset Markets, and the Pattern of Savings and Investment

If Partnership Markets were successful, they would have important impacts not only on the housing markets, but also on a broad set of markets of public policy interest. Among the most important indirect impacts would be those likely to be felt throughout the asset markets in the risk profiles of individuals and the economy as a whole. This would also involve effects on the costs of the different kinds of capital and the level of saving and capital accumulation.

Inasmuch as Partnerships would reduce the amount of mortgage debt overall, we would expect increases in other forms of debt. The altered risk structure to private portfolios would be very important and could be expected to lower catastrophic risk for those who sold part of their home to Limited Partners. This change in private-household asset and risk characteristics would accompany a change in consumption demand, as the house poor became free to make the purchases they are currently unable to make.

The increased flow of funds into the Partnership Market would have crowding-out effects on other assets. This would be important in the context of the interest rate on government debt and the level of private-sector investment. The international context would also be important. These effects are very difficult to predict.

There would also be an overall effect on the savings rate, depending on whether the reduced need for "forced" savings by existing owners was offset by the new savings of the additional group of owners, and also on how much trading up took place. For interesting analyses of the interaction between the housing market and the savings rate, see Engelhardt (1995) and Hayashi, Ito, and Slemrod (1988).

17.3 "Optimal" Housing Finance Markets

The introduction of Partnership Markets would also act as a spur to other institutional developments. We have alluded to some of these above, such as changes in rental contracts and possible new forms of insurance. In this section we try to step back to an even more rarefied level of abstraction and think about some long-run prospects for institutional change.

One interesting starting point for this discussion is the institution-free approach suggested by pure economic theory. To get a better picture of the way the markets would develop, we step back to a simpler scheme of optimal ownership stripped of certain realistic institutional features. Although our review of the institutional history of the housing finance market in the next chapter does not lead us to believe in a pure optimality theory, the pursuit of such a vision represents an interesting idealized case to illustrate the far broader menu of possibilities for reforming the housing market and housing finance institutions. The simple view that results from envisioning a fully optimal system of the housing finance market may help point to directions in which the market is likely to evolve.

We follow the standard method of approximation favored by many economists that involves assuming the existence of a complete set of markets for all future periods and all states of the world. In the case of housing, there would have to be markets for the right to receive the rental payments on the house in any possible future state of the world. For example, it would be possible to buy a certificate entitling the holder to "one dollar of rental payment in ten years' time should the following sequence of events have occurred between now and then," and even to payments of a fraction of a dollar.

This "Arrow security" would be traded in a market immediately, and everyone would in this way be able to bid for any contingent share of the rental payments on the housing asset in which they were interested. To separate use of the asset from ownership, the occupant would pay rent in all future states of the world to whoever owned the rights to receive rent in that state of the world. In this abstract picture, the issue of who owned the house would have a very complex answer and would involve a description of the entire economy-wide pattern of ownership of the contingent rental payments.

From the viewpoint of optimal asset diversification, there would seem to be no reason for the home occupant to own any significant share of their house. Why not follow the logic above and achieve total asset diversification by having each household own a tiny share of each home and pay rental payments out to the population in proportion to their ownership shares? A little reflection shows that this would not be an ideal asset allocation plan, since it would leave the occupant with some risks that they could diversify away by increasing their asset holding in their own home. The simplest logic for explaining the demand for ownership of a housing asset is to think of it in terms of an underlying desire on the part of households to reduce consumption risk.

The reason for this underlying desire is that if the occupant believes they will wish to continue to occupy the given property for some considerable time, they will desire to reduce uncertainty concerning future rental payments. A very high level of market rent will force the household either to move or lower its nonhousing consumption. To avoid this and to insure their levels of housing and nonhousing consumption, the occupant would be willing to pay a current premium to take some form of ownership stake in their house to preclude their having to pay the higher rent corresponding to the home's increase in value. Currently, the only available method of insuring against these rent increases is full ownership.

What would determine the optimal pattern of ownership in such a world? One of the key determinants of the pattern of ownership would be household views about their likely pattern of home occupancy and its correlation with their patterns of earnings and income generation. The simplest world to consider would be one in which the entire future pattern of housing occupancy is determined simultaneously with ownership. If it is commonly known that a household will live in the house for five years and then move, an optimal scheme would involve this household's owning all the rental rights for this period of time. The next occupant would then purchase all rental rights for their period of occupation, and so on. Of course, this simple vision would have to be adjusted to provide incentives for home maintenance.

The current market is a far cry from this idealized picture and can be viewed most simply as a contingent contract market operating with two massive constraints. The first constraint is that the ownership rights cannot be unbundled. Rather than having a market in which one person can own 10% of the rent in state one and 20% in state two, ownership is an all-or-nothing affair. The second constraint is that the current market lacks any ability to separate ownership from asset use.

Our Partnership idea is designed to help soften both constraints. Much more can be done to improve things even beyond this, including changes in rental and mortgage contracts. At the very least, it seems that market performance could be greatly improved by increasing the availability of sophisticated rental contracts. A more sophisticated set of contracts would allow for considerable variation in the length of terms, in the nature of the rental payment stream, in the qualification criteria for renters, and in the information developed to screen renters according to past behavior. To fully develop these ideas would take another entire book.

18   Institutional Angles on Partnership Markets

It is unduly narrow to see the impact of Partnership Markets in terms of the classical economic framework. Partnership Markets would be a fundamentally new set of market institutions and must be seen and interpreted in this context. A discussion of this aspect of the markets has the additional speculative component that so little is known concerning the nature and evolution of market institutions.

18.1 The Institutional Infrastructure of Partnership Markets

Market institutions are not static entities. The U.S. housing finance market is very different today than at the turn of the century, and these changes have resulted from a great many forces, such as the development of financial services and the changing role of the federal government, which have had a parallel impact on a great many other businesses. This suggests that the institutions of housing finance are best seen in something of an evolutionary perspective. In this light, we believe that technological forces exert important influences on market evolution, and this forms part of the basis for our belief that the time may have come for Partnership Markets, particularly in the United States.

We see at least three key areas in which the United States has particularly well-developed preconditions for Partnership Markets: technological and informational preparedness, financial-market preparedness, and legal preparedness. We refer to these and all other aspects of preparedness as forming the "institutional infrastructure" of the Partnership Markets, since we regard them as defining many basic elements necessary for the ultimate development of these markets.

Technological and Informational Preparedness
With respect to information technology, the U.S. financial markets are generally well poised in terms of developing the necessary technological

basis for Partnership Markets. Some modification of existing systems and procedures would be needed to facilitate the servicing and origination of Partnership Agreements, but the pace and commitment to innovation in this part of the market would make this a rather easy transition.

In particular, these markets would rely on the wide availability of data on the behavior of individual households in the housing and financial markets. U.S. firms have been highly successful in this area, with credit information services far ahead of those in other countries, based on extensive use of computer-aided technologies.

Some examples of the advance of computer-based information systems in housing finance are

• *Client server and file imaging.* The mortgage application process is heavily computerized, and many lenders have given their salespeople laptop computers to use in taking loan applications. The documents are then sent and stored as file images on the servicers' computers. We believe that it would be possible to implement similar front-end application programs in the Partnership Market. Such programs would be designed to assist customers in selecting the appropriate form of Partnership Agreement, and the optimal ownership share. The standardization of the Partnership Contract would make it easy to enter the relevant information into a computer file.

• *Credit bureaus.* In the United States there are three major repositories of computerized credit information (TRW, Equifax, and Transunion). Each month, the major lenders supply these bureaus with information on the loan payment performance of their customers. Every time a potential borrower applies for a new loan, the lender first gathers information from the existing credit files of that borrower. The same process could be used to track the performance of potential or existing Managing Partners.

• *Credit scoring.* Both the credit bureaus as well as certain independent firms (FICO, MDS) use the historical credit bureau data to create predictive models of consumer behavior. Similar modeling techniques could be used to predict Managing Partner behavior, particularly regarding the Managing Partner's desire to maintain their real assets.

• *Computerized auto-dialers.* The servicers of consumer loans make heavy use of computers in answering customer questions, handling pay-offs, and collecting on delinquent accounts. The same technology could be used for the Limited Partner for procedures as diverse as ordering appraisals, replying to requests for improvements, responding to requests to alter the ownership share, and assisting the Managing Partner in the event of a breach.

It is interesting to note that these technological innovations have occurred in areas where the private mortgage market firms do not compete directly with the agencies. Perhaps the private firms are reluctant to commit capital in areas of head-to-head competition with the agencies.

Financial Market Preparedness

The current competitive structure of the financial services sector in the United States also bodes well for the Partnership Market. Financial institutions are accepting of the need to pool their resources and experience in order to form a new market, as in the secondary mortgage market, or make a market more efficient, as in the case of credit bureau reporting. The success of the credit bureaus is a particularly interesting case, since it took some time for creditors to overcome their initial hesitancy and report their information to the bureaus. In the early days various financial institutions saw their information as a source of competitive advantage. The value of this private information was gradually eroded as the bureaus gathered information from an ever broader set of participants.

Another important feature of U.S. financial markets is that the key firms have experience in forming various types of associations and other legal entities in order to form a new market. Important examples are the Visa and Mastercard consortia—associations formed by the banks to create the credit card market, partly as a competitive response to the charge card companies (American Express, Diners Club). Other important examples are the automated teller machine (ATM) networks formed by the banks (NYCE, MAC, CIRRUS, etc.) to jointly exploit the new payment technologies. We believe that Partnership Markets would be likely to stimulate some even more creative forms of cooperation among the major financial institutions.

Legal Preparedness and the Endogeneity of the Law

The U.S. legal structure also appears to have developed in directions that would be quite accommodating to Partnerships. In fact, lawyers have been recommending the benefits of the partnership form of ownership for residential real estate for quite some time (see Nelson and Whitman 1985). The Uniform Partnership Code would be directly valuable. Of course, a number of fine points of the legal code might need to be adjusted to handle issues specific to Partnerships in residential real estate.

There would be significant uncertainty about many legal fine points in the early stages of market development, and this uncertainty may slow the development of the market. But we do not regard it as likely that the legal code would significantly constrain the development of the market. One reason for this is that we are not aware of any significant legal impediments to the Partnership Market in the current legal code. Even more important is the fact that the legal code itself is not static. In the past, federal agencies have used arguments based on economic efficiency to initiate changes in the legal code, and we would hope that the same far-sighted approach would apply in the case of Partnership Markets.

An interesting example of a federal agency influencing the legal structure is the "due on sale" clause in mortgage contracts. As a general matter, all loans are assumable, in the sense that debtors generally have the right to find a third party to pay off their debts. The due on sale clause in the mortgage contract states that the mortgage debt must be paid off when the mortgagee sells their house, which means that the buyer of the home is not allowed to assume the debt, but rather must apply for a new mortgage. In 1976, the Federal Home Loan Bank Board (FHLBB) specifically authorized all federal savings and loan associations to automatically enforce all due on sale clauses in mortgage contracts. This ability was challenged by the states, and the case went to the Supreme Court, where the position of the FHLBB was upheld (see Bruce 1985, p. 108).

18.2   Inertia in the Housing Finance Market

While technology does influence institutions, we do not view market structure as a purely technological phenomenon. We believe there is a great deal of inertia in a wide variety of institutions. A simple indication of history's importance in determining the nature of housing finance institutions comes from comparing the current U.S. housing finance market with the radically different finance systems in other advanced industrialized economies.

The underlying issue concerns the degree of inertia in the housing finance market. Change does not happen by itself, but instead needs to be actively pursued, especially in a market as complex as the housing finance market. In fact, one of the most striking features of the U.S. housing finance market is the lack of innovation in contract form. Innovation is so uncommon that a change in terms, from FRMs to ARMs, is often heralded as the major new product of the last fifty years. There are also several examples of the market's failure to develop beneficial new contracts even in situations in which the change required to introduce the new contract is remarkably small.

One simple contract idea that never took off was the price level adjusted mortgage (PLAM) widely proposed in the inflation of the late 1960s and early 1970s (see Fabozzi and Modigliani 1992). During an inflationary period, nominal interest rates rise to offset the reduction in the real value of nominal debt that inflation produces. One indirect result of this increase in nominal rates is a front-loading of the repayment schedules on nominal debt. A household that takes out a fixed interest-rate mortgage at a high nominal interest rate is in effect being required to pay back some of the real value of the loan early in the form of additional interest. To counter this, it was suggested that the United States introduce loans in which the real value of the outstanding principal was indexed to prevent inflation from having an impact on the pattern of real borrowing. After much public discussion, the idea was shelved and has received little attention in the low-inflation period that has followed.

Another simple example of a contract innovation with the potential to produce a Pareto improvement that has not happened lies in the area of mortgage refinancing. Earlier work by three of us has shown that many home owners are locked out of the refinance market when rates are declining by the need to requalify on the LTV and credit guidelines on their loans (Caplin, Freeman, and Tracy 1993). A simple solution would be to offer mortgages carrying an explicit refinancing guarantee at time of origination, and allow the market (institutional investors) to price this feature.

The profound level of inertia in the housing finance market makes it hard to imagine a small-scale, low-cost introduction of Partnership Agreements being particularly successful. In fact, several attempts have already been made to launch contracts that have certain features in common with the Partnership Agreements outlined in this book, each with limited success. Among these are:

• a crude variant of a Partnership Agreement written by the real estate brokers ERA,

• the shared-appreciation mortgage (SAM) explored at the time of high inflation,

• a variety of relative investment schemes,

- university and other employer-based schemes, and
- equity-sharing schemes.

The ERA Contract

In the early 1980s, ERA real estate brokers made a brave effort to introduce a crude form of partnership agreement. Unfortunately, the contract had several poor covenants that probably ruled out a successful launch. Many of these incentive problems and uncertainty existed because the limited partner made no equity investment but instead gave the consumer a discount on the interest payments in the first few years and took joint responsibility for maintenance expenditures. Unfortunately, the contract foresaw dangers in that the limited partner might not honor their commitment to maintenance expenditures in a declining market but did not suggest a compelling way around this problem. The managing partner forwarded the cash for maintenance, the limited partner was not personally liable for any debts they incurred, and the managing partner had to go to court to try to force collection of the unpaid debts. In fact, the limited partner had a tremendous incentive to walk away from the contract if house prices fell, leaving the household with uncollected bills.

In fact, the contract's main structural point was to allow the limited partner to benefit from the tax subsidy on debt for owner-occupied housing. For this reason the contract contained numerous clauses to comply with the perception of what the IRS wanted to see. In fact the contract's apparent status as a scheme for tax evasion would doubtless have provoked IRS scrutiny and possibly a challenge in court.

The SAM

The SAM was proposed in the 1970s (see Dougherty, Van Order, and Villani 1982 for an introduction and Murphy 1993 for a recent discussion). The contract allows households to increase their purchasing power by attaching an option to the lender allowing the lender to participate in any nominal price appreciation. In the classic contract, the borrower is offered a one-third break in their interest payments for a one-third share in the house's appreciation. One big reason the proposal was made in the 1970s was that it appeared to offer a way to reduce the very high interest payments caused by the high nominal interest rates and the failure to adopt PLAMs. Note that the discount on the rate causes a significant incentive problem in terms of the length of tenure, which resulted in considerable uncertainty regarding the capital gains or losses to both parties.

In a low-inflation environment, the longer the borrower remained in the property, the greater the extent of their subsidy, and any unexpected event triggering mobility (prepayment) caused the home owner to lose. Therefore SAMs represents consumers' betting on the accuracy of their estimates of tenure and refinance opportunities.

In addition, as written, the contract's attractiveness depends critically on the inflation rate. With no inflation in house prices, all borrowers would have wanted the program and no lenders would have offered it. With hyperinflation, all lenders would have wanted it but no borrowers would. In fact, the program did not take off in large part because the period of discussion extended beyond the period of inflation. Note that even at this time, one of the main grounds for concern was fear of the underlying incentive problems (see Frieberg 1982).

Relative Investment Schemes

Closely related to these contracts are a variety of schemes aimed at facilitating capital contributions from relatives to younger generations in return for some equity (see Guenther 1985). For the most part, this activity appears to have been limited to relaxing the agency guidelines on the sources of cash at closing, which is a somewhat narrow focus. It is difficult to judge the potential of these programs since they carry a fee that can frequently be avoided by finding cheaper ways to overcome the cash-at-closing restrictions, which is not terribly difficult. As with the ERA contract, an important aspect of these schemes has been the attempt to take advantage of the tax subsidy by structuring the program as a capital lease.

University and Other Institution-Specific Schemes

A variety of institutions, such as universities, make private deals with their employees to help with the purchase of a home in exchange for a certain portion of the equity. Typically, these schemes operate on a very small scale, and their terms may differ from individual to individual. They are frequently inspired by features of the tax code or by the desire to offer differential rewards to different employees while keeping their salaries the same. These schemes are the closest that can be found to Partnerships and would be very much worth studying for future development of the contract. But they are rather special in the sense of being tied to a special set of institutions: universities and their tenured employees.

Equity Sharing Schemes

There are a variety of equity sharing schemes that have gained acceptance on the fringes of the housing finance market. Some examples of such schemes are written up by Diana Bull and Elaine St. James in *The Equity Sharing Book* (Penguin Books, 1990). They describe contractual procedures for individual transactions in which a given investor writes a form of equity sharing arrangement with an individual buyer. Various different contract forms have been used in these negotiated deals, and the authors report that by 1990 more than 300 such deals had been completed. Some other similar schemes are reported in Levin and Roberts (1981).

While there are many differences between our proposed Limited Partnership contract and the various contracts used in existing equity sharing schemes, we regard the issue of developing an institutionally supported mass market as the heart of the matter. Most of the current efforts are brokered transactions where both the investors and owner-occupants are individual households who engage in highly individualized negotiations over contract terms. Such complex and costly transactions will not give rise to a mass market. Given the high level of transactions costs and the absence of secondary markets, the role of the market in diversifying risks remains very limited. The thin market also reduces the ability of the market to "learn by doing," which is needed to improve both the alignment of incentives and procedures for monitoring and bonding.

The inertia in the housing finance market contrasts sadly with the dynamism of the commercial property market, as shown by:

• *Limited partnerships.* The commercial cousin of the contract that we propose already exists in the commercial property market, although there are significant differences in the contract covenants.

• *Sale and leaseback.* This contract form allows the commercial market to effectively separate the ownership from the use of a commercial property.

• *Leasehold mortgage.* This mortgage allows the holder of a commercial lease to borrow money using the value of the lease rights as the collateral.

• *Ground lease and space lease.* These leases allow the commercial market to separate the right to use the underlying property (ground) from the right to use the structures built on that ground (space).

• *REITs.* These securities allows the commercial market originators to bundle the standardized commercial real estate contracts for sale to third party investors.

• *Syndications and loan participations.* These allow the originators of loans secured by commercial real estate to sell off parts of those loans to third party investors.

Why is the commercial property market so much more dynamic than the residential property market? Part of the answer may lie in the vast sums of money involved in individual commercial property transactions. Given the large amount of money at stake, the transactions costs involved in writing sophisticated contracts are less of a constraint for commercial transactions than they are for residential transactions. Viewed in this light, the relatively primitive state of residential real estate finance may result from the small amounts of money at stake in individual real estate transactions.

While nothing can be done to change the relatively small scale of individual real estate transactions, a great deal can be done by recognizing that such transactions have sufficient common elements to be handled in a highly standardized fashion. When looked at from the macroeconomic perspective, residential real estate is a massive financial resource, and improvements in real estate finance would be hugely beneficial to the economy. But changes to this market cannot always come from the ground up. Standardization is necessary to keep transactions costs at a reasonable level, and the development and implementation of broadly acceptable standards is a complex and costly process that calls for a great deal of coordination among key market players.

18.3   The Importance of Market Leadership

Given the historic difficulties involved in launching new ideas in the housing finance market, we believe that it will require a major shift by some market participants if the Partnership Markets that we propose are to take off. After all, we are proposing changes that would affect almost every player in the housing market and housing finance market. We believe that some institutions would have to take a leading role in promoting the widespread changes needed for Partnership Markets to take off.

The leading institutions' most important role would be in the coordination of change and in fostering public, political, and broader institutional awareness and support for the markets. This would be a difficult and expensive role, and the institutions would have to be compensated by the possibility of deriving significant profit from a successful market launch.

The institutions' reward would consist of being in a position to become market makers, originators, and servicers. The market leaders might wish in turn to carve out major roles for other financial institutions to help ensure that the adjustment would take place in a timely manner, foster a healthy level of competition, and increase the alignment of private and public interests.

Given that the lead institutions would likely want to become the market makers, it would be important for them to consider how to standardize and package the housing Partnerships. As in the current secondary market, market makers would be responsible for putting together standards of acceptability for Limited Partnerships they would be willing to purchase. Included in this would be details of a package of information associated with the deal together with guidelines on such issues as the nature of the appraisal on the property and other pertinent details. In addition, they would get to specify the standard contract clauses.

In addition to their role as standard setters, the market leaders, in their role as market makers, would also have the crucial role of bundling the Partnerships into pools against which PREFERS would be issued. As the discussion in chapter 10 indicates, the nature of the underlying pools might be important to the later development of derivative securities and therefore to the possibilities for insurance based on local property values. More generally, the pools not only would begin to provide investment and hedging vehicles but also would become a source of information for all market participants. We believe that this information might ultimately have important consequences for the dynamic behavior of the housing market.

Another important role for the market leaders would be facilitators of the information flow. At various stages it would be important for market participants to have access to data on other market players' performance. For example, potential Managing Partners would need to know the terms different potential Limited Partners have offered and would also like to know how different Limited Partners have carried out their contractual obligations in the past. On the other side, potential Limited Partners would want to know as much as possible about the relevant past behavior of different Managing Partners. While one would expect this information to gradually be made available in reasonable form as the market evolved, the market maker might play an important role in guiding the development of appropriate forms of information and specifying the kinds of information each party must stand willing to supply.

The lead institutions would also be important in overcoming inertia due to standardization. A main feature of this type of market would be that the participants in this process of standardization would want all the uncertainties of the new Partnership Agreements addressed before endorsing the change rather than allowing them to develop over time. This in turn would require at least some significant investment in new knowledge prior to change. Therefore the inescapable conclusion is that many market participants would likely incur very large costs in investigating the form of the new agreements and the surrounding institutions, let alone in launching the product on any large scale.

Even if institutions did step forward to take the leadership role, this would not guarantee that the markets would take off. For a reform effort to be successful requires the cooperation of all major parties in the market. Among other things, data and institutional knowledge that only insiders have is needed to spot any flaws in a proposed new market structure. The need for market insiders' cooperation and information raises highly complex issues:

• Would it be possible to get enough momentum for reform without the current market players' early and explicit cooperation?

• Could they all be induced to provide good information, or would some balk when they realized the information they provided could accelerate their loss of competitiveness?

• Would they withhold support in the hope of striking a bargain for a better market position at the end of the reform process?

Although there would undoubtedly be some frictions in this process, past experience shows that the financial markets' competitiveness works well against this barrier, as indicated by the success of the credit bureaus and of competitive alliances such as VISA, Mastercard, and the ATM networks described in section 18.1.

Another important way of preparing the information needed for Partnerships to flourish would be through further economic analysis. With study, researchers might be able to provide guidance on rational directions for change and therefore make it worth the cost. Without study, the uncertainties would almost certainly exacerbate the existing inertia. But this serves to reemphasize the point that the existing market players would need to cooperate. For the economic analysis to be valuable, it would be necessary to gather information from the players currently best informed about the market structure and conditions.

18.4 The Agencies: Part of the Problem or Part of the Solution?

A market central to public policy with such a long history of federal involvement also needs strong political underpinnings to develop and maintain momentum in the reform process. Here is one of our deepest causes for concern. Does the United States today have a political climate conducive to rational discussion of reform, or is the political system likely to be more part of the problem of institutional inertia than part of the solution?

The agencies are by far the largest, and in the case of FNMA and Freddie Mac the most profitable, players in the mortgage finance market, with a cost advantage over all competitors because of their government sponsorship. The agencies derive their profit from their essentially monopolistic positions as standard setters and market makers in the secondary markets.[3] In light of their history and the value of their political franchise, the agencies have an intricate mix of economic and political motivations. This is not surprising given their unusual origin and the subsidies they receive by virtue of their special relationship with the federal government.

The quasi-governmental nature of the institutions of housing finance certainly appears to have helped develop the secondary markets, but it has not been such a creative force in the more recent period. In fact, Fabozzi and Modigliani (1992) place the responsibility for the lack of development of PLAMs right on the government's doorstep, stating that in their opinion in the United States:

... no innovation in home financing has been possible without some sanction from government regulators, and regulators have been unimaginative. (pp. 131–32)

In a similar vein, we believe that such a simple innovation as the automatic refinancing clause outlined in section 18.2 would become fraught with agency concerns over how institutional investors would react to changing established standards of allowable refinances. Rather than correcting the root of the problem, the agencies prefer to negotiate in private with the various political and regulatory groups over where to set the maximum LTV whenever a group of consumers appears trapped.

Viewed from this perspective, the federal government's central role in the housing finance market is one of the key reasons the market needs something of an overhaul. We are hardly the first to suggest that corporations with federal charters need a bit of a shake-up and that they do not have the strongest record of innovation in service.[4] The U.S. housing finance market is more closely analogous to the U.S. Postal Service than to the dynamic corporate-finance and high-technology sectors in which private innovation is so pervasive.

Against this, the examples of the thirty-year mortgage and secondary markets illustrate the agencies' opposite side, in which they encourage and direct change the private markets are not producing. Not all the inertia in the housing finance market results from the federal role. It took several decades to get the secondary market to take off, and it really occurred as a result of federal persistence and something of a trial-and-error approach. By taking the leadership role in the Partnership Market outlined in this section, the agencies could reestablish their role as market reformers.

Concluding Remarks

What do we see as the broad contribution of this book? It is not the fact that we have posed an interesting question about the housing finance market, nor is it that we have proposed a new set of products. Many different people have proposed and written about equity markets in housing for many years. As pointed out in chapter 18, various small-scale equity sharing schemes already exist for residential real estate, and legal scholars have long since understood that there are a vast number of contractually feasible forms of home ownership other than outright ownership by the occupant (e.g., Nelson and Whitman, 1985, pp. 784–785). Within the field of real estate economics, the idea of joint ownership has previously been discussed by Miles (1994), Geltner, Miller, and Snavely (1995), Caplin, Freeman, and Tracy (1994), and others.

Rather than posing new questions, our contribution in this book is a new approach to addressing the existing ones. We have described in a broad conceptual, institutional, and statistical manner the functioning of the current market. Based on this, we have suggested a new market structure that appears capable of greatly improving the functioning of the housing finance market. We have also used this as the basis for speculating on the performance, in many dimensions, of our proposed market structure. The novelty of our approach lies in the profound effort we have made to explore the many ramifications of our proposal, and to connect theoretical constructs with institutional realities.

A major conclusion of this book is that the housing finance market is far from perfect, and recognizing that it is at a crossroads may greatly improve its performance. By this, we mean that the surrounding institutions have developed to the point that the housing finance market could take an entirely new and more fruitful direction.

We do not believe that the current U.S. housing finance market is the only market at a crossroads. On the contrary, we believe that the basic forces that call for renewed attention to the institutions of housing finance are universal. In a world subject to massive shocks, institutions of all kinds need to be continuously reengineered. Unfortunately, many institutions have a tendency to become outdated, and therefore it is important for researchers to focus attention on possible directions for improvement. Archaic institutions will ultimately arrive at their own crossroads and be forced to change. We believe that the manner and the timing of the change may be influenced by ideas, and it is in this spirit that we have written this book.

Unfortunately, economic theory is largely silent on the definition, nature and evolution of market institutions. There is no compelling model of what can go wrong with institutions, or even of the rational basis for institutional inertia. Absent any powerful unifying perspective, examples of institutions that adapt in an apparently slow manner are seen as anomalous, the exception that proves the rule. This is connected to the defensive posture of claiming that such examples are illusory, and that they result from the researcher's lack of understanding of the "true constraints" that make the apparent lack of adaptation fully optimal.

In this sense, our book represents only a very small step forward. We have documented as carefully as possible one example of a market at a crossroads. This has helped us gain insight into the forces responsible for inertia in this market. With more such examples studied, we are confident that the broad nature of institutional inertia would become better understood. We believe that social scientists stand to learn a tremendous amount by joining in a struggle to gain deeper understanding of institutional inertia. We ourselves may be standing at an important crossroads.

Notes

Chapter 1

1. It is important to understand that Partnership Agreements are not to be viewed as an alternative to standard mortgage finance, but rather as a complementary form of finance.

2. Such common property limitations are often a serious issue in townhouses and condominiums because almost everything outside the physical building is common ground. Although the exact restrictions vary substantially from property to property, the use and control of these common property areas is quite restricted.

Chapter 2

1. For a careful empirical analysis of the impact of demographic factors on tenure choice, see Henderson and Ioannides 1989.

2. See Weiss 1978 for a theoretical treatment of this bias. The bias is to some extent offset by the tax treatment of owners of rental property to the extent that landlords avail themselves of depreciation and other similar tax deductions. However, the Tax Reform Act of 1987 significantly reduced the tax deductions available to landlords, which increases the potential for this bias.

3. See the Internal Revenue Service publication *Statistics of Income—1991* for detailed breakdowns of home mortgage interest deductions by household income.

4. Interpreting these results presents a potential causality problem. Empirically it is difficult to fully control for the quality of a house. Rental properties may systematically be of a lower quality even after controlling for observed differences in housing characteristics. In this case, the negative price effect is picking up a quality differential, not a negative rental externality.

5. As the detailed market analysis of chapter 3 indicates, none of the three items above operates as an isolated absolute constraint on borrowing; instead they tend to be a group constraint. For example, underwriters will be willing to trade off weaknesses in one item against excess strengths in another. These are commonly referred to in the industry as "compensating factors."

6. It is rather unfortunate that the industry has adopted the somewhat confusing nomenclature of grading both credit history and paper on a scale of A through D. But one should keep

in mind that having an A credit history is one component of eligibility for an A paper mortgage, the other two being loan-to-value ratio and ability to pay.

7. It is worth noting that one of the government's affordable housing initiatives revolves around relaxing this income constraint by allowing underwriters to include rent substitution as a component of income in low-income areas.

8. We describe these additional costs in chapter 3.

9. See Varady and Lipman 1994 for an extensive analysis of the NAR data.

10. Recent buyers in eighteen cities are sampled. Chicago Title and Trust Co. 1993.

11. For the period 1975–77, a predicted binding wealth constraint reduced the probability of home ownership by 61%, a predicted binding income constraint by 32%. See also Zorn 1989 and Duca and Rosenthal 1991 for related studies.

12. The United States is divided into twenty-seven areas.

Chapter 3

1. Congress has instructed these agencies to stand ready to purchase mortgages issued in accordance with their guidelines in all areas of the country at all times. The agencies group these mortgages into pools and provide credit enhancement on the pools before selling them to investors. The ability to immediately sell conforming mortgages in a liquid market allows the smaller originators to benefit from the agencies' ability to broadly diversify the credit risk by holding a national portfolio. In terms of the underlying economics, the main service that the agencies provide is insurance: they guarantee investors against losses caused by default on mortgage payments. For this reason, most screens and tests required for a mortgage to be conforming are designed to reduce the probability of default and the default costs that the agencies could end up bearing.

2. Fannie Mae (1996a) and Freddie Mac (1996a).

3. Fannie Mae (1996b) and Freddie Mac (1996b).

4. Currently defined in the Agency Sellers Guides as loans over the principal amount of $207,200.

5. Although this is somewhat dependent on the individual originators guidelines.

6. It is telling that the PMI companies will often call for reappraisal of the property, and may well reject applications acceptable to the mortgage originator. Property appraisals by PMI companies are widely regarded in the industry as upholding a higher standard than those of the mortgage originators, mainly because the PMI companies will suffer the most immediate losses in the event of a default. There is a very limited reinsurance market for PMI contracts, so the responsibility for loss stays with the PMI company.

7. See Sirota (1994) for a detailed introduction to FHA mortgage products and pricing, and DeBoth (1995) for a detailed description of differences between FHA mortgages and conventional mortgages.

8. In fact, some special FHA programs allow for LTVs of 100% and above. These products have a particular narrow focus, however, and are not available to the majority of buyers.

Chapter 4

1. There is an extensive literature on the accuracy of self-reported house values. Kain and Quigley (1972) and Thibodeau (1992) find no evidence of systematic bias in large data samples.

1. Vacation and investment real estate is counted in the household's total assets, but is not included in the numerator of this ratio.

3. The current LTV is calculated as the ratio of the current mortgage balance to the household's self-reported current house value.

4. Households with significant nonhousing debt (i.e., education loans) may also have to pay down these obligations in order to meet the back-end PITI ratio outlined in chapter 2.

5. We incorporate the tax deductibility of mortgage interest but ignore the deductibility of property taxes. We also assume that the entire mortgage payment is deductible (both principal and interest), which is not a bad approximation in the early years of the loan.

6. Liquid wealth includes checking and other bank accounts, stocks, interest-earning assets, mortgages owned, and money due from the sale of a business.

Chapter 5

1. See Mary Voboril, "The Dutchess County Blues: IBM Cutbacks Lay Low a Company Town," *Newsday*, August 29, 1993.

2. The wage data is produced by the Bureau of Labor Statistics, *Employment and Earnings: States and Areas*. We chose the manufacturing wage since it was reported for all of our forty-two SMSAs. For each SMSA, we computed annual wage changes for as many years between 1975 and 1994 as were available in the data.

3. Typically, about 10% of all borrowers surveyed whose loans are delinquent are preparing to file bankruptcy (see Survey Report on Consumer Collection Trends, Western Union, 1995); and holders of 50% of all loans more than ninety days delinquent file bankruptcy.

4. Although much has been made recently of the ability of borrowers who have previously declared bankruptcy to access some credit, as we have pointed out, these borrowers are no longer A-credit customers and therefore often must pay the substantially higher borrowing costs of the D-paper market.

5. Bankruptcy is like anything else in this life: You get what you pay for. Although some firms charge low transactions fees, the filing is "cookie cutter," and one is not likely to gain much advantage over creditors from a standard filing. Far more costly to lenders are bankruptcies in which the filer files a nearly endless series of challenges and other actions, getting maximum advantage from the stay provisions.

6. Many credit counseling services report, however, that this stigma is declining.

7. The baseline loan is a thirty-year fixed-rate conforming conventional loan with an LTV of 75%, A credit, and standard PITI ratios.

8. Chan (1996), Genesove and Mayer (1993), and Stein (1993).

9. See Caplin, Freeman, and Tracy (1993), and Archer et al. (1996) for details.

10. We use historical asset returns as a simply proxy for ex ante assessments of future returns, which is the traditional approach in this type of analysis.

11. See chapters 6 and 10 for a more complete discussion of data sources and methods.

Chapter 6

1. See Kocherlakota (1996) for a recent summary of this literature.

2. Most real estate diversification benefits would come at the SMSA level. However, regional risk could be further diversified by allowing Limited Partners to purchase contracts across different regions.

3. To reiterate, this assumes that other risk factors such as maintenance risk and holding-period risk have been mitigated through the Partnership Contract and/or the market structure.

Chapter 7

1. The specific calculations are given in chapter 3.

Chapter 8

1. We incorporate the tax deductibility of mortgage interest, but ignore the deductibility of property taxes. We also assume that the entire mortgage payment is deductible (both principal and interest), which is not a bad approximation in the early years of the loan.

Chapter 9

1. Associations often impose significant additional restrictions on the use of or access to these common properties. They also reserve the right to increase an individual home owner's obligation (dues, fees) in the future. These limitations are often a serious issue in town house and condominium complexes, because almost everything outside the physical building is common ground.

2. Examples might include items such as sheds, decks, swing sets, pools, landscaping, and the like.

3. Such information would include but not be limited to builder's concessions, seller's points, builder drawdown financing, seller-prepaid expenses, seller financing, assumptions, and so forth.

4. Discovery could occur upon any application by the Managing Partner to sell or to invest more in the property or at prespecified time periods over the life of the Partnership. From the point of discovery, the Managing Partner would first be given a reasonable amount of time to complete the necessary repairs.

5. Possibly a mechanic's lien would be used in this circumstance.

6. Traditionally a lender charges anywhere from 25 to 50 bps more for a mortgage on an investor (not owner-occupied) property. However, this proves difficult to monitor going forward under a traditional mortgage, because the right to rent out a property is considered a mortgagor's basic right under real estate law. As one can imagine, mortgagors have a tremendous incentive to misrepresent their intentions to get the lower rate. Those who do so are known in the industry as "hidden investors."

7. The list could be expressed in terms of percent of dollar cost. Also, one should note that various trade associations representing realtors and home improvement contractors already compile lists of the increase in value for certain categories of home improvements.

8. This would be similar to the list of reasonable and customary charges used in health care insurance.

9. However, with the advent of an active secondary market for trading Partnership Agreements (see chapter 10), the need for the Managing Partner to buy or sell an interest in their own residence for portfolio reasons should substantially diminish.

10. These conditions would be the buyer's ability to obtain financing, a satisfactory engineering inspection, that the structure meets the building code, and that it has a clear title.

12. Ten days might be a standard period.

13. How right of first refusal would be exercised is specified in the next section.

14. One relatively easy way to enact such monitoring would be for Limited Partners to include Managing Partner performance in their credit report.

15. Partition of the Partnership would be somewhat similar to a court-authorized liquidation.

16. "Actual notice" is desired, as opposed to "constructive notice," in which the public recording or filing serves as notice, or "inquiry notice," in which notice is served by producing the note at redemption.

17. Events requiring such notice would include but not be limited to default, foreclosure, foreclosure auction, subrogations, statutory redemptions, short sales, leases with an option to buy, and seller-financed sales.

18. Traditional mortgage lenders often lose 15% to 20% of the value of a property through a combination of neglect and malicious damage during the foreclosure process.

Chapter 10

1. It is too difficult for private companies to compete head to head with the agencies for conforming product, but for jumbos and other nonqualifying loans it can be quite profitable.

2. The traditional fee for this is 25 bps.

3. Several interesting securities law issues would of course arise, such as whether these PREFERS would need to be registered with the SEC, what fund disclosures would be necessary, and so forth.

4. Another interesting issue here would be to try to have PREFERS classified as a "prudent" investment under the Trust and Investment Act of 1940, so that the large funds might purchase them without violating their fiduciary duty.

Chapter 11

1. Today commercial banks commonly own mortgage origination subsidiaries and also operate an internal mortgage origination service.

2. This clause is important because the offer from the buyer is usually given with a deposit, and the buyer wants to guarantee that money will be refunded if financing is denied.

3. This is a tricky phase, particularly for the self-employed, whose incomes are hard to verify except on the basis of past tax returns, which are easily forged. If the income statements are verified, then the mortgage originator computes income using their own methodology and uses these calculations to check the debt-to-income ratios.

4. Interestingly, agency guidelines now require a merged report that contains the credit information from all three bureaus.

5. Note that although the criteria used in screening applications are both easy to understand and reasonably designed in the general sense of embracing the goal of reducing risk, they are not guaranteed to be fair to all groups. An important set of current questions concern sources of discrimination in lending arising from the screens' possible unintended side effects and also from the use of judgment by the individual lending officers.

6. Such an increase reduces the amount of the loan to be granted.

7. A teaser rate is a below-market rate an adjustable rate mortgage carries for the first reset period. Usually this teaser rate only marginally improves the borrower's chance of passing the debt burden underwriting screen, because the ARM is underwritten using the payment after the first reset.

8. An interesting new practice is to offer ARM borrowers the option to convert their loans to fixed-rate loans. These options are quite difficult for the consumer to value because they (1) have long times to maturity, (2) are often European calls exercisable only in window periods around resets, (3) often charge some application fee, although the fee is usually less than a comparable refinance charge, (4) may not convert into the most competitive market rate and in fact are often expressed as a spread above the agencies' buy rate, and (5) are dependent for the value of their conversion not only on the absolute level of interest rates but on the steepness of the yield curve.

9. Seasoning has occurred when a mortgage has been on the lender's books for enough time to reassess its risk by reviewing the history of its payment performance. Typically the rating agencies consider five years to be sufficient time for seasoning to improve the rating of a mortgage pool.

10. Source: Groves and Prigal, Mortgage Finance Review (1995).

11. Source: Groves and Prigal, Mortgage Finance Review (1995).

12. Often a mortgage originator will originate a loan at a loss of 50–75 bps in the origination fee to generate the servicing fee, which can be sold with the mortgage for a typical fee of 125–190 bps depending on the type of mortgage (because of varying prepayment expectations by type).

Chapter 12

1. The law currently requires adverse-action reasons when a loan application is turned down. Although the Partnership would not be a loan, such consumer protection would eventually appear.

2. Such costs are outlined in chapter 7.

3. Examples of such other experiences with maintaining assets are car leases, apartment rentals, appliance leases, library records, and the like.

Chapter 14

1. As one would imagine, the fallout ratio varies greatly by geography, wealth levels, and market conditions.

2. Such calculations also give the agent a good idea of what the buyer will be able to afford.

3. Typically a buyer's agent receives a 3% commission on the sale of the house. Often 1.5%–2% of this commission goes to the buyer's agent's firm (broker) to pay for overhead. So if a seller offers a 4% commission to the buyer's agent, the financial incentive is quite significant, often doubling the profit to the buyer's agent. By law the buyer must be informed of these extra commissions, but few buyers notice or realize their significance.

4. States keep publicly available records of where many toxic waste sites are located.

5. Often when talking among themselves real estate professionals use the term "net price" when comparing offers, which excludes perks, seller's points, commissions, overages, and the like.

6. However, as a matter of practice in many states this deposit is very hard for the seller to seize if the buyer does back out. Often the amount of damages is limited to the reasonable losses incurred until another buyer is found at a similar price.

7. When used in this context we are referring to the function of mortgage origination, not what type of legal entity the originator operates under (e.g., mortgage origination license, commercial banking license, thrift license, and so forth). Today the question of legal entity can be quite confusing (e.g., many commercial banks own mortgage origination subsidiaries that buy loans from mortgage brokers). Usually in this book we use "mortgage originators" to refer to any licensed institution originating loans and "mortgage banking" to refer to a function or strategy for running the business.

8. As we have mentioned, each guarantor has a manual of standards for accepting mortgages (seller's guide) that covers all the screens as well as a detailed standard of appraisal. The guarantors also keep lists of approved appraisers, who often have been certified by the National Association of Appraisers.

9. This standard varies quite a bit depending on the property's location.

Chapter 15

1. These certificates would be forwarded to the Managing Partner's mortgagee if used to secure a loan.

2. Perhaps any improvement under a certain amount, such as $500, would be considered a repair.

3. Today the borrower must live in the property to get the benefit of the stay, which also prolongs the opportunity to damage the property.

4. Often in down property markets no third-party bidders show up for the auction. This means that the mortgagee bids on the property, but is limited in bidding the maximum of the loan balance, accrued interest, and various expenses. The lender then owns the property. Any remaining money owed is usually awarded as a deficiency note to the mortgagee. Lawyers often worry that the lender might have an incentive to artificially lower the bid to boost the amount of the deficiency, although in practice this risk is minimal.

5. Many critics of this law say it is ineffective because it forces "good" third-party bidders at a foreclosure auction to decrease bids for a property. The risk that the mortgagor will exercise their right of statutory redemption over the mandated time period creates an expected opportunity cost that the bidder must try to recoup with a commensurately lower bid. Seven states currently have this type of law, and the typical time period is one year.

6. Foreclosure costs can be quite high, often around 15%.

7. Typically this period is three months, but sometimes the mortgagee will request another fixed time such as six months.

Chapter 16

1. A "housing association" in this context is a non-profit or quasi-governmental organization that aims to provide housing for low-income households.

2. This is the most local level of government in the United Kingdom.

3. These loans often matured in five to seven years and were nonamortizing.

4. This means they are private in the sense of having equity ownership but get to borrow at the federal interest rate. They also remain inextricably entwined with federal housing goals since their monopoly position and continued high profits depend on their political standing and could readily be removed if they were to displease Congress. For this reason the discussions of the stock analysts who follow FNMA and Freddie Mac often dwell on the organizations' lobbying efforts.

5. A conventional mortgage is one that is not federally insured.

6. Jumbo mortgages are discussed in chapter 7.

Chapter 17

1. The potential effect has been analyzed by Chan (1994), Genesove and Mayer (1993), and Stein (1993).

2. See for example Case and Shiller 1989.

3. See Berkovec and Goodman 1993, Kluger and Miller 1990, and Janssen, Kruijt, and Needham 1994.

Chapter 18

1. They also take advantage of essentially risk-free borrowing because of the implicit federal guarantee.

2. It is sometimes argued that the fact that FNMA and Freddie Mac are privately held removes the major incentive problems and makes them profit-maximizing competitors. There is some truth to the idea that these corporations compete, but they are still profoundly influenced by federal policy makers, and respond strongly to "hot-button" political issues.

Acronyms

ATM	Automatic teller machine
BPO	Broker price opinion
CBO	Congressional Budget Office
CES	Consumer Expenditure Survey
CSO	Conventional shared ownership
DIYSO	Do-it-yourself shared ownership
ED	Household with education debt
ELS	Equity loan scheme
FHA	Federal Housing Administration
FHLBB	Federal Home Loan Bank Board
FNMA (Fannie Mae)	Federal National Mortgage Association
FHLMA (Freddie Mac)	Federal Home Loan Mortgage Association
GNMA	Government National Mortgage Association
HUD	Department of Housing and Urban Development
LTV	Loan to value ratio
MBS	mortgage-backed security
NAR	National Association of Realtors
NED	Household with no education debt
NHS	National Housing Survey
PITI	Principal, interest, taxes, and insurance
PITIM	Principal, interest, taxes, insurance, and maintenance
PLAM	Price-level adjusted mortgage

PMI	Private mortgage insurance
PREFER	Partnership real estate funds with equity returns
PUD	Planned urban development
REIT	Real estate investment trust
SAM	Shared appreciation mortgage
SCEPTRE	Secondary partnership markets in real estate
SIPP	Survey on income and program participation
SMSA	Standard metropolitan statistical area
TAPS	Targeted partnership subsidies
VA	Veterans' Administration

References

Archer, Wayne R., Ling, David C., McGill, Gary A. 1996. "The Effect of Income and Collateral Constraints on Residential Mortgage Terminations." *Regional Science and Urban Economics* 26(3–4): 235–261

Berkovec, James A., and Goodman, John L., Jr. 1993. "Turnover Rates as Measures of Demand in the Market for Existing Homes." Working paper, Board of Governors of the Federal Reserve System.

Better Homes and Gardens. 1995. "Home Buyer's Guide." Special Interest Publications.

Bruce, John. 1985. "Real Estate Financing in a Nutshell." West Publishing Co. St. Paul, MN.

Brueckner, Jan K. 1994. "Consumption and Investment Motives and the Portfolio Choice of Homeowners." Paper presented at the National Bureau of Economic Research conference on Public Policy and the Housing Market. Kiawah Island, S. Carolina, Fall 1994.

Bull, Diana, and St. James, Elaine. 1990. *The Equity Sharing Book: How to Buy a Home Even If You Can't Afford the Down Payment.* New York: Penguin Books.

Canner, Glenn B., Passmore, Wayne, and Mittal, Monesha. 1994. "Private Mortgage Insurance." *Federal Reserve Bulletin* (October): 883–99.

Caplin, Andrew, Freeman, Charles, and Tracy, Joseph. 1993. "Collateral Damage: How Refinancing Constraints Exacerbate Regional Recessions." Working paper no. 4531, National Bureau of Economic Research.

Caplin, Andrew, Freeman, Charles and Tracy, Joseph. 1994. "Housing Partnerships: A New System of Housing Finance." Working paper, Columbia University.

Case, Karl E., and Shiller, Robert J. 1987. "Prices of Single Family Homes Since 1970: New Indexes for Four Cities." *New England Economic Review* (September/October): 45–56.

Chan, Sewin. 1996. "Spatial Lock-In: Do Falling House Prices Constrain Residential Mobility?" Working paper, Rutgers University.

Chicago Title and Trust Corporation. 1993. "Who's Buying Houses in America?" Chicago: Chicago Title and Trust Corporation.

Clements, Jonathan. 1995. "Home Improvements or Repairs?" *Wall Street Journal*, 7 November.

Colden, Anne. 1996. "Insurers Try 'Managed Care' for Autos Amid Competition, Technology Changes." *Wall Street Journal.* August 25.

Cunningham, Donald F., and Hendershott, Patric H. 1984. "Pricing FHA Mortgage Default Insurance." *Housing Finance Review* 3(4): 373–92.

DeBoth, James R. 1995. "FHA Can Mean 'Fine Help Available' for Cash-Strapped Home-buyers." Villa Park, IL: Mortgage Market Information Services.

Del Boca, Daniella, and Lusardi, Anna-Marie. 1996. "Debt Commitment, Housing, and Family Allocation of Time." Working paper, ICER, University of Turin.

Department of the Environment. 1995. "An Appraisal of Shared Ownership." London: HMSO.

DiPasquale, Denise, and Wheaton, William C. 1996. *Urban Economics and Real Estate Markets.* New Jersey: Prentice-Hall.

Dougherty, A., Van Order, R. and Villani, K. 1982. "Pricing Shared Appreciation Mortgages." *Housing Finance Review* 1(4): 361–75.

Duca, John V., and Rosenthal, Stuart S. 1991. "An Empirical Test of Credit Rationing in the Mortgage Market." *Journal of Urban Economics* 29(2): 218–34.

Eilbott, Peter, and Binkowski, Edward S. 1985. "The Determinants of SMSA Homeownership Rates." *Journal of Urban Economics* 17(3): 293–304.

Engelhardt, Gary V. 1994. "Consumption, Down Payments, and Liquidity Constraints." Working paper, Dartmouth College.

Engelhardt, Gary V. 1995. "House Prices and Home Owner Saving Behavior." Working paper no. 5183, National Bureau of Economic Research.

Engelhardt, Gary V., and Mayer, Christopher. 1994. "Gifts, Down Payments, and Housing Affordability." Working paper no. 94–5, Federal Reserve Bank of Boston.

Engelhardt, Gary, and Mayer, Christopher. 1996. "Intergenerational Transfers, Borrowing Constraints, and Savings Behavior: Evidence from the Housing Market." Working paper, Dartmouth College.

Fabozzi, F., and Modigliani, F. 1992. *Capital Markets: Institutions and Implements.* New Jersey: Prentice-Hall.

Fannie Mae (Federal National Mortgage Association). 1996a. "The Fannie Mae Sellers' Guide." Washington, D.C.: U.S. Government Printing Office.

Fannie Mae. 1996b. "The Fannie Mae Servicers' Guide." Washington, D.C.: U.S. Government Printing Office.

Fannie Mae. 1994. "Fannie Mae National Housing Survey." Washington, D.C.: U.S. Government Printing Office.

First American Title Insurance Co. 1996. "Residential Refinance, Title, and Escrow Cost Estimates State by State." First American Title Insurance Co.

Freddie Mac. 1996a. "The Freddie Mac Sellers' Guide." Washington, D.C.: U.S. Government Printing Office.

Freddie Mac. 1996b. "The Freddie Mac Servicers' Guide." Washington, D.C: U.S. Government Printing Office.

Freiberg, L. 1982. "The Problem with SAM: An Economic and Policy Analysis." *Housing Finance Review* 1(1): 73—92.

Geltner, David M., Miller, Norman G., and Snavely, Jean. 1995. "We Need a Fourth Asset Class: HEITS." *Real Estate Finance*: 71—81.

Genesove, David, and Mayer, Christopher J. 1993. "Equity and Time to Sale in the Real Estate Market." Working paper no. 4861, National Bureau of Economic Research.

Glink, Ilyce. 1995. "100 Questions Every Home Seller Should Ask." Times Books. New York.

Glink, Ilyce. 1994. "100 Questions Every First Time Home Buyer Should Ask." Times Books. New York.

Goetzmann, William N. 1995. "The Effect of Seller Reserves on Market Index Estimation." Mimeograph, Yale School of Management.

Goetzmann, William N. 1993. "The Single Family Home in the Investment Portfolio." *Journal of Real Estate Finance and Economics* 6: 201—22.

Goetzmann, William N., and Ibbotson, Roger G. 1990. "The Performance of Real Estate as an Asset Class." *Journal of Applied Corporate Finance* 3(1): 65—76.

Grauer, Robert R., and Hakansson, Nils H. 1995. "Gains From Diversifying into Real Estate: Three Decades of Portfolio Returns Based on the Dynamic Investment Model." *Real Estate Economics* 23(2): 117—59.

Groves, Tiffany, and Prigal, Debby. 1995. "Do You Know Your B's & C's?" *Mortgage Finance Review* 3(2): 3—4.

Guenther, Robert. 1985. "All-in-the-Family Mortgages Start to Show Some Promise." *Wall Street Journal*, 29 May.

Gyourko, Joseph, and Linneman, Peter. 1993. "The Affordability of the American Dream: An Examination of the Last Thirty Years." *Journal of Housing Research* 4(1): 39—72.

Hayashi, Fumio, Ito, Takatoshi,and Slemrod, Joel. 1988. "Housing Finance Imperfections, Taxation, and Private Saving: A Comparative Simulation Analysis of the United States and Japan." *Journal of the Japanese and International Economies* 2: 215—38.

Hendershott, Patric H., and Schultz, William R. 1993. "Equity and Nonequity Determinants of FHA Single-Family Mortgage Foreclosures in the 1980s." *AREUEA Journal* 21(4): 405—30.

Hendershott, Patric H., and Waddell, James A. 1992. "The Changing Fortunes of FHA's Mutual Mortgage Insurance Fund and the Legislative Response." *Journal of Real Estate Finance and Economics* 5: 119—32.

Henderson, J. Vernon, and Ioannides, Yannis M. 1989. "Dynamic Aspects of Consumer Decisions in Housing Markets." *Journal of Urban Economics* 26(2): 212—30.

Henderson, J. Vernon, and Ioannides, Yannis M. 1983. "A Model of Housing Tenure Choice." *American Economic Review* 73(1): 98—113.

Hymer, Dian. 1996. "What Is Supposed to be Disclosed to Buyers?" Oakland, CA: Inman News Features.

Ibbotson and Associates, Inc. 1996. *Stocks, Bonds, Bills and Inflation: Yearbook*. Chicago: R.G. Ibbotson and Associates.

Internal Revenue Service. 1994. "Statistics of Income—1991." Washington, D.C.: U.S. Government Printing Office.

Janssen, Jos, Kruijt, Bert, and Needham, Barrie. 1994. "The Honeycomb Cycle in Real Estate." *Journal of Real Estate Research* 9(2): 237–51.

Jones, Oliver, and Grebler, Leo. 1961. *The Secondary Mortgage Market: Its Purpose, Performance, and Potential*. Los Angeles: Real Estate Research Program.

Jones, Ted C., and Hart, Larry. 1995. "Closing Costs: How Much and Who Pays?" *Tierra Grande*, the Real Estate Center Journal. Texas A. & M. University.

Jud, G. Donald, and Seaks, Terry G. 1994. "Sample Selection Bias in Estimating Housing Sales Prices." *Journal of Real Estate Research* 9(3): 289–298.

Kain, John F., and Quigley, John M. 1972. "Note on Owner's Estimate of Housing Value." *Journal of the American Statistical Association* 67: 803–6.

Kennickell, Arthur, and Shack-Marquez, Janice. 1992. "Changes in Family Finances from 1983 to 1989: Evidence from the Survey of Consumer Finances." Federal Reserve Bulletin. Washington, D.C.

Kluger, Brian D., and Miller, Norman G. 1990. "Measuring Residential Real Estate Liquidity." *AREUEA Journal* 18(2): 145–59.

Kocherlakota, Narayana R. 1996. "The Equity Premium: It's Still a Puzzle." *Journal of Economic Literature* 34(1): 42–71.

Lederman, Jess. 1987. *The Secondary Mortgage Market*. Chicago: Probus Publishing Company.

Levin, M., and Roberts, P. 1981. "Future Forms of Financing—Lending Devices Addressed to Inflation and Tight Money." American Bar Association.

Linneman, Peter, and Wachter, Susan. 1989. "The Impacts of Borrowing Constraints on Homeownership." *AREUEA Journal* 17(4): 389–402.

Mayer, Christopher J., and Simons, Katerina V. 1994. "Reverse Mortgages and the Liquidity of Housing Wealth." *AREUEA Journal* 22(2): 235–55.

Merrill, Sally R., Finkel, Meryl, and Kutty, Nandinee K. 1994. "Potential Beneficiaries from Reverse Mortgage Products for Elderly Homeowners: An Analysis of American Housing Survey Data." *AREUEA Journal* 22(25): 257–99.

Miceli, Thomas J. 1989. "Housing Rental Contracts and Adverse Selection with an Application to the Rent-Own Decision." *AREUEA Journal* 17(4): 403–421.

Miles, David. 1994. *Housing, Financial Markets and the Wider Economy*. New York: John Wiley & Sons.

Murphy, J. Austin. 1993. "A Practical Analysis of Shared-Appreciation Mortgages." *Housing Policy Debate* 2(1): 43–48.

Nelson, Grant, and Whitman, Dale. 1985. *Real Estate Finance Law*. West Publishing Co. St. Paul, MN.

Peek, Joe, and Wilcox, James A. 1991. "The Measurement and Determinants of Single Family House Prices." Working paper no. 91–7, Federal Reserve Bank of Boston.

Poterba, James M. 1992. "Taxation and Housing: Old Questions and New Answers." *American Economic Review* 82(2): 237–42.

Quigley, John M., and Van Order, Robert. 1991. "Defaults on Mortgage Obligations and Capital Requirements for U.S. Savings Institutions: A Policy Perspective." *Journal of Public Economics* 44(3): 353–69.

Rasmussen, David W., Megbolugbe, Isaac F., and Morgan, Barbara A. 1995. "Using the 1990 Public Use Microdata Sample to Estimate Potential Demand for Reverse Mortgage Products." *Journal of Housing Research* 6(1): 1–23.

Razzi, Elizabeth. 1996. "Buying a Home in a Buyer's Market." *Kiplinger's Personal Finance Magazine* (April): 63–70.

Rohe, William M. 1995. "Converting Public Housing to Cooperatives: The Experience of Three Developments." *Housing Policy Debate* 6(2): 439–79.

Romano, Jay. 1996. "Warning to Sellers: Let the Buyer Be Aware." *New York Times*, 1 September.

Rosen, Harvey. 1995. *Public Finance*. 4th edition. Boston: Irwin.

Rosenbaum, David, Goren, Thomas A., and Jacobs, Laurence H. 1995. "Risk and Benefit: Structural Efficiency in Senior Home Equity Conversion." Walnut Creek, CA: Lifetime Security Plan.

Secondary Mortgage Markets. 1996. "Data Insert, 1996." Secondary Mortgage Markets (November).

Shiller, Robert J., and Weiss, Allan N. 1994. "Home Equity Insurance." Discussion Paper 1074. Cowles Foundation for Research in Economics, Yale University.

Sirota, David. 1994. "Essentials of Real Estate Finance." Real Estate Education Co. Chicago, IL.

Stein, Jeremy. 1995. "Prices and Trading Volume in the Housing Market: A Model with Downpayment Effects." *Quarterly Journal of Economics* 110(2): 379–406.

Stevenson, Richard. 1996. "Report Skeptical of U.S-Backed Home Mortgages." *New York Times*, 30 May.

Terry, Rachel. 1996. "Changing Housing Markets: The Case for Flexible Tenure and Flexible Mortgages." London: National Federation of Housing Associations.

Terry, Rachel. 1995. "Funding Shared Ownership: From Complexity to Simplicity." York, U.K.: Joseph Rowntree Foundation.

Thibodeau, Thomas G. 1992. "Residential Real Estate Prices: 1974–1983." Mount Pleasant, MI: The Blackstone Company.

United Homeowners Association. 1995. *Partnership Agreement with the National Partners for Homeownership*.

Varady, David P., and Lipman, Barbara J. 1994. "What Are Renters Really Like? Results from a National Survey." *Housing Policy Debate* 5(4): 491–531.

Venti, Steven F., and Wise, David A. 1991. "Aging and the Income Value of Housing Wealth." *Journal of Public Economics* 44(3): 371–97.

Voboril, Mary. 1993. "The Dutchess County Blues: IBM Cutbacks Lay Low a Company Town." *Newsday*, 29 August.

Wang, Ko, Grissom, Terry V., Webb, James R., and Spellman, Lewis. 1991. "The Impact of Rental Properties on the Value of Single-Family Residences." *Journal of Urban Economics* 30(2): 152–66.

Weiss, Yoram. 1978. "Capital Gains, Discriminatory Taxes, and the Choice between Renting and Owning a House." *Journal of Public Economics* 10(1): 45–55.

Western Union. 1995. "Survey Report on Consumer Credit Collection Trends." Western Union Commercial Services.

Yates, Judith. 1992. "Shared Ownership: The Socialisation or Privatisation of Housing?" *Housing Studies* 7(2): 97–111.

Zorn, Peter M. 1989. "Mobility-Tenure Decisions and Financial Credit: Do Mortgage Qualification Requirements Constrain Homeownership?" *AREUEA Journal* 17(1): 1–16.

Index

age-tenure profile, 21–24
American Express, 231
Amerin, 40
appraisers, 151, 192–194
Archer, W., 247
Arrow security, 226
as-is clause, 131, 203
ATM Networks, 231, 239

bankruptcy, 78
Berkovec, J., 252
Better Homes and Gardens, 203
Binkowski, E., 23
broker price opinion (BPO), 206
Bruce, J., 232
Brueckner, J., 90–93
Bull, D., 236

Canner, G., 40
Caplin, A., 233, 243, 247
Case, K., 72, 89, 169–170, 223, 252
Chan, S., 247, 252
Chicago Title and Trust Co., 32, 246
Citi Mae, 144
Clements, J., 134
CMAC, 40
Colden, A., 134
consumer expenditure survey, 50, 69–70
credit bureau, 29–30, 150–151, 230
credit rating, A–D, 29–30, 154–155
credit score, 30
Cunningham, D., 210

death of spouse, 201
DeBoth, J., 246
debt/income test, 31, 151–152
Del Boca, D., 221

Department of Housing and Urban Development (HUD), 38, 210–211
Diners Club, 231
Dipasquale, D., 25
divorce, 201
Doctrine of Waste, 131
Dougherty, A., 234
Duca, J., 246
Duff and Phelps, 78

Eilbott, P., 23
Engelhardt, G., 32, 52, 80–81, 225
Equifax, 230
equity premium puzzle, 176
ERA, 234
escrow, 133, 194

Fabozzi, F., 233, 240
Federal Home Loan Bank Board, 232
Federal Home Loan Mortgage Association
  (Freddie Mac), 30, 38, 143, 217, 240, 246
Federal Housing Administration (FHA), 38, 217
Federal National Mortgage Association
  (FNMA), 28, 38, 145, 217–218, 240, 246
FICO, 230
Finkel, M., 64–65
foreclosure, 202–203
Freeman, C., 233, 243, 247
Frieberg, L., 235

Geltner, D., 243
Genesove, D., 247
Glink, I., 186, 204
Goetzmann, W., 73, 167–170
Goodman, J., 252

Goren, T., 162
Government National Mortgage Associa-
  tion (GNMA), 38, 143, 218
Grauer, R., 170
Grebler, L., 217
Grissom, T., 28
Groves, T., 29, 250
Guenther, R., 235
Gyourko, J., 35

Hakanson, N., 170
Hart, L., 42
Hayashi, F., 225
Hendershott, P., 210
Henderson, J. V., 245
house price index
  FHA/Freddie Mac, 92, 170–178
  futures market, 223
  hedonic, 166
  repeat sale, 166
  self-selection, 167–168, 180–181
Hymer, D., 190

Ibbotson, R., 73, 168–169
Ibbotson and Associates, 92
insurance
  forced place, 133
  home owner, 135, 203
Ioannides, Y., 247
IRS Schedule 1099B, 134, 163
Ito, T., 225

Jacobs, L., 162
Janssen, J., 252
Jones, O., 217
Jones, T., 42
Jud, G. D., 167

Kain, J., 247
Kennickell, A., 81
Kluger, B., 252
Kocherlakota, N., 176, 248
Kruijt, B., 252
Kutty, N., 64–65

Lederman, J., 144
Levin, M., 236
Ling, D., 247
Linneman, P., 33, 35
Lipman, B., 32, 246
loan to value ratio (LTV), 31, 51, 66, 78,
  151–152

lock-in, geographic, 79
Lusardi, A-M., 221

Mastercard, 231
Mayer, C., 32, 65, 80–81, 247, 252
McGill, G., 247
MDS, 230
Merrill, S., 64–65
Megbolugbe, I., 64
MGIC, 40
Miceli, T., 27
Miles, D., 243
Miller, N., 243, 252
Mittal, M., 40
Modigliani, F., 233, 240
Morgan, B., 64
mortgage
  adjustable rate (ARM), 153, 232
  amortization, 153
  assumability, 153
  backed security (MBS), 143–144
  balloon, 153, 216
  broker, 149
  conforming, 38, 150–153
  conventional mortgages, 38
  default, 78, 181–182
  FHA, 38, 210–211, 217
  government, 38
  interest deduction, 24, 209
  jumbo, 38
  maturity, 153
  nonconforming, 38, 153–155
  originator, 149
  prequalification, 149, 188–189
  price level adjusted (PLAM), 233, 240
  quality, 29, 154–155
  refinancing constraint, 81, 233
  servicing, 155–156
  shared appreciation (SAM), 234–235
  standardization, 144
  VA, 31, 38, 210–211
Murphy, J. A., 234

National Association of Realtors, 32–33,
  246
National Housing Survey, 32
Needham, B., 252
negative equity, 67, 119, 120
Nelson, G., 231, 243

Panel Survey of Income Dynamics (PSID),
  52, 80

partnership
    cross-breach of contract, 139
    direct breach of contract, 139–140
    right of first refusal, 137
    short-term rental, 133, 201–202
Passmore, W., 40
Peek, J., 166, 172, 178
Poterba, J., 209
Prigal, D., 29, 250
principal, interest, taxes, and insurance (PITI),
    31, 50, 66
    and maintenance (PITIM), 103
private mortgage insurance (PMI), 38–40,
    194
public housing, 210

quick sale price, 206
Quigley, J., 182, 246

Rasmussen, D., 64
Razzi, E., 187, 189
real estate agent, 185–191
real estate investment trust (REIT), 89
Roberts, P., 236
Rohe, W., 216
Romano, J., 204
Rosen, H., 209
Rosenbaum, D., 162
Rosenthal, S., 246

St. James, E., 236
Schultz, W., 210
Seaks, T., 167
secondary mortgage market, 143–144, 217–
    218
secondary partnership market, 145–148
Shack-Marquez, J., 81
shared ownership, U.K. scheme, 213–216
Shiller, R., 72, 89, 169–170, 223, 252
Simons, K., 65, 81
Sirota, D., 246
Slemrod, J., 225
Snavely, J., 243
Spellman, L., 28
Stein, J., 247, 252
Stevenson, R., 211
structural engineer, 194
survey of consumer attitudes, 67–68
survey of income and program participation
    (SIPP), 33, 81

targeted partnership subsidies (TAPS), 211–
    212

Tax Reform Act of 1987, 245
Terry, R., 215–216
Thibodeau, T., 247
Tracy, J., 233, 243, 247
Transunion, 230
TRW, 230

United Homeowners Association, 211

Van Order, R., 182, 234
Varady, D., 32, 246
Venti, S., 63
Veterans Administration (VA), 38
Villani, K., 234
Visa, 231, 239
Voboril, M., 247

Wachter, S., 33
Wadell, J., 210
Wang, K., 28
Webb, J., 28
Weiss, A., 223
Weiss, Y., 245
Western Union, 247
Wheaton, W., 25
Whitman, D., 231, 243
Wilcox, D., 166, 172, 178
Wise, D., 63–64

Yates, J., 213

Zorn, P., 246